The Development of Pottery Technology from the Late Sixth to the Fifth Millennium B.C. in Northern Jordan

Ethno- and archaeological studies: Abu Hamid as a key site

Nabil Ali

BAR International Series 1422
2005

Published in 2016 by
BAR Publishing, Oxford

BAR International Series 1422

*The Development of Pottery Technology from the Late Sixth to the Fifth Millennium B.C. in
Northern Jordan*

ISBN 978 1 84171 861 3

BAR Publishing is the trading name of British Archaeological Reports (Oxford) Ltd.
British Archaeological Reports was first incorporated in 1974 to publish the BAR
Series, International and British. In 1992 Hadrian Books Ltd became part of the BAR
group. This volume was originally published by Archaeopress in conjunction with
British Archaeological Reports (Oxford) Ltd / Hadrian Books Ltd, the Series principal
publisher, in 2005. This present volume is published by BAR Publishing, 2016.

Printed in England

BAR
PUBLISHING

BAR titles are available from:

BAR Publishing
122 Banbury Rd, Oxford, OX2 7BP, UK
EMAIL   info@barpublishing.com
PHONE   +44 (0)1865 310431
FAX   +44 (0)1865 316916
www.barpublishing.com

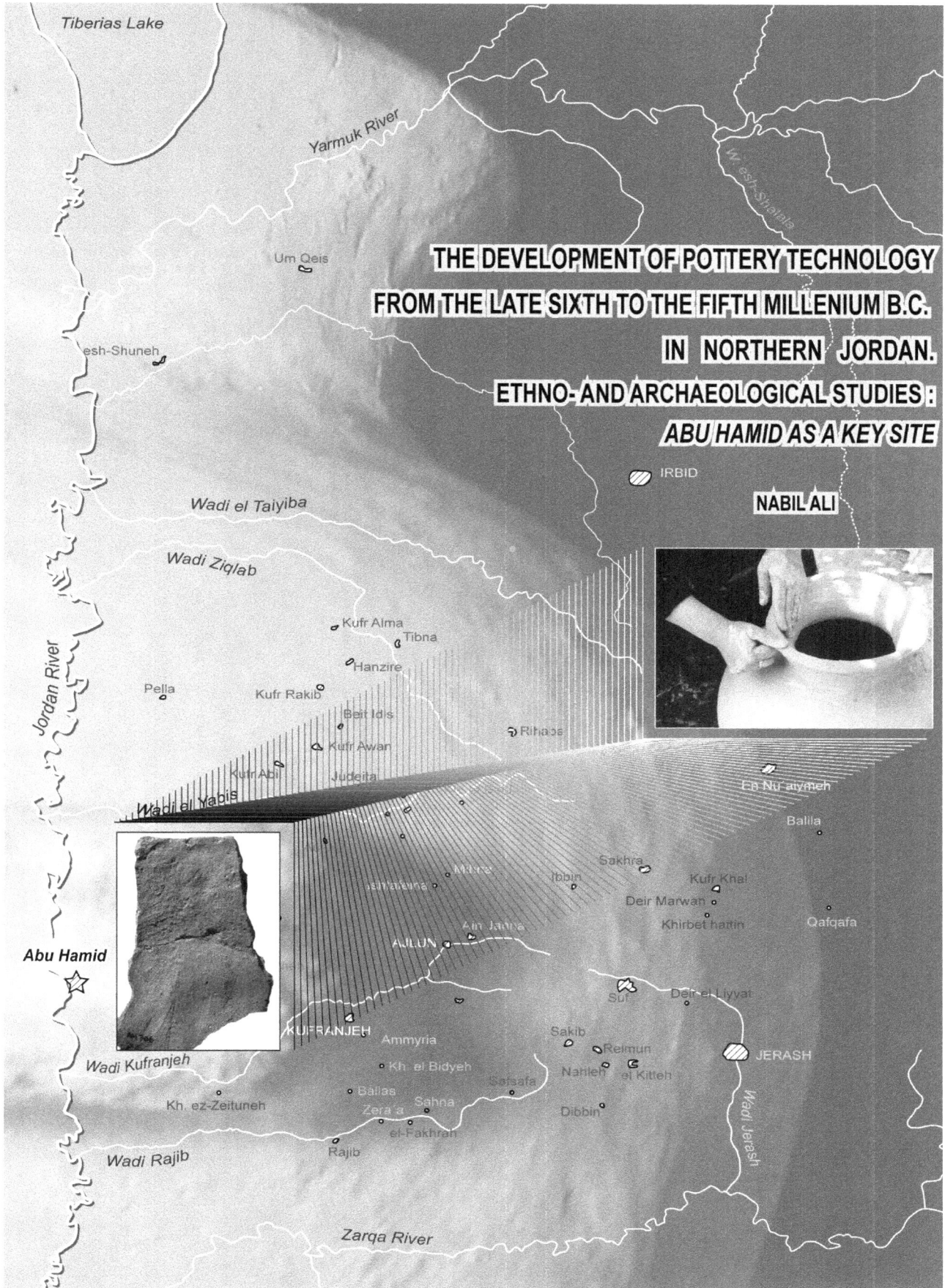

Tiberias Lake

Yarmuk River

W. esh-Shatala

Um Qeis

THE DEVELOPMENT OF POTTERY TECHNOLOGY
FROM THE LATE SIXTH TO THE FIFTH MILLENIUM B.C.
IN NORTHERN JORDAN.
ETHNO- AND ARCHAEOLOGICAL STUDIES :
ABU HAMID AS A KEY SITE

esh-Shuneh

IRBID

NABIL ALI

Wadi el Taiyiba

Wadi Ziqlab

Kufr Alma

Tibna

Pella

Hanzire

Kufr Rakib

Beit Idis

Rihaba

Kufr Awan

El Nu`aiymeh

Kufr Abil

Judeita

Balila

Wadi el Yabis

Sakhra

Mhre

Ibbin

Kufr Khal

sin areina

Deir Marwan

Ain Janna

Khirbet hattin

Qafqafa

Abu Hamid

AJLUN

Sui

Deir el Liyyat

Sakib

KUFRANJEH

Ammyria

Reimun

JERASH

Nahleh el Kitteh

Kh. el Bidyeh

Safsafa

Ballas

Wadi Kufranjeh

Sahna

Dibbin

Kh. ez-Zeituneh

Zera a

Wadi Jerash

el-Fakhran

Wadi Rajib

Rajib

Jordan River

Zarqa River

Contents

PARTII: FROM STATIC TO DYNAMIC CONTEXTOFARCHAEOLOGICALPOTTERYPRODUCTIONATABU HAMID: LATE 6TH–5THMILLENNIUM BC

List of Figures

List of Tables

List of Maps

Acknowledgements

This study is based upon my PhD Thesis, which was completed at the "Freiburg Universität" / Germany (2003). I am very grateful to many people for helping me bring this research here to fruition. I am especially indebted to Prof. Dr. M. Heinz, my advisor, whose continued support and advice has been extremely important to me. Her broad knowledge and valuable experience and her patient instruction have improved my research skills and supported me to finish my study. Also my special thanks are forwarded to Prof. Dr. Z. Kafafi (Faculty of Archaeology and Anthropology – Yarmouk University / Irbid), the second advisor, for his advice and unlimited help which are more than appreciated.

For her efforts and invaluable assistance, special thanks to Dr. G. Dollfus (CNRS, UMR 7041 / Paris). By her valuable comments and discussions, this study has been enriched. For both Dr. G. Dollfus and Prof. Dr. Kafafi, the co-directors of Abu Hamid Project, special gratefulness are due for granting me the permission to study the pottery assemblages from the archaeological site of Abu Hamid.

My special thanks are for Dr. V. Roux (CNRS, UMR 7055 / Paris), as an advisor on my work from its initial stage. Many thanks for her support and permission to study the material from Abu Hamid at the "Université Paris 10 – Nanterre".

I would like to express my gratitude to every potter in Jordan, who allowed me to stay and follow their work. Without their help, understanding, kindness and pleasant friendship this work would not be possible.

Deep thanks are due to Prof. Dr. Dr. A. Beck, from the "Universität Klinikum / Konstanz", for his excellent technical assistance in conducting some of the pottery xeroradiography. To him and his assistances many thanks.

I benefited from discussions with many scholars and I acknowledge a special help from the following: Dr. Prof. S. Seitz ("Völkerkunde Institut / Freiburg"); Dr. A. Gelbert for her goodwill and invaluable discussion while I was studying the pottery assemblages at the "Université Paris 10"; Dr. J. Lovell (Sydney University), Dr. M. Al-Naddaf (Yarmouk University) and Dr. S. Kulemann-Ossen ("Freiburg Universität").

I am especially indebted to C. Kohlmayer for drawings and layout of several figures and maps, and for preparing the editing papers. Many thanks for her endless patience, encouragement and support.

I would like to express my gratitude to every one in the "Orientalisches Seminar – Freiburg Universität" for their assistance and for pleasant friendship, especially M. Izadpanahi, Ph. Coy and E. Wagner.

My thanks are due also to Jordanian friends N. Hindawi and J. Telfah. My gratitude goes also to all my friends in the Faculty of Archaeology and Anthropology (Yarmouk University) for their assistance and help, especially to Mr. N. Qadi. I would like to express my thankfulness to Prof. Dr. Z. Al-Sa'ad, head of the Faculty of Archaeology and Anthropology (Yarmouk University), who facilitated the administrative process for studying the material of Abu Hamid at the institute.

In addition, I am grateful for the German Academic Exchange Service ("DAAD") for giving me the chance to follow my study in Germany. Especially I am grateful to H. Albertin and R. Nagel for their help. Special thanks also go to Mrs. Klaus from the "Katholische Hochschule Gemeinde / Freiburg".

Special thanks are due to Mr.. David Davison for his assistance and help.

I wish to record my sincere appreciation and thanks to my family and friends for their spiritual support, love, patience and encouragement throughout my study.

Nabil Ali
Department of Near Eastern Archaeology
University of Freiburg / Germany

Zusammenfassung

Diese Arbeit befasst sich mit Methoden und Techniken des Keramikaufbaus. Das untersuchte archäologische Material stammt aus der Siedlung Abu Hamid/ Jordantal und wird in das 6. und 5. Jahrtausend v. Chr. datiert. Die Keramik entstammt zwei Hauptperioden der Siedlung. Dabei können drei Untergruppen eingeteilt werden, von denen zwei mit den ‚Lower Levels' von Abu Hamid in Verbindung gebracht werden. Diese Schichten entsprechen dem Kulturhorizont ‚Post-Yarmoukian' (LN2). Die letzte und dritte Keramikgruppe gehört zu den sog. ‚Middle Levels', die dem Wadi Rabah Horizont gleich zusetzten sind (Frühes Chalkolithikum).

Um die technischen Prozesse der Keramikherstellung zu untersuchen, wurde eine ethnoarchäologische Studie in Nordjordanien durchgeführt. Mit Hilfe einer solchen Studie kann die Beziehung zwischen menschlichen Verhaltensmustern und deren Materialisation in der Keramiktechnologie, besonders in Bezug auf Aufbautechniken, betrachtet werden. Darüber hinaus kann mit Hilfe der ethnoarchäologischen Forschung die Beziehung kultureller, also ökonomischer und sozialer Aspekte, zur Keramikproduktion nachvollzogen werden.
Die Formung der Keramik aus Abu Hamid wurde mittels der Wulst-, Pinch-, Model-Technik(en) durchgeführt. Alle diese Techniken sind für die ‚Lower Levels' nachgewiesen, wohingegen für die ‚Middle Levels' nur die Wulsttechnik belegt werden konnte.

In den ‚Lower Levels' wurde die Keramik per Hand hergestellt. Für die Herstellung der Keramik in den Middle Levels hingegen konnte die Verwendung eine kreisende kinetische Energie (im Folgenden als RKE = rotative kinetic energy bezeichnet) nachgewiesen werden., wobei diese Energie nur für Ränder genutzt wurde.

Anhand der technologischen Klassifikation der drei erwähnten Keramik-Assemblagen können technische Unterschiede, sowohl innerhalb einer Gruppe als auch zwischen den Gruppen, nachvollzogen werden. Aus diesen Gruppen erschließen sich Hinweise auf ökonomische und soziale Aspekte. Auf Grund des architektonischen Befundes kann festgestellt werden, dass es keine permanente Besiedlung in Abu Hamid während der ‚Lower Levels' gab. Dieser Umstand scheint, Einfluss genommen zu haben auf technische Charakteristika der Keramikproduktion. Die identifizierten technischen Gruppen können einen Hinweis darauf sein, dass Keramik zur direkten Nutzung und nicht im Voraus hergestellt wurde. Darüberhinaus ist es möglich, die drei unterschiedlichen, technologischen Gruppen mit verschiedenen ‚levels of know-how' zu parallelisieren.

In den ‚Middle Levels' etablierte sich eine permanente Siedlung. Für diese Phase können wir zwei technischen Kategorien identifizieren: eine Technik verwendet RKE, während die andere sich auf alte Traditionen stützt. Auf Grund unterschiedlicher technischer Gruppen und Formungstechniken kann man annehmen, dass es eine Veränderung in der Organisation der Keramikproduktion gab. Produzenten und Konsumenten sind nicht mehr identisch mit denen des ‚Lower Levels'. Dies könnte ein Hinweis auf eine Spezialisierung innerhalb der Produktion sein.

Introduction

I. Background

Pottery was designated as a *fossil*-technological mark by early anthropological evolutionists such as Tylor (1871) and Morgan (1877). It was considered a basis for distinguishing hunter-gatherer societies from agricultural ones. The correlation between this particular technological innovation and the development of an agricultural, sedentary society was, according to Childe (1951: 175), a component of the "Neolithic Revolution". However, later archaeological research has shown that, chronologically, pottery followed at least 2000 years the domestication of plants and animals. Furthermore, pottery was not necessarily limited to only sedentary societies but could be made and used by mobile groups as well, (Aikens 1995; Arnold III 1999; Hoopes and Barnett 1995; Kenyon 1979; Moore 1995; Rice 1999). Nonetheless, pottery remains a significant material culture that helps to explain cultural diversity, on the one hand, and for studying cultural change, on the other. This stems mainly from the fact that pottery is one of the rare objects that are used in so many daily activities of social groups.

From the time of its invention, by the mid-eighth millennium BP, pottery remains one of the dominant artefacts found at most the archaeological sites in the Near East (Moore 1995). The study of pottery follows two, mostly separate trends. The first centres primarily on a cultural-historical approach and seeks to establish chronological sequences and the spatio-temporal framework of pottery distribution. The second focuses on the technological characteristics of the pottery. This technological approach employs several types of hard-ware analyses (e.g., paste compositional analysis, chemical analysis, and Neutron Activation Analysis) in order to define the location of production, the system of exchange or trade, and nonetheless pottery forming techniques (Davidson and McKerrell 1976, 1980; Vandiver 1986, 1987; Franken 1974).

The socio-economical loci of most pottery technological studies in south-western Asia and the Near East have been complex societies. This is due in part to the nature of archaeological research, which, historically, has more or less focused on the development of the city-state. Hence, several studies have based their hypotheses on the role of exchange and trade, or of specialization, as a mechanism of social complexity. Pottery studies tend to evaluate these hypotheses by focusing on the compositional analysis of pottery.

However, research on prehistoric pottery technology has recently expanded (Vandiver 1987; van As and Wijnen 1989/1990; van As, Jacobs and Wijnen 1996/1997; Roux and Courty 1998). The loci of these studies have been on either small-scale societies (Late Neolithic) or, to a large extent, on *pristine* complex ones (Late Chalcolithic: the stage that preceded the city-state phase) (Vandiver 1987; Roux and Courty 1997; Al-Saa'd *et al.* 1997). The pottery repertoire of small-scale societies has been less studied in a coherent, systematic way. Likewise, a reference source stemming from pottery ethnoarchaeology has also been less emphasized. Such an emphasis would aid in understanding the dynamic interrelationship between pottery manufacture and production.

II. The problem

The use of pottery in Jordan as utilitarian objects dates back to 5500 BC (Kafafi 1991, 1995) and is still made and used in Jordan. The same trends in pottery study noted above can also be ascribed to the case of Jordan. However, the technological study of prehistoric pottery can be defined by two basic trends. One focuses on the provincial and technological characteristics of pottery as an artefact; that is, technological explanations outweigh cultural ones (e.g. Al-Saa'd *et al.* 1997). The second trend is more contextual in nature. Technological data is examined in order to shed light on the economic and sociological dimensions of pottery production (Roux and Courty 1997, 1998). This kind of study attempts to shed light on its technological development, for example, the use of the wheel in fashioning pots, and its socio-economic manifestations (Roux and Courty 1997), and the analysis of pottery as a means of measuring social identity and/or boundary (Roux and Courty in press). Both studies use hard ware analysis in terms of petrographical techniques to help in their technological explanation. In addition, experimental studies were conducted as a source of reference and as an analogical tool.

A survey of the literature on prehistoric pottery technology in Jordan brings to light two further research needs. These are a) the need for a detailed study of the pottery-forming technology at single site, such that the initial stages of pottery production are documented; and b) the needs for an ethnoarchaeological study in order to provide a source of reference for understanding the sequences of pottery production and its cultural manifestations. These two archaeological inquiries with respect to pottery studies in Jordan are here postulated as research aims.

This work stems from the main hypothesis that techno-economical and demographic factors affected and/or determine socio-cultural variability (Harris 1968; Schiffer

1983). Such variability reflects, among other things, pottery production. The term variability will denote here two things: a) the technological information that potters participated in a given society with respect to the production of its pottery needs. In this case, variability might be reflected in the operational sequence(s) employed in pot forming, the produced pot forms, and the types of wares, and b) the significance of the socio-cultural context and the conditions of production. In this case, variability will be reflected in the quality and quantity of production.

The above hypothesis will be evaluated and tested using two scales. The first is through an ethnoarchaeological study of the pottery, and the second through an archaeological pottery analysis. The former was conducted on hand-made pottery in Jordan. The archaeological pottery repertoire came from the archaeological site of Abu Hamid in the Jordan Valley. The assemblages here analysed date from the late sixth to the late fifth millennium BC. They are ascribed to two main cultural Horizons: the "post-classical Yarmoukian" Horizon (Late Neolithic 2) and the Wadi Rabah one (Early Chalcolithic). During these phases, the societies seem to be on a small-scale. They precede the cultural stage that leads to urbanism.

III. Approaching the problem

"Technology" either in its materialist or cultural dimensions is the central pillar of this research. This enhancesl 2 approaching it from a theoretical paradigm and a methodological one, both of which embrace our understanding of pottery production. Related to this problem also are the theoretical approaches that have dealt with the problem of technological change.

III.1 The theoretical debates on "Technology"

In the history of anthropological research, two main theoretical positions have dominated the discussion concerning relationship between technology and society. These stem from the discourse on the locus of culture - that is, whether human behaviour, as a component of culture, is determined by natural laws or not (Service 1985).

With the re-emphasis on evolutionary/cultural ecological theory in anthropology during the late 1950's (White 1959; Steward 1955), the normative theory was de-emphasized. Culture was defined as "man's extrasomatic means of adaptation" (White 1959) and its locus was displaced from the minds of individuals. Instead, emphasis was placed on culture as an adaptive system, and the focus shifted to understanding the mutual interaction between organisms and their environment (Steward 1955:30). As a system, culture has been arbitrarily partitioned into three subsystems – technology, social organization and ideology – that aim at a systemic understanding of the mode of integration of these subsystems and how they function (White 1959).

However, neo-evolutionists such as White, Steward and Harris, emphasized causal explanations of cultural differences and similarities. In the analysis of a culture's environment, the locus of explanation is assumed to be its techno-economical factors (food, shelter and tools). Otherwise, social and ideological systems are seen as responses to environmental and technological conditions (Harris 1976, 1987; Steward 1955). In this way, cultural practice is seen as the adaptive production of materials for use in functioning cultural systems, whereas technology is seen as a means of adaptation existing beyond the limitations of social constraints.

This materialist approach with respect to cultural explanations has been adopted in archaeology. This process began with what is called the "New archaeology" or "processaul archaeology" (Binford 1962, 1965; Fritz and Plog 1970; Watson et al. 1984). Emphasis was on culture as an adaptive, dynamic, and systemic concept, a view that has been evaluated by a combination of cultural ecology with system theory (Clarke 1968; Flannery 1972). To be significant for archaeological explanation, culture as an adaptive system is divided into three interrelated subsystems: technology, social organization and ideology (Binford 1962). In keeping with the mainstream, the locus of technological system centres on the notion of its cultural ecological function being a determinant of other cultural features.

This new archaeological phase went side by side with the establishment of different methods, techniques and means of explanations. Anthropological data and new ethnoarchaeological studies provided a basis for archaeological hypothesis testing (Binford 1977; Watson 1980) for explaining the functioning and interrelationship of material items in their cultural subsystems. This has had a clear impact on pottery studies. Less attention is paid to pottery as a chronological tool. Instead pottery has been studied with an eye toward inferring cultural dynamic aspects, such as social organization (Deetz 1965; Longacre 1968; Whallon 1968). Archaeologists have also applied the culture ecological approach to the study of ceramic production (Matson 1965). Ceramics may be regarded as part of the technological subsystem, and as such, effort has been directed at defining the interrelationship between pottery, the environment, and other cultural subsystems (Arnold 1985; Rice 1981, 1987). This is evident in the gathering data on the local environment in which potters work and the natural resources which they use (Arnold 1985, 1993; Kolb 1989).

Pottery-making has been generally considered an economic activity, one based in seasonal timing, local resources, and the laws of supply and demand. The potter then is an individual who operates under different types of constraints – physical, chemical and economic – in achieving his/her final product (Arnold 1985; Franken and Kalsbeek 1975; van der Leeuw 1977; Rice 1987). Material constraints are considered as having the prime effect on the technology which the potter utilizes in fulfilling other cultural needs.

This materialist approach has been, more recently, challenged by structuralism or postmodern thought. This shift in thinking began in the1960s, but it was not until the 1980s that it found its place in the archaeological discourse (Hodder 1982; Bintliff 1991; VanPool and VanPool 1999). This theoretical model emerged as a critique of the processual school, and became known as post-processualism, and saw a shift in emphasis from the study of culture as an adaptive system to a focus on the role of ideas and symbols as modes of social integration. Instead of focusing on functional explanation, post-processualists emphasized social interpretations (Hodder 1992; VanPool and VanPool 1999), and archaeological data has been evaluated on the basis of hermeneutics and contextualism forms (Hodder 1986, 1991, 1997; Preucel 1991, 1995).

The main influence of this theoretical movement is reflected in the way technology is perceived as a cultural or social constructed phenomenon (Lemonnier 1986; Pfaffenberger 1992). Physical constraints are seen partly as affecting techniques and technologies compared with the cultural or symbolic representations of social group (Lemonnier 1986, 1989, 1993). These have been the main critiques of the ecological approach. An understanding of the social systems that contain the technology and its role in the society was called for (Pfaffenberger 1992: 495). This leads to an emphasis on techniques and technology for their own sake – an "anthropology of technology" (Lemonnier 1986) or a "social anthropology of technology" (Pfaffenberger 1992). These approaches, though different in name, share in common the notion of a *reciprocal* relationship between the two realms – those of nature and culture – as opposed to one where influence only runs in one direction.

The other main concept evaluated using anthropology of techniques concerns technological choices. These choices refer to options, either in terms of matter or social choices, with respect to which artisans must operate (Lemonnier 1986). These choices

> (result) in the recourse to a given material, the use of a particular tool, the application of a sequence of actions, or the mobilization of specific technical knowledge (Lemonnier 1986: 153).

This notion concerning technological choices has been discussed in order to explain the causes underlying why different techniques are adopted between social groups even where they share similar environmental conditions. Cultural explanation – such as ethnic differentiation, cultural markers, ritual and ideology – rather than material ones can explain technological heterogeneity either within or among social groups.

Technological activity is considered as forming a system. This system in turn consists of four elements: matter, tool or the "means of work", including the human body itself; gestures and movements organized in operational sequences, and finally, knowledge either conscious or unconscious (Lemonnier 1989: 156).

The social anthropological approach to techniques and technology has a special role in pottery studies. It emphasizes techniques as behaviour acquired through social dimensions, and not merely on the basis of material constraints (van der Leeuw 1993: 240). Techniques

> can not be studied in static terms, but should be seen as the locus of transformations in a dynamic relationship between ... the forces and social relations of production and collective representations and... the laws of matter and energy which form the background for social behaviour (van der Leeuw 1993: 240).

Coming from this perspective, a potter is seen as mediating between the matter and cultural constraints through his/her knowledge and approach. These is reflected in the choices the potter makes about the use of the environment and raw materials, the choice of tools, and finally on the basis of his or her technical capabilities (Pritchard and van der Leeuw 1984; van der Leeuw 1993: 241).

These two theoretical approaches to technology differ on the following points:

1- The relationship between culture and society: In the anthropological discourse, cultural materialists stress the conception of technology as a natural force, and place its locus in the environment. Social anthropologists maintained that technology is a cultural construct, and place its locus within the social dimensions.

2- Material versus cultural constraints: Technology is an adaptive subsystem and its components reflect certain physical constraints. For the social anthropologists, technology is shaped not only by material constraints but by cultural ones as well.

3- Technology and social organization: The ecological approach to technology holds that technology affects social organization. The anthropology of technology emphasizes the fact that there is no distinction between technical and social phenomena.

3

These two theoretical approaches on technology and society evaluate not only the approach to pottery studies but also the analytical methods and tools involved. The latter statement stems from the point of emphasis on each approach and the elements of its explanatory tools (see below section 2 and 3). In the next two sections, the focus will be drawn on the methods and techniques that use in pottery technological reconstruction, and the ones used in measuring pottery variation. The latter will be evaluated based on the dichotomy of style and technique.

III.2 Reconstruction of the operational sequence of pottery manufacture

Archaeological pottery studies may be categorized as belonging to two kinds: one focuses on the decorative and morphological characteristics of pottery, while the second emphasizes the technological dimension. Each can be adopted to solve a given research problem. The one emphasizing the technological dimension can be adopted to define the operational sequences – *chaînes opératoires* – undertaken in pottery manufacture – that is, to define the series of operations that are performed to transform raw material into finished products (Creswell 1996; van der Leeuw 1993). Analysed are: the physical characteristics of the raw materials, the various methods and techniques of pottery-shaping, of firing, and of decoration. These multi-variable analytical aspects reflect the technological difficulties in reconstructing the stages of pottery-making. Hence, technological studies of archaeological pottery generally emphasize one aspect over others depending on the particular research question. The concern here is on defining the operational sequences involved in transforming the clay body into a final product.

Reconstructing the methods and techniques of pot-shaping is a complex and interlinked task. Its difficulty lies in the nature of the forming process, whereby later actions taken by the potter wiped out those previously taken. The action of finishing, for example, constitutes the final stage of forming and usually erases the previous stages. Reconstruction of the different stages of pottery-shaping has generally been approached through the direct observation of macro-traces preserved on the pots' faces (Franken and Kalsbeek 1983; Shepard 1965). Such studies have been criticized inasmuch as they don't reveal detailed information about the different stages of the forming process (Courty and Roux 1995; Gelbert 1994; van der Leeuw 1977). Other methods of pottery-forming analysis involve the microscopic observation of clay, or the orientation of temper particles (Shepard 1965). The focus on non-plastic orientations as an indication of forming-technique has been taken further by the application of radiographic methods. These methods define the orientation of both temper and voids in the pottery ware, which can be correlated with pressure techniques applied to the clay

during forming (Carr 1990; Rye 1977, 1981; Vandiver 1986, 1987). Such methods reveal information about the segments used in the forming of a pot, and the joining methods used between segments (Vandiver 1987).

However, reconstruction of the different stages involved in archaeological pottery forming should be correlated with a source of reference (Rye 1981). The reference source is necessary for determining the kind of behaviour that produced the static traces observed in the archaeological sherds. Usually, in pottery studies, this reference source can be established through either experimental studies (Franken and Kalsbeek 1983; Vitelli 1984) ethnoarchaeology / ethnographic studies, or semi-experimental studies (Courty and Roux 1995, 1998; Roux 1994). Pottery ethnoarchaeology is particularly important when conducted in the same region as where the archaeological site being excavated. It involves, as do the semi-experimental studies, the fine observation of the different stages involved in pot-forming, and the kind of traces associated with them. Moreover, ethnoarchaeological studies are significant when conducted at the regional scale where variability in the different stages of forming can be defined.

The other stage that correlates with pottery-forming is surface treatment. This refers either to the finishing of pot surface – through smoothing or polishing – or the application of decoration-painting and incisions. The purpose of ethnoarchaeological or experimental studies is to define the variety of surface finishing methods and techniques, and/or decoration techniques (Gelbert 2000).

The final stage of pottery production is firing. This includes the determination of firing technique and an analytical measuring of temperature (Matson 1939; Shepard 1965; Rice 1987). In addition to determining the firing temperature, new approaches have been developed by which the kind of fuel and the firing temperature may be correlated.

Reconstruction of the different operation sequences – *chaînes opératoires* – of archaeological pottery manufacture is, then, the first and primary step before any further explanation can be attempted. This strategy allows for a fine analysis of the technological variation within a given potters community.

III.3 Measuring pottery variation: style vs. technology

Recently, the social dimension of material culture has been re-emphasized by evaluating the significance of the concept of style. It has been previously argued that material culture attributes can be addressed under three dimensions: function, style and technology. Technology has been considered more under raw material characteristics and production steps, a technology that more adheres to environmental conditions. Style as social information carriers has been assumed to reside in object's formal or decorative attributes (Binford 1965; Dunnell 1980). However, the concept of "style" has been the subject of intensive discourse with respect to its definition, locus and function (Carr and Neitzel 1995; Conkey and Hastorf 1990; David and Kramer 2000: 168-224; Hegmon 1992, 1998).

Style is simply defined as "a way of doing / making" (Hodder 1990; Sackett 1990; Wiessner 1990). Style, then, is defined as a kind of behaviour, but there is disagreement about the dualistic nature of behaviour, and where behaviour resides in material culture. Two kinds of behaviour have been postulated. The first reflects what people do of their own free will and the second what people do because they have to (Bettinger, Boyd and Richerson 1996: 133).

Within anthropology and archaeology, from a materialistic point-of-view, style is considered a component of material culture, but one that has a non-utilitarian function (Arnold 1985; Binford 1965; Dunnell 1978; Wiessner 1983: 256, 1990: 108; Wobst 1977). Style has been correlated with artefacts' formal attributes, such as decorative elements or design. These attributes shed light on both the spatio-temporal dimension and the social context in terms of learning and social interaction (Arnold 1985; Binford 1965: 209; Dunnell 1978). Nonetheless, a contradiction remains between technology and style – the latter is seen as independent of the former (Dunnell 1978). The assigning style to such a passive role has since changed, and functions ascribed to it have been extended. Wobst (1977) expanded the concept of style and its functioning in the cultural system. He argued that attributes of material culture may function in a social context as a means of information exchange / communication (Wobst 1977:321).

The work of Wobst (1977) helped furnish and extend the discourse concerning the social aspects of style and material culture variation (Hodder 1982; Sackett 1982; Wiessner 1990). Style as a concept has been expanded to include not only its relevancy to social communication between social groups but also within a single social group. Artefact's formal attributes can yield information on the social groups and the boundaries between them (*emblemic* style, or on the individual identities and their expression, *assertive* style (Wiessner 1983, 1990).

The emphasis on the formal attributes of artefacts as reflecting social or ideological behaviour ignores the importance of production systems in explaining artefact variation (Lechtmann and Merrill 1977; Conkey 1990; Davis 1990; Lemonnier 1986, 1993; Sackett 1990). Several researches showed the significance of technique as a socially informative system, underpinning the set of choices that artisan undertook in producing the artefacts,

and not to see them as reflecting an environmental pressure. These choices assumed to lead to the same end in making an artefact that will have the same use. This approach is known as the *isochrestic* approach to style (which means equivalent in use) (Sackett 1990). The concept of isochrestic variation has been expanded to include both the cultural choices embedded in artefact production as well as decorative choices (Lemonnier 1986, 1993). It emphasizes the importance of the choices within which artisans operated and the operational sequence of artefact production. The social role of style extended then to include technology and not only the formal characteristics of artefacts, (Gosselain 1998, 2000; Hegmon 1998; Stark 1998), especially those steps undertaken in the operational sequence of pot forming and having stable characteristics.

The discourse on the social and cultural dimensions of artefact variation (style versus technology) expanded the kind of inferences that can be approached by studying pottery. The use of style to refer to manufacture technique and its execution would increase the social information that can be inferred from prehistoric pottery studies. This is for two reasons: a) the larger part of prehistoric pottery is sherds – this sets limitations as far as conducting comprehensive study of decorative attributes; and b) the prehistoric archaeological record is more dominated by plain wares rather than decorative ones. Therefore, a focus on decorative attributes limits the range of cultural information that can be inferred from the pottery. In this context, technological style provides not only technological information but also sheds light on the social dimensions of pottery manufacture, such as the learning environment, skill, and socio-economical factors. A focus on technological rather than decorative style helps us better understand how technological information is manipulated by a society to fulfil their needs through the manufacture of different pottery forms. Variation within a given technological style, moreover, may be correlated with socio-cultural variations.

III.4 Explaining pottery technological change

A concern with change, as a phenomenon, is the *raison d'être* of both anthropological and archaeological researches. This phenomenon has been addressed from different theoretical point stands. From the ones that just focus on simple classification procedures to define what has been changed to others which tackle the different mechanisms and processes that could cause change. The proposed theoretical models, however, that deal with the phenomenon of change focus mostly on explaining the relation between technology and society. The locus of change has been addressed under the directional relation of technology to society or the multi-mutual relations between them. Most commonly, in the anthropological and archaeological discourse, is the application of the social anthropological paradigms and the evolutionary approaches to study change.

III.4.1 The evolutionary approaches to change

Under the evolutionary paradigms to change, two theoretical stands should be at the outset of this discussion distinguished. These are the cultural evolutionary theory to change and the biological Darwinian theory.

The cultural evolution approach regards changes in culture as the product of adaptations, mainly to the natural environment. The main components of this approach to study change stemmed from the work of White (1949, 1959) and Steward's culture ecological approach (1955). Despite the fact that these two theoretical stands emphasized different cultural scale, they have in common the emphasis on adaptation to external factor as a cause of change. Both approaches view change as a transformational process – that is, change is seen as the functional transformation of interdependent systems as an adaptation mechanism. The main mechanism of adaptation has been identified with the technological factor. This implies that cultural change can be measured by the increase in technological efficiency (White 1959: 42). Hence, technology becomes a primacy means for both measuring the degree of cultural adaptation and cultural progress. As this approach changes the emphasis on transformation of the system components, the task has been furthered to define the extent to which the change in technological realm can affect changes in other components of the system such as the social and ideological ones. This process of defining the technological change is important to understand the changes in other parts of the systems.

On the archaeological explanatory level, culture ecology has been adopted to explain cultural change (Binford 1962). Changes in the cultural system were regarded as adaptive responses to different environmental conditions. Furthermore, archaeologists adopted the general system theory to give structural and quantitative rigor to explanations of change. The aim of this combination is to identify the direction and strength of positive and negative feedback connections between the components of cultural systems (Flannery 1967; Watson *et al.* 1971: 61-87). These feedbacks have been identified with energy, information and goods, whereas energy has been given a central role.

Interestingly, the cultural evolutionary approach has been employed to study the technological changes in material cultures esp. the pottery (Arnold 1985, 1993; Rice 1981; van der Leeuw 1977). Clearest is the study of Rice (1981) to the evolution of pottery production systems. The attempt has been made to evaluate the interrelationship between techno-economical and social change and com-

plexity. This trial model of pottery evolution has shown the interrelatedness of social and economical changes with the scale of pottery production: from the one that was household-based on one that was centralized (Rice 1981: 223).

The second main trend in studying cultural evolution stemmed from the Darwinian biological theory (Dunnell 1980, 1989). This approach can be described as homologous to culture and evolution. It emphasized on developing a theory of cultural evolution that confirms Darwinian principles. Central to this approach is the emphasis on natural selection as mechanism of cultural change. Contrary to the cultural evolutionary paradigms, selection, as cause of change, has not a progressive character. Selection, which functions on empirical variability, can result in a change either toward complexity or not, that is de-evolution. Furthermore, change has not been seen as transformational of the system's components, but as adaptive and opportunistic one (Dunnell 1980).

As the main focus of evolutionary approach on variability, the attempt has been made to identify the mechanisms of variability transmission. This emphasis gives the Darwinian approach to change its historical depth. Learning, as an inheritable mechanism, transmitted behaviour. This mechanism causes variation in the frequency of transmitted traits. Selection, then, will operate on the *fittest* human behaviour.

The application of this approach will be found more in studying pottery technological change. It stresses on the identification of those traits that can be regarded as functional, and the ones that stylistic, i.e. neutral. In studying pottery technological change two scales have been investigated. These are the technological historical scale and performance scale. Selection occurres on the pottery performance characteristics such as temper. The change of given performance characteristics is driven by selective environment which causes change in the maker's and user's behaviours (O'Brien *et al.* 1994: 261).

Several studies have applied the biological approach to study pottery technological change (Braun 1987; O'Brien 1996; Neff *et al.* 1997). For example, Braun (1987) attempted to study the causes of changes in cooking pot temper size and type. As the causes of such changes ought to be found external to the studied phenomenon, he explained such changes as a subsistence driven selection that enhances better firing effects and cooking durability.

These two approaches to cultural change have been rigorously criticized. Several scholars are in favour of socially, contextually, and historically oriented approaches to study the relation between society and technological change.

6

III.4.2 Social anthropology to change

The cultural evolutionary approaches to change and how they have been applied to study technology have longer historical traditions compared with the socially or culturally directed approaches. However, to present a unified theoretical theory of change which can be assigned to these later approaches is a difficult task. This is due mostly to the fact that these approaches have been developed in isolation from each other. These include, among others, the post-processual, postmodern, Marxist and Neo-Marxist approaches (Loney 2000: 651). However, these approaches have in common several elements concerning change: all are contextually and historically oriented in terms of research; all avoid general model building around the issue of technological change; all reject the concept of progress (the key concept in evolutionary studies, denoting change as indicative of an increase in efficiency); and all re-evaluate the relationships between technological change and cultural complexity.

It has been assumed that pottery production and change cannot be understood without taking into account the contextual and historical events that influence production. In this sense, less emphasis is placed on ecological factors as a determinant of change. Instead, cultural factors, especially social ones, are proposed as influencing pottery production (Annis 1984). The idea that technological change automatically corresponds with increased production efficiency is considered as one sided. Change must also take into account choices that are open to potters in terms of effectiveness and life expectancy (van der Leeuw 1993: 241).

The contextual study of pottery production has also revealed the nature of the relationship between technology and cultural change and complexity. It has been shown that cultural change, such as that related to socio-political complexity, does not always correlate with technological complexity (Loney 2000: 652). Pottery manufacture techniques tend toward stasis in spite of changes in the social and political realms. As Loney argues, such cultural changes do not affect the scale of production; e.g., the change from household to workshop production (Loney 1995: 75-77, 243-249, cited in Loney 2000: 652-3).

The above presentation of different theoretical driven perspectives on change would raise a major question: could we treat these approaches as complementary or separately ones? We would see in these approaches complementary strategies to understand and explain the causes of general human behavioral patterns and extending these to explain the heterogeneity of these behaviors in a given context.

IV. Methodological consideration

IV.1 Ethnoarchaeology

The use of ethnographic data to better understand the nature of the archaeological record does not represent a new trend in the history of archaeology. The data was used to find a kind of confirmation on the basis of the practice of contemporary traditional societies observed archaeological phenomena. The adoption of ethnoarchaeology as research strategy took place in the middle of last century (Kleindienst and Watson 1956; Thompson 1958), though only becoming well-formulated in 1960s and 1970s (Ascher 1962; Gould 1968; Binford 1978; Kramer 1979; Watson 1979; Yellen 1977). More recent studies have seen this strategy more from unstructured ethnographic analogies to a more systemized examination of causal relationships between human behaviour and material culture.

The general goal of ethnoarchaeology is to establish hypothetical models that will aid in explaining archaeological phenomena. The significance of such ethnoarchaeologically-derived models is that they expand the degree of inferences that can be made about human behaviours; they also provide the archaeologist a means for evaluating his or her methods of investigation (Binford 1978; Kramer 1979; Watson 1979; Watson and Gould 1982). This area of "archaeological thought" is devoted to hypothesis-testing and the building inferences about past human behaviour. Whatever the model postulated, the main issue is the way it is used for archaeological interpretations. Analogy and correlation, for example, are two such means of interpretation. This entails recognizing similarities between present phenomenon and that represented in the archaeological record. More specifically, similarities must be measured if patterns between them are to be recognized. Finally the nature of the relationship between the two must be inferred (Dark 1996: 60; Gamble 2001: 84). Several types of analogies have been designated for such purpose, though only two are generally used. The first is termed "direct historical analogy" (Steward 1955; Ascher 1961), and refers to the use of ethnographic or ethnoarchaeological analogical reasoning where a continuity from the prehistoric to the historic period is evident. This kind of analogy is considered useful for archaeological purposes where cultural continuity is exceptionally marked, such as in the Near East (Hole 1979; Watson 1979). The second type of analogy is termed "new analogy" (Kramer 1979) or "general comparative analogy" (Ascher 1968), and involves the use of ethnographic analogies derived from different geographic regions as the archaeological data (Kramer 1979: 2).

The use of analogy for archaeological interpretation has generated disagreement among archaeologists (Binford 1967, 1978; Hodder 1982; Wobst 1978; Wylie 1985,

1988). Some maintain that analogy can be used in cases in which there are similarities in environmental (Ascher 1961), or economic conditions. Others see analogy, not as means of explanation, but as providing a clue in thinking about the past (Binford 1968, 1978; Childe 1956). The latter view is justified on the basis of not limiting our knowledge to what we know of the present – the past has features not represented in the present. To overcome this potential problem, a middle-range theory has been developed (Binford 1978, 1983). The related methodology does not consider ethnographic data irrelevant, but seeks a logic bridging the static nature of the archaeological record (material data) and the dynamic of past human behaviour (i.e., interpretation) (Dark 1996: 40). It seeks to enable an understanding of how a particular pattern in the archaeological record is created (Binford 1978, 1983; Trigger 1989: 389). Moreover, it does not seek to define the past strictly on the basis of the ethnoarchaeological / anthropological data. Instead, data is manipulated to build models of behaviour-material cultural interactions and identify the principles that condition these interactions (Deal 1998). Hence, the emphasis is not on formal similarities but on analogies of process that define types of inter-relationships between the entities being compared (Arnold 1993).

IV.2 Bridging pottery ethnoarchaeology and archaeology: a dynamic approach of pottery manufacture

Several ethnoarchaeological studies have revealed certain dynamic interrelationships related to pottery production (Arnold 1985; Arnold 2000; Costin 2000; Kramer 1985, 1997). These related to their manufacture, distribution, use, and change. Others studies focus on the learning environment of pottery craft (Hayden and Cannon 1984), and the identification of pottery production locations (Deal 1988, 1998; Stark 1985). The significance of ethnoarchaeological studies has been expanded to include new approaches to the study of ceramics (van der Leeuw 1991, 1993); likewise, the evaluation of pottery analytical techniques with respect to cultural transmission (Arnold *et al*. 1991; Arnold 2000). These studies have aided in modelling approaches to archaeological studies – for instance, in defining the techno-economical context of pottery production (Rice 1981; Arnold 1985) or in the examination of the cognitive structure of pottery activity (van der Leeuw 1993; Wright 1993).

A systemic and dynamic approach to the study of pottery production has been developed from a culture ecological perspective (Arnold 1985, 1993; Kolb 1989; Kolb and Lackey 1988; Matson 1965). This known as the "ceramic ecology" approach (Matson 1965) which was later refined and combined with the system theory approach (Arnold 1985, 1993). This theoretical combination allows for a coherent study of pottery production. It focuses on the relationship of ceramics with the environment on the one hand, and with cultural subsystems on the other. It defines the technological strategy and its associated behavioural pattern employed in exploiting the environment as the basis for an understanding of the conditions of production.

This approach to ceramic studies also emphasizes the systemic interrelationships between ceramics as a component of a techno-economical subsystem and other cultural subsystems, such as social and ideological ones. In this way, as part of techno-economical subsystem, ceramic production is adapted to and modified by the environment to meet the society's cultural needs. The place of ceramics within the techno-economical subsystem facilitates the study of its relation to the remaining part of the subsystem on the one hand, and to ideological and social structural subsystems, on the other (Arnold 1985: 16, 1993).

The ceramic ecological approach to the study of pottery allows for a dynamic understanding of pottery production through a focus on potters as units of analysis (Arnold 1993). Defining potters as such is significant as it allows for an analysis of the technological information or knowledge that potters usually share. They are also the units through which technological strategies of production can be explained in terms of the exploitation of raw materials, preparation, manufacture, use and finally, discard. Moreover, they are the units through which are transferred the social and other cultural manifestations in pots.

In this study, this particular unit of analysis is broadened to include decision-making, as reflected in the operational sequence – *chaîne opératoire* – and whereby potters function as carriers of technological knowledge. This step of the investigation will help to define the extent of the information pool possessed by potters and shared through social interaction and learning.

This ecological, systemic approach to ceramics also helps us to better understand ceramic change. As a component of a techno-economical subsystem, one in which potters are defined as constituting units of analysis, this approach helps us to understand how potters adapt to new techno-economical conditions, as well as how such adaptation is reflected in this subsystem's relationship to other cultural subsystems.

IV.3 Classification and sampling procedures

One of the characteristics of archaeological pottery is its large quantity and tendency toward heterogeneity. These raise the methodological problem of defining the starting point of one's analysis of a given assemblage. The direct relationship between research aims and classification or sorting procedures needs first to be identified (Rye 1981; Rice 1987; Neff 1993). Since the concern here is on pottery variability and variation with respect to technical operations (mainly shaping techniques), the sorting or grouping process should reflect how operation processes are expressed in ceramic.

However, the classifying procedure followed in both ethnoarchaeology and archaeological studies focuses on maximized intra-group similarities and inter-group difference with respect to shaping techniques (Dunnell 1986: 151-152, cited in Neff 1993: 29). The intuitive-grouping procedure (Neff 1993) is adopted to signify a stratifying heterogeneity, with respect to operation sequence of pottery shaping; it is generated by the technological knowledge *shared* by potters on the one hand, and behavioural variation between potters on the other.

The archaeological pottery assemblage will sustain the above groupings if it is defined in a spatio-temporal framework. Thus, each pottery assemblage is spatially and temporally defined. Sorting procedures take into account two main variables: the operation sequence of shaping and the pot-form. Therefore, one technological group is not constrained by pot form, but rather by the operation sequences employed in their shaping. Based on this, a collection of 800 sherds were sampled from the archaeological site of Abu Hamid. These included bases, body sherds and rims.

IV.4 Methods of investigation

There should be a convergence between the stated archaeological problem or aim and the method and technique chosen for pottery analysis (Rice 1987). The preliminary aim of this study is to define the actions taken by the potter in transforming the clay body into finished product. Two methods of investigation have been employed to achieve this aim. These are: by visual examination – that is, identifying the macro-features of pottery sherds – and the use of X-radiography.

IV.4.1 Surface-features examination

This is one of the means by which archaeologists are able to define pottery forming operations and techniques (Rye 1981; Franken 1974; Shepard 1965: 53-7; Vandiver 1986, 1987). This form of analysis can be achieved with little or no specialized tools or techniques (Rye 1981). It entails identifying surface features (such as drag marks, the direction and type of striation, and smoothing techniques) and fracture patterns as evidence of forming operations. The main tool of investigation is the hand lens.

Individual notes were taken and measurements (thickness, diameter) made on the 800 sherds. The examination aimed at isolating those surface features and joining patterns which, if found to be repetitive, can lead to a reconstruction of the pattern of manufacture of the pot.

IV.4.2 X-radiographic analysis

A sample of 43 pottery sherds was chosen and subjected to radiographic analysis at Konstanz hospital. This technique, when applied in ceramics studies, can provide data on forming techniques (Carr 1990, 1993; Braun 1982; Loney 1995; Rye 1977, 1981; Vandiver 1987). It is an extremely effective way of producing an image of the internal features of an object. These features are differentiated on the basis of their composition, gravity, and thickness, features defined by their capacity to transmit X-rays. When applied to ceramics, the internal features of a radiographed part, such as temper particles, voids, voids between modelled segments (coils or slabs), and fracture systems, can be observed (Carr 1993: 14).

IV.5 Presentation of the study

This study is divided into two main parts. Part one presents the ethnoarchaeological study that has been conducted on pottery production in northern Jordan. It includes the location and environmental setting of the study area (Chapter 1), the context of pottery production with reference to potters' socio-economical contexts, and their identity. It also includes the context of pottery production and a description of the technological traditions that have been identified among the potters. Two chapters (4 and 5) have been devoted to measuring and explaining the causes of technological similarities as well as differences in the potters' out-put.

Part 2 presents the archaeological study. It includes a description of the site of Abu Hamid and its environmental setting. Moreover, it presents the chronology and the sequence of occupation at the site, as well as the spatial and temporal contexts of the sampled pottery sherds. Further, it presents morphological and metric descriptions of the pottery assemblages. Two chapters (8 and 9) are devoted to the identification of archaeological pottery forming techniques and the measuring of the technical variations among them. The last chapter presents the explanations of these technical variations.

PART I:

FROM DYNAMIC TO STATIC CONTEXT OF POTTERY PRODUCTION IN NORTHERN JORDAN.

AN ETHNOARCHAEOLOGICAL STUDY

Chapter One: **The social and economical context of potters' population in northern Jordan**

Before addressing an analytical description of the ethnoarchaeological pottery production in Jordan, the environmental setting under which the potters in the region operate, their social and economical organizations, and finally their identification in terms of age, gender and the learning environment of pottery activity, will be presented.

I. Environmental setting of the study area

I.1 Location of the study area

The present ethnoarchaeological field study in Jordan (29° 30 and 32° 31 N) has been carried out in the northern part of the country. This area is limited to the south by az-Zarqa river, to the north by the Yarmouk river, whereas to the west it is adjunct by the Jordan valley and to the east by the plateau and the steppe (**Map 1**). It is usually referred to as the Ajlun Mountain. This area falls sharply approaching the Jordan valley and slopes gently to the east. The elevation varies between 1200 and 1500 m. These north-south chains are cut by three major wadis

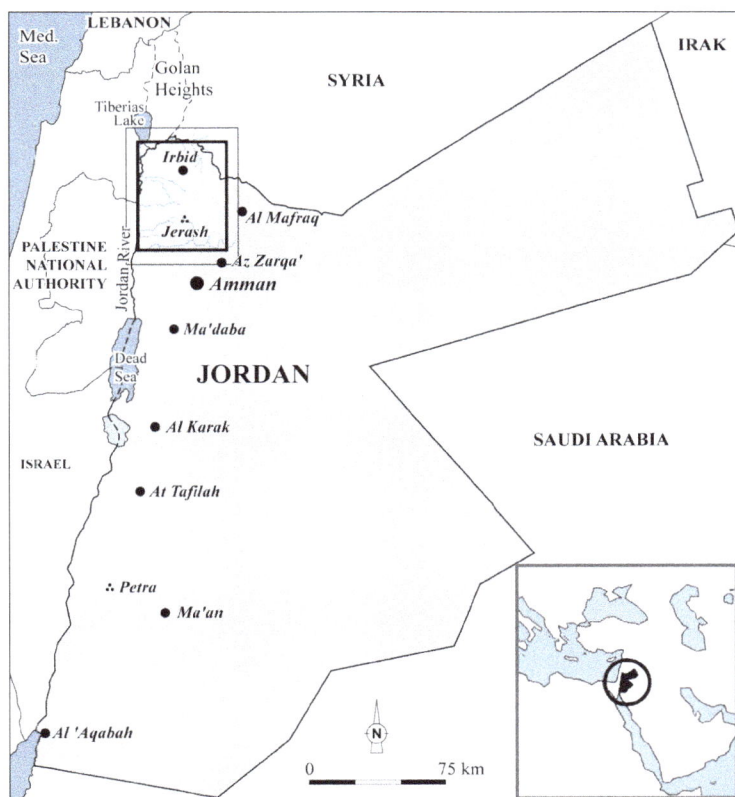

Map 1: The location of ethno-archaeological study area

running east-west – wadi Rajib, wadi Kufranjeh and wadi el-Yabis; reaching their lowest elevation in the Jordan Valley, ca. 242 m below sea level (**Map 2**, see III.1). These wadis provide water resources for the area.

I.2 Geological setting

Geologically speaking, the region covered in this study belongs to what is termed the Ajlun Group. It is characterized by calcareous strata deposited in a neritic environment. It has marl-limestone deposits in the lower beds and hard crystalline limestone in the upper beds (Bender 1974). The latter is of a marine origin and is composed of chalky formations intersected by cherty limestone and phosphate beds (Beaumont 1985: 291). The marl limestone deposits are an important source of clay, and dominant types in the Ajlun area. Marl in its natural state is mixed with varied amounts of calcite. Generally, the closer one gets to the surface, the more abundant the calcite.

Several faults are observed in the region, especially along slopes. The eroded sections at these faults show the uppermost organization of the geological strata. Top down, they consist of a *terra rossa* layer, hard limestone deposits and marl-limestone.

I.3 The present climatic conditions

There is a strong relation between the topography and climate elements, such as temperature and rainfall. The Ajlun Mountain is located in a transitional climate zone, between the Mediterranean climate zone to the west and the arid ones to the east and south (Shehadeh 1985: 25). It is characterized by sub-humid Mediterranean bio-climate, which means rainy winters and mild summers (Shehadeh 1985: 34; Ahmed 1989).

The Ajlun region receives the highest amount of rainfall in the country ranging between 400-600 mm (Al-Eisawi 1985: 45). The rainy season begins in October-November and reaches its climax in January. The amount of rainfall begins to decrease in March, and stops in May. Almost 95% of the region's rainfall occurs from November to March, with a concentration of 70% during December, January and February. The number of days during which it rains ranges between 30 to 50 days per year, with an average daily rainfall of between 10 mm to

100mm (Beaumont 1985: 93). During January and February, precipitation may take the form of heavy snow.

From the end of September, the cloud's cover increases, reaching its climax in January and February. Moreover, the relative humidity also increases from October through May. The mean minimum temperature recorded in winter, during January the coldest month, ranges between 2 to 5°C.

The summer season is characterized by warm and sunny days. The average temperature, during August, the hottest month, is 27°C. The temperature, however, differs in the valley such as el-Yabis where it reaches 37,9°C in August. During summer, there is a variation in temperature based on the amount of rainfall. When the latter increases the mean temperature will decrease and *vice versa* (Al-Eisawi 1985: 50).

I.4 The vegetation cover

The Ajlun highland belongs to the so-called Mediterranean vegetation zone dependant to a large extent of the climates, and soil types. Red Mediterranean soil is dominant in the Ajlun highland. This soil is suitable for the cultivation of various crops and forests (Ahmad 1989).

Most of the highland is covered by extensive forest of different species of trees. These include pine, herbaceous, evergreen oak, and deciduous oak. The most dominant type is the pine (Al-Eisawi 1985: 51-52).

Besides the wild vegetation cover, the mountainous areas are suitable for the cultivation of domestic crops: cereals, grapes, olives, kernel- and stone-fruits. Significant in this respect is the land along the wadis that intersected the mountain chains. Several orchards are distributed along these wadis which are cultivated with different summer crops such as figs, apples, vines, and pomegranates.

In Ajlun Mountain deforestation is the main process affecting vegetation cover. Several areas have been completely cleared for agricultural purposes. These have been mainly cultivated with wheat, barely, and olive trees. Beside that, herding activities in fact constitute another main factor that affects the vegetation cover in the region (Beaumont 1985: 294).

II. The socio-economical contexts of the potter population

In this part, we will address two interrelated cultural issues with respect to pottery production: these are the characteristics of the social organization of potters, and the types and kinds of economic practices that are conducted by them.

II.1 The social organization of the potters in Ajlun region

The settlements in the Ajlun region are mountainous villages. The social structure of most of them has been greatly influenced by various historical factors. During the eighteenth and nineteenth centuries, several families re-settled in this region. They came from nearby countries: Egypt, Palestine and southern Syria. The Ajlun region has been chosen because geographically it is an isolated region and a secure place to live in for families or individuals who escape from social feuds, over-taxations of the Ottoman government, or attacks of the nomads (Lewis 1989; Mershen 1992: 409). In the study area, among the potters such a re-settling pattern has been observed among three potter's families living in two villages, Arjan and Ammyria. In the latter, the potter's family claimed descendent from Egypt, whereas in the case of the Arjan potters, one family claimed its descent from Palestine (Potter 3) and the other from southern Syria (Hawran) (Potter 1).

Apart from the above historical circumstances, these mountainous villages are socially organized around clans. Each clan in turn is composed of lineages that share the same ancestor. Families are patrilineal. Correspondingly, the residence pattern is patrilocal, and women are required to move and settle in the husband's house or village.

The smaller social unit is the household either of nuclear or extended families. The latter family type is the most frequent. It consists of the father, mother, their unmarried sons and daughters and their married sons. There is a correlation between the extended family type and the changes that can occur in the spatial organization of the household that take place to cope with an increase in the number of family members of the married sons. When it is the case, new rooms are built either off the main house or as a second floor.

Endogamy is most common. It takes place either between members of the same lineage or between lineages of the same clan. The former tends to be more prevalent and often involves marriage between cousins. Endogamy has been found among all potters communities in Ajlun area with one exception. Only at Kufranjeh a potter (2) claimed to originate from another village. Nonetheless, exogamy exists but to a lesser extent.

II.2 The economical context of potter population

Generally speaking, the mountainous villagers in the Ajlun area have an agro-pastoral economy. For their households income, the inhabitants of these villages depend largely on cultivation of several crops (either winter or summer crops), and on raising animals: goats, sheep, and to lesser extent cows. Based on the spatial distribution of the ecological zones in the Ajlun area, this agro-pastoral economy can be well evaluated and studied. It is possible to get an idea of the way each village divides its surrounding environmental space and related exploitation patterns according to the mountain chains and the valleys that cut them. These two ecological zones enhance different exploitation patterns.

The historical record for land registration during the nineteenth century in the Ajlun district explains the structure of space in each village on the basis of ecological variation (Roger 1999; Mundy 1994). Each village is divided into: a) space where houses are constructed, b) shareholding land which surrounds the village, c) land used for olive tree cultivation, and d) small plots such as gardens, vineyards as well as grain field (Mundy 1994: 70). Small plots refer mostly to the land located along the valleys. This land organization pattern reveals an important economical practice given to olive tree cultivation that, until now, plays a major role in the income of the household. In the early twentieth century, it was a source of conflict between the villages (Hütteroth and Abdulfattah 1977).

The higher areas are cultivated with cereals and olives, whereas the lower zone is used for mixed cultivation of summer crops, orchard products that include figs, vines, pomegranates, chickpeas, okra and other stone-fruits. These crops depend on irrigation, the source of which is derived from the nearby valleys.

Beside these general practices, a close look at the individual household unit reveals different economical cycles. This will be addressed here only to the potter's households. The gathered information in Ajlun area shows that not all of the potter's household share the same activities in the same way or to the same degree.

1- Agricultural activities
Agricultural practices play a vital role in the household income especially for the ones who own a plot of land. Three potters (Arjan: potter 1; Kufranjeh: Potter 1; and Anjarah: Potter 1) claim to own their lands. These households practice winter as well as summer cultivation. Crops include wheat, barley and other supplementary products such as okra and chickpeas. Also these households practice gardening on land-plots within the house structure where are cultivated mainly fig trees as well as summer crops.

2- Animal husbandry
The second main capital among the agro-pastoral communities is domesticated animals: goats, sheep, cows, and to a lesser extent, chickens. The potters' households are differentiated one from the other on the basis of the kind of the animal they have. Sheep and goats are kept by five potters' households, two in the village of Ammyria (Potter 1 and 2), two at Bilas and one at Anjarah. Others, keep cows instead of goats and sheep such as potter 1 at Arjan.

For some households animal husbandry forms a primary source of capital. They depend on selling secondary products to support the household income. These products, such as milk, are sold to the shops in the villages. In some cases, sheep and goats are themselves sold either in the villages, or in the near-by town, during the time of Islamic feasts.

3- Coal-making activity
The cycle of economic activities of few potters' households includes the production of coal. This activity involves cutting pine trees, which are then subjected to a process of atmosphere reduction to produce the coal. The time-schedule of this activity is between March and April. It usually takes place outside the village area in the upper attitude zone. Coal production has been attested only by two potters' household at the village of Arjan (Potter 1 and 2). The sale of the end-product constitutes another source of income, especially for landless household units.

4- Orchard-leasing
The land along the valleys in the Ajlun region is a vital area for agricultural production. Orchards, cultivated mainly with summer crops for commercial benefits, are distributed along these valleys. Families, who own such orchards and have no the time to take care of them, attempt to lease them. One potter's household in Arjan (Potter 2) uses to lease orchards along Wadi el-Yabis from June to September. This practice, however, requires that the household unit settle temporally in the vicinity of the orchard. The cultivated products are either sold directly to consumers who come to the orchard or through middlemen.

5- Wag-labour
The economical cycle of potter's household includes also the practice of wag-labour. Activities such as olive collecting, plough and harvesting can be considered the most practiced wag-labours. The olive-collecting season starts in October / November and lasts for almost a month. This activity is labour intensive, and is undertaken either in the vicinity of the village, or when required, entails moving to a nearby camping site. Household units who do not own a land depend largely on this activity to supplement their economic income (Arjan: Potter 1; Amyria: Potter 1). The economical return of these wag-labours can be either in a form of a payment or a payment kind.

Based on oral information, plough and harvesting are another source of income. These usually include preparing the land for cultivation and harvesting. Both activities involve a seasonal settling in the working area.

In addition to the above economical practices, governmental jobs can be another source of income. All these economic activities carried out by each household reflect a remarkable variation.

II.3 The schedule of pottery activity

Several ethnoarchaeological studies on pottery production emphasize on the correlation between environmental factors, scales of production and subsistence strategies (Arnold 1985, 1993; Deal 1998; Kolb 1989). These studies show the extent to which environmental conditions, such as weather and climate, and the practice of different subsistence strategies can reduce the scale of pottery production to a part-time activity.

In Ajlun region, pottery making is a seasonal activity. It is practiced between June and September. Due to climatic and weather conditions, the craft is a part-time rather than a full-time activity. The climatic conditions in Ajlun region are characterized by a harsh winter with heavy rainfall and occasional snow. The temperature decreases sharply and the humidity increases. These factors have a direct effect on different pottery segmental activities. Rainy days hinder the collecting of clay as it becomes more difficult to unearth deposits. Likewise, such climatic conditions have a negative effect on clay preparation. Usually, clay should be left to dry before grinding; this requires sunny, dry days. Such constraints are evident in pot forming. Pots are formed using coiling techniques which require a sufficient drying interval between and during each phase of pot forming. Low temperature and high humidity will hinder the forming process and may cause the collapse and/or cracking of the pot because of the moisture that remains in the clay for a longer time than necessary.

These circumstances influence also the working location of pottery-making which takes place outside the living area (Ali 2005). It may be undertaken in courtyard, in a garden or in the seasonal camps (orchards). Rainy days, therefore, are not consistence with pottery making. Moreover, there is a limited living-space and this hinders people from making pottery inside the house or even from using it to store the unfired pots.

Another major constraint with respect to pottery making has to do with firing and where it is located. Pottery is fired in pits which are usually dug near the house. Potters, however, avoid firing pots in moist pits as animal dung – the main fuel – absorbs humidity from earth, thus causing the pots to crack as a result of absorbing part of this humidity.

Technological innovations related to problems of space-availability and artificial drying facilities can overcome the problem of seasonal constraints. Only one ex- potter,

in Arjan, described the circumstances under which pottery-making might be produced off-season. A motivation for such a development would be the increasing demand for pots. To meet this end, pottery-making can be conducted in a roofed area – the basement of a house for example – which can also function as a storage space. This would also ensure the availability of enough space for pot forming. Pots can be stored unfired, the potter waiting until the beginning of summer to fire them. Other related changes aiming at overcoming climatic constraints extant during winter concern the drying process. After pots have been formed, they can be dried by placing them near the hearth. However, these adaptive mechanisms have not been observed in any of the visited villages in Ajlun region. Nonetheless, this kind of information is significant as far as understanding the potential adaptive behavior aimed at overcoming weather constraints in pottery production.

Pottery activity is related, in a way or another, to the economical cycle of the household. It is an activity conducted to supplement the household incomes. Its schedules can be best understood when they are correlated with other subsistence strategies. The practice of summer and winter cultivation can explain such a correlation. Summer cultivation, for many households in the Ajlun region, is an important economical source. During this season a priority is given to the set of activities related to crop gathering, even if it is during peak time for pottery production. Such a constraint between these two economical activities reduces the time left for pottery making.

Another economical practice that has a constraint on pottery production is olive-collecting. This activity takes place between October and November. It also involves a full day work from morning to afternoon. In this case, despite the relative sunny days of these two months, potters usually stop producing pots.

The schedule of pottery making in Ajlun region sheds light on two interrelated issues. The first is the type of relation between this potting activity and other economical practices for the household unit. The type of capital and the economical practices of potter's household affect to some degree the intensity of pottery production per season. The second is the constraint of environmental factors on this activity. These factors play an important role in relating this activity to a part-time one.

III. The identification of the potter population

In the previous pages, the attempt has been to present the natural and cultural contexts under which the potters in northern Jordan operate. In the following pages, the main concern is to go into details on the following points: the identification of the villages where pottery is still produced, the number of potters in each village, the identity of potters and finally the learning environment.

III.1 The location of pottery production

In a survey of northern Jordan, pottery production has been mainly concentrated on Ajlun region, more specifically along the wadis that intersected the mountain chains. These are from south to north: wadi Rajib, wadi Kufranjeh, and wadi el-Yabis (**Map 2**). Along these wadis pottery is still produced at a limited number of villages. The practice of pottery making has been attested only at five villages. This number is minimal compared with the size of the region, and the number of villages found in it. The area to the north of wadi el-Yabis, for example, has been included in the survey, but no pottery production was identified there. This, despite the fact that Mershen (1985) in her study of this area, has reported a number of pottery production villages. It seems that the techno-economical development in Jordan as a whole, constitutes a major factor that underlies the great reduction in pottery making, whereas household containers are made of other raw materials such as plastics and aluminium.

In the five identified villages, there is a variation in terms of the number of active potters, their maximum number in one village (Arjan) being three. The number decreases to two such as at Kufranjeh, Ammyria and Ballas. The number of potters per village seems to have changed drastically during the past two or three decades. Oral information indicates that in the village of Arjan, the number of potters during the 1970s was fifteen. Currently, this number does not exceed three. As mentioned above, the techno-economical factors play a major role in this change.

Further attempts have been made to re-construct the spatial distribution of pottery production in northern Jordan, according to two sources: the work of Mershen (1985, 1991) and oral information. The latter source is important as it sheds light on the location of villages where pottery production has ceased. Several retired potters form the basis of this information. They were interviewed either in villages where pottery is still produced or in villages where such practice has now disappeared. This source of information enabled the identification of two more villages where pottery has been produced. These are Kufr Khall and Safsafa.

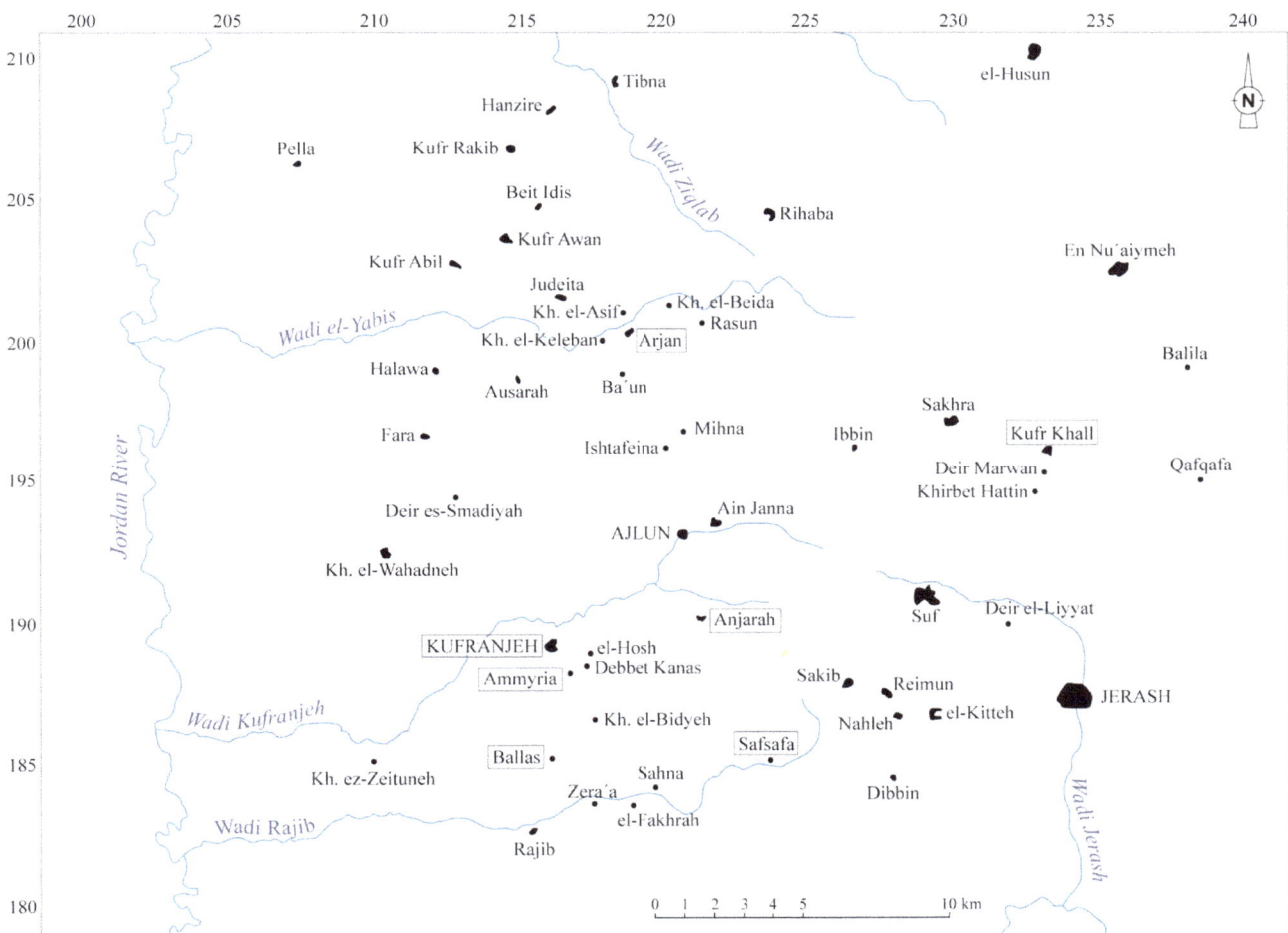

Map 2: The location of visited pottery production villages

17

III.2. Potters identity

By potter's identity we refer to three aspects: the potter's gender, age and social class. Gender identification is a significant aspect with respect to the organization of labor. It sheds light on division of labour at the household unit or social group level. Pottery making in Ajlun region is a female activity. The allocation of the tasks related to pottery making is in the hand of women. Potters work independently of other household members; the need for other assistance is often due to their old age or poor physical conditions.

The second main aspect related to the potter's identity is age. The emphasis on age identification helps in attesting the potter's skill. In the Ajlun region, a precise identification of the potter's age was a difficult task, and potters themselves estimate their age within a given range. However, all the observed potters are more than fifty years old. They can be classified under two main groups (**Table 1**). One group represents potters whose age ranges between 50-65 years old. The second group includes potters who are between 65-75 years old. These two age ranges, however, are an indication of the discontinuity in learning the craft in the Ajlun region.

Village Name	Potter No.	Estimated Age
Arjan	Potter 1	≥55
	Potter 2	≥50
	Potter 3	≥70
Ammyria	Potter 1	≥55
	Potter 2	≥75
Kufranjeh	Potter 1	≥55
	Potter 2	≥75
Ballas	Potter 1	≥65
	Potter 2*	≥50
Kufr Khall	Potter 1*	≥55
Safsafa	Potter 1*	≥70

Table 1: The estimation of potters' age in different villages.
Note: * indicates cases where the information gathered was
from potters who had stopped making pottery

Another aspect that relates to potters' identity is the social status. Several ethno-archaeological studies show that in some regions in the world potters belong to a special caste and or class (i.e. Arnold 1985). The relation between crafted people and other segments of society, for example in terms of marriage, is limited. With respect to the potters in Ajlun region such a social distinction is not evident. Potter households are not related to a specific caste or class because of the practice of pottery production. The social distinction between these potters and other members of the community is based mainly on an economical factor, which is the main factor that makes a differentiation bet-

ween the different households. It depends on the degree to which pottery production can aid the household income. Either pottery production relates to the main economic cycle of the household or the practice of this activity is oriented to gain some additional benefits. This is the case among the potters household who own a plot of land.

III.3 Learning environment

Learning environment of pottery making is one significant aspect to understand the degree of similarities and differences of pottery *style*(s) (Kramer 1985). In a given community, the practice of pottery-making is to be found within a given group of social members. They are the basis of the technological knowledge of pottery-making. The practice of this knowledge, however, is subjected to variation among the potters. This is due to personal motivation and experience, the source of learning, and the age at which the potter began learning.

In most of the cases observed in Ajlun region, potters learned the craft after marriage. This is indicative of two significant social phenomena. It reflects the age at which the craft is learned and the source of learning. As mentioned above, the residence pattern in the villages of Ajlun region is patrilocal. To a large extent, this determines the pattern of social interaction to which a potter is accustomed (**Table 2**). A potter will generally tend to associate socially with her husband's family or lineage. As so, she will more likely learn the craft from her husband's closed kin who lives nearby: the husband's sister (potter 2, Arjan), the husband's first wife (potter 3, Arjan), grandmother's line (potter 1, Anjara). In the case of exogamy (potter 1, Kufranjeh), the source of learning has been the husband's sister who lives close.

Village Name	Potter	Learning line
Arjan	Potter 1	Mother-line
	Potter 2	Husband's sister
	Potter 3	Husband' first wife
	Potter 4*	Mother-line
Ammyria	Potter 1	Husband's kinship
	Potter 2	Husband's kinship
Kufranjeh	Potter 1	Husband's kin
	Potter 2	Mother-line
Anjarah	Potter 1	Father'/ Mother's kin (grandmother)
Ballas	Potter 1	Mother-line
	Potter 2	Mother-line
Kufr Khall	Potter 1*	Mother line
Safsafa	Potter 1*	Village neighbourhood

Table 2: The learning sources of potters
in northern Jordan.
Note: * indicates cases where the information gathered
was from potters who had stopped making pottery

The above cases have in common the learning of pottery-making after marriage. The age at which the women get married ranges between 15-18 years old. However, the potters claim to learn the craft at the age of thirty. This is an indication that one main reason for learning pottery-making depends mostly on economic reasons.

To a lesser extent, the source of learning among the potters in Ajlun region is to be the mother's line. In such a case, there has been a correlation between the age at which the potter learned the craft and the locus / source of learning. These potters learned the craft before moving to their husband's houses. The average age for learning, consequently, is younger than in the group mentioned above.

Pottery learning also has a direct relation to the circumstances of the household's economic system which, to some extent, determines patterns of social interaction. Spatially, this refers to the cultivation of the surrounding fields around the village. Participants in these activities were either resident household members and/or wage-labourers who settled seasonally in the fields. Under such circumstances, one of the potters at Safsafa learned the craft while participating with her husband, as a wage-labourer, ploughing and harvesting activities in another village. This seasonal movement enabled her to contact other people who had settled close to them. The source of pottery learning in this case came as a result of interaction with individual from other villages.

To sum up, the learning model with respect to pottery-making in Ajlun region can be classified at the village-scale into: a) daughter / mother; b) wife / husband's sister; c) grand-mother's line; and d) second wife / first wife. A significant source of learning pottery is through the economic interaction with other villages.

The mechanism of learning is another important aspect that should be addressed when the training environment is considered. This refers to the stages of learning on which a potter bases his/her learning to manipulate the know-how and gestures of pottery making. Three stages can be distinguished: a) identification and preparation of raw materials; b) acquiring and performing gestures related to pot-shaping; c) learning of the firing technique. All these stages are acquired through direct observation; no verbal learning form is mentioned. For example, potters often report that they first became involved in the preparation of raw materials. After that, the teacher will shape the pots. During this stage, apprentices have the chance to observe the gestures involved in pot-shaping. Then they replicate these gestures by forming small pottery objects. This stage is generally one of trial-and-error. These shaped pots are fired with the pots made by the teacher. Here again, the final stage of learning can be directly observed. Its

replication is again a process of trial-and-error; each time there is an error, the teacher evaluates the causes so that they might be avoided during the next attempt. The time-span for this training is hard to evaluate. Moreover, it is difficult to correlate the duration of learning with the source of learning; for example, whether the duration of learning within the family locus, i.e. the mother's-line, differs from that after marriage. Based on the potters' information, the learning process lasts 2–3 years. This might be translated into two or three working seasons. This should be differentiated, however, from the maximum time for acquiring motor habit as reflected in the maintenance of a special technological style.

Chapter Two: The context of pottery production in northern Jordan

This part of the study entails a detailed discussion of pottery production in northern Jordan. It aims to define the technological knowledge or information that potters practice to exploit their environment, as well as to make their product. Identifying this kind of "information flow" is significant in evaluating the spatial segregation of technological choices, either between or within potter groups. This helps us to understand the exploitation pattern with respect to the environment and the techniques embedded in the production of pots. Consequently, production variability can be plotted on the geographical distribution.

I. Background

The system of pottery production can be analysed by defining, among other factors, the means of production; that is to say, by defining the means of raw-material exploitation, preparation and forming technology (Costin 2000). The first involves defining the relationship between the potter and his/her environment in terms of the exploitation and selection of natural resources. These resources include clay, temper, raw material needed for decoration and fuel. Defining such a relationship will help to explain the processes and motivations involved in choosing specific raw materials, both of which will be reflected in the similarities and differences across wares (Arnold 1985, 1993, 2000; Neupert 2000; Stark *et al.* 2000). The exploitation pattern of raw materials might be well affected by both natural and cultural factors. These include, among others, erosion of clay deposits, accessibility to sources and landownership (Arnold 1985).

The second main factor with respect to the means of production is the technique(s) embedded in pot forming. This involves defining the processes of pot forming, finishing and decoration. Methodologically, these processes can be analysed by evaluating the concept of *chaîne opératoire* (operating sequences or enchainments), which is defined as: "the series of operations which transforms a substance from a raw material into manufactured product" (van der Leeuw 1993: 239-40; see also Roux 1994). The concept of *chaîne opératoire* enables a systemic reconstruction of the different sequences of pot forming. Each sequence is distinguished in terms of technique and method. The forming method is defined as a "complex sequence of forming, which involves phases, stages and operations, each of which can be achieved through different techniques" (Roux 1994: 46; Roux and Courty 1998: 763). Phases are designated as the forming of each functional part of the pot (base, body, and orifice). The fashioning of each phase can be reduced to three stages: forming of the *roughout*, forming of the *preform,* and of the *finishing*. The roughout

entails different operations, thinning operation for example, which can be defined as the "hollow volume, which does not represent the final geometrical characteristics of the pot" (Roux 1994: 46). The second stage of fashioning, the *preform*, is defined as "a pot with its final geometric characteristics" (Roux and Courty 1998:763). The main operation involved in the *preform* is shaping.

In the following pages, these two main factors of the means of pottery production will be addressed. First, the exploitation pattern of environment in terms of raw material gathering and selecting, and the natural and cultural factors that play a role in this process will be described. This will be followed by the methods and techniques embedded in raw material preparations to the transformation of these raw materials into the final product.

II. The Interrelationship between potters and their natural environment

Pottery production is associated with the availability of three main natural resources: clay, water, and fuel (for firing). The northern part of Jordan, especially the Ajlun region, is rich in these raw materials. The following pages focus on the spatial distribution of these sources and the access potters have to them.

II.1 Clay and temper: defining spatial relations (**Table 3**)

The potters in Ajlun region exploit the clay beds that are located along the steep slopes of *wadis* or near springs. Due to the geological and topographic characteristics of the Ajlun region, erosion processes are evident in winter along the wadis. These processes allow for the creation of faults along the steep slopes, which in turn expose the clay beds. These locations are suitable to collect clay. At Arjan, for example, potters exploit the clay beds in the vicinity of their respective village which is exposed due to heavy rains. The same practice has been observed at Ammyria. Heavy rains create a fresh deposits exposure along the sides of wadi *tin es-Sabil*. The potters take advantage of this natural factor to obtain their clays.

Besides the nature exposure of clay-beds, clay allocation has been correlated with the presence of springs (Arabic: 'Ain). The Ajlun region is well known for the distribution of several water springs. These are distributed along wadi el-Yabis, wadi Kufranjeh and wadi Rajib. Clay sources can be found along the cutting-stream or near water springs. A pit is dug to extract the clay from these sources, contrary to the nature exposure caused by heavy rains. At the village of Arjan, potters extract also the clay sources along cutting-stream of wadi el-Yabis, or near Ain el-Beida. The same can be said in the case of the potter at Anjarah, who prefers the clay source from wadi Rajib (**Map 3**).

Human factors also facilitate the allocation of clay sources. Construction activities, such as house building, may expose clay beds. One of the potters in Ammyria, for example, was exploiting clay beds exposed as a result of the construction of a gas-station. In the same village, another potter was exploiting clay beds exposed as a result of the construction of a water pipe net. These clay sources, however, are usually limited in duration, and are exploitable for one season.

Landownership, however, is a factor that often hinders the potters' ability to exploit these locations (Arnold 1993: 64). This is particularly evident where clay is found on agricultural lands. At Arjan, for example, potters reported that they used to exploit clay from the steep slope of wadi el Yabis (el-Rayan). This was a common source for all potters in the village – they called this place *ma'alaka*, the

adjective form of *ma'alak*, which means clay. Landowners cultivating this area, however, prohibited the potters from exploiting the clay. As a result potters had to search for clay sources far from agricultural lands. This practice has continued until now. This factor effectively increased the distance between potters' households and clay sources.

The second main raw material for pottery making is the temper. The potters in Ajlun region use three types of tempers in pot making. These can be grouped as major and minor ones. The major temper types include grog and calcite. Minor ones include goat-hair and less frequently, chaff. Unlike the case with clay, grog can be collected without restrictions. It is usually collected from the surfaces of archaeological sites. Modern pottery sherds are seldom re-used as temper. However, the ready availability of archaeological sherds makes them valuable resources. This availability is due mainly to the large number of archaeological sites in the vicinity of the villages or even within them (**Map 3**).

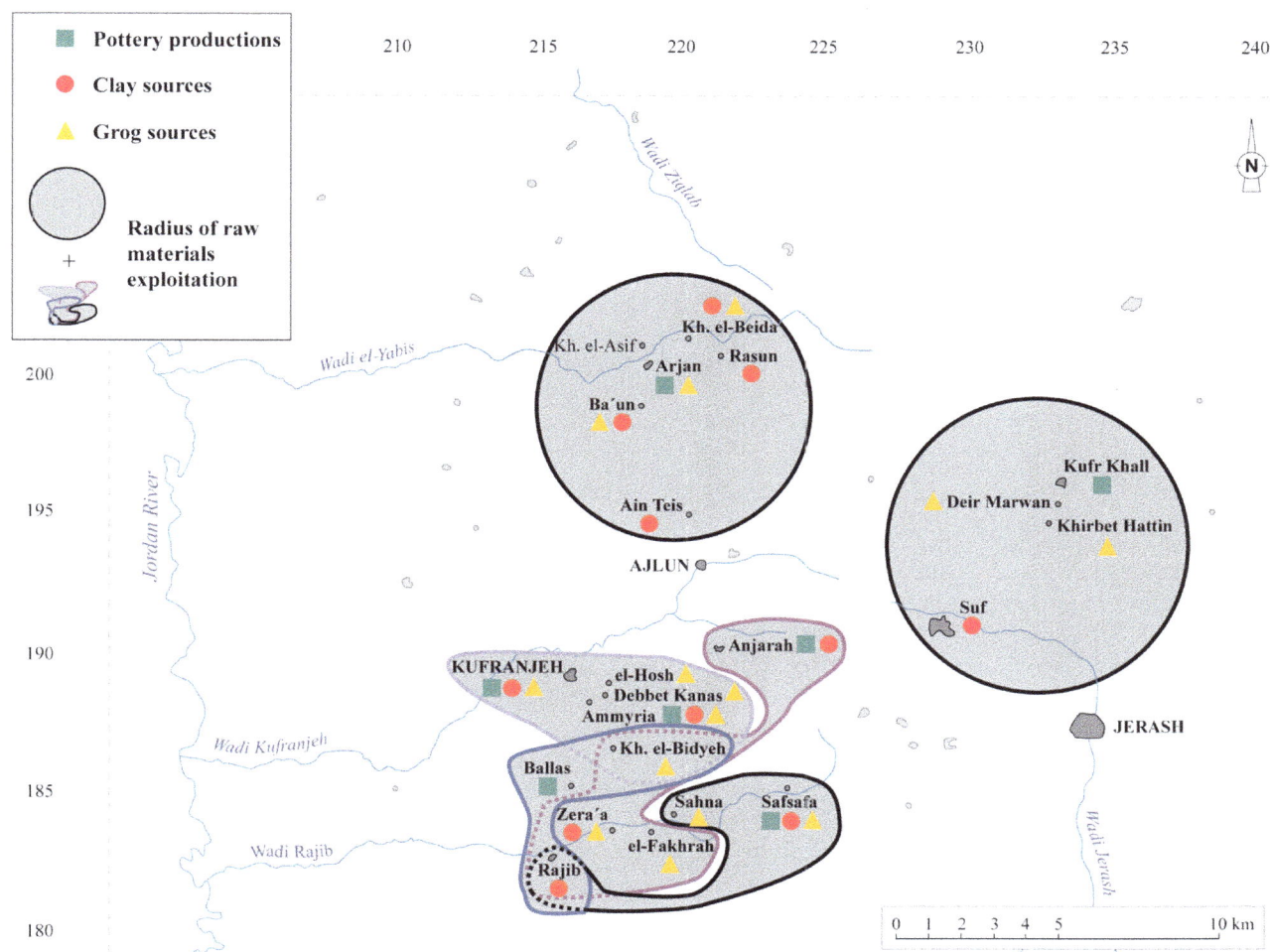

Map 3: The distribution of raw material sources to the potters' villages

Village	Potter	Clay source(s)	Grog source(s)
Arjan	Potter 1	'Ain Teis, Wadi el-Yabis, Ba'un	Arjan, Khirbet el-Beida
	Potter 2	'Ain el-Beida, 'Ain Teis, Wadi el-Yabis	Khirbet el-Beida, Arjan
	Potter 3	'Ain Teis, near the village	Arjan
	Potter 4*	'Ain Teis, Ain el-Beida	Ba'un, Khirbet el-Beida, Arjan, Tiara
Anjarah	Potter 1	Zera'a, Anjarah, Rajib	el-Fakhrah, Zera'a, Khirbet el-Bidyeh
Ammyria	Potter 1	'Ain Ammyria, Kufranjeh	Ammyria, Khirbet el-Bidyeh, Debbet Kanas, el-Hosh
	Potter 2	'Ain Ammyria	Ammyria, Khirbet el-Bidyeh
Kufranjeh	Potter 1	Kufranjeh	Kufranjeh, Kh. el-Bidyeh
	Potter 2	Kufranjeh	Kufranjeh, Kh. el-Bidyeh
Ballas	Potter 1	Rajib	Khirbet el-Bidyeh
	Potter 2	Rajib	Khirbet el-Bidyeh
Khirbet Safsafa*	Potter 1	Rajib, wadi Safsafa	Sahna
Kufr Khall*	Potter 1	Sūf	Deir Marwan, Khirbet Hattin

Table 3: The geographical distribution of potters and the location of raw material resources.
Note: * indicates that information was gathered from potters who had at that point stopped producing pottery

At Arjan, in the village itself, archaeological sherds are abundant. These date back to the Umayyad, Abbasid, and Mamluk periods (Mittmann 1970: 69-70). To the west, at about 0.75 km from Arjan, there is another archaeological site, *Khirbet el-Keleban,* which dates back to the early Iron Age, the late Hellenistic-Byzantine period, and finally, to the Mamluk period (Mittmann 1970: 70). Moreover, there is to the north and north-east of Arjan at about 1,75 km, another archaeological site – *Khirbet el-Beida* – dating back to the EB I-III, LB, IA, the Late Hellenistic period, the Late Byzantine period, and the Umayyad period (Mittmann 1970: 70). These archaeological sites are the sources of pottery sherds that can be used as temper. Potter 2 at Arjan, while settled in her orchard, collected sherds from the nearby olive fields, which are not more than 10–20m away. These most likely came from the *Khirbet el-Beida* archaeological site. Other potters in the village collected sherds from *tinat um Swuileh,* which is located within the village.

Grog sources at Ammyria are also abundant. Pottery sherds are found either in houses' gardens or within a close distance from the village. Besides the village itself, pottery sherds are collected from the nearby archaeological sites *Khirbet el-Bidyeh* and *Debbet Kanas.*

The choice of grog source is determined mainly by the distance between the location of a potter's house and the source and this depends on the topography of the village. Potter 1 at Ammyria, for example, could collect grog from the agricultural fields close to her house or from as far away as 0.5 km to the north, at *Debbet Kanas.* The other potter at Ammyria, Potter 2, prefers to collect sherds from *Khirbet el-Bidyeh.* The reason for this has to do with the topography of the village. The location of potter's (2) house is higher than that of potter 1, and this makes it

difficult to collect the sherds from the lower course of the slope. Hence, she prefers to collect pottery sherds from *Khirbet el-Bidyeh,* which is within reach.

Potters in other villages, such as Anjarah and Ballas, also collect archaeological pottery sherds from *Khirbet el-Bidyeh,* which is considered the main source for grog.

The second type of temper is calcite. It is collected in chunks from nearby wadi beds like wadi el-Yabis, Rajib and Kufranjeh. Calcite chunks are distributed randomly in wadis and only potters can identify them.

The minor temper types such as goat-hair or chaff are found within the household. The availability of goat hair is directly related to the subsistence strategy of potters. As noted above, each potter's household has a number of goats that supplement their income. Therefore, potters do not need to travel to get this particular source of temper. The same can be said with respect to chaff.

II.2 Raw materials for decoration

The potters in Ajlun region use different raw material for pots decoration. These can be classified as either organic or inorganic sources. In the case of the latter, this includes *terra rossa* and mineral oxide, and are obtained from several sources. The former, organic sources, represents by the cortex of oak root (which locally is called *dbagh*).

Of these raw materials, only mineral oxide – known locally as *sfera* – requires a variable traveling distance; in some cases it is within 2-5 km from a potter's household. Potters at Arjan, for example, walk as far as 2 km to get this material. The distance was greater for other potters, such as those from Ballas and Anjarah, who travel up to 3-5 km. Other potters – for instance, in Ammyria – claimed that they found this material within clay deposits. Thus they had to travel only 40 m from home to acquire mineral oxide. The source for *terra rossa – hireth –* could be obtained within the household area. Potters only had to dug a small pit of 30 cm deep to get this.

II.3 Fuel sources

In the Ajlun region, potters use two kinds of fuel. These

are wood and animal dung. All potters in the study area make use of cow dung as fuel. They purchase this fuel i.e. dung from different sources, like relatives who own cows in the village, from cow-farms in the vicinity of the village and, no less frequently, from the potter's own cows if any. The potter's cows usually may not provide a sufficient amount of fuel (dung), because she may not have enough cows. At the village level, one finds that not many households raise cows. Consequently, there is always a problem of finding fuel (dung) in the village itself. Potters may therefore have to purchase fuel from cow-farms, thus lessening the amount of fuel they use. This is due mainly to the fact that potters have to pay for dung if they get it from farms.

Wood could be a more abundant source of fuel; since most of the villages are located in a forested area. The most dominant species are pine and oak. However, the use of wood in pot firing meets only one type of pot (see below). Therefore, animal-dung can be considered as the main source of fuel because it is used for firing different pot types.

III Variability of *chaînes opératoires*

At the out-set of this part it is worth re-mentioning an important issue. The visited villages in Ajlun region are located along the three main wadis – el-Yabis, Kufranjeh and Rajib – that cut the mountains. In each of these wadis, at least one production centre has been identified. In this section we will analyse the technological variability between the different villages in terms of the operational sequences – *chaînes opératoires* – of pottery production. In the Ajlun region, the use of this methodological concept allows a classification of the pottery repertoire into two technological traditions. These two traditions are differentiated in terms of raw material selection, clay body preparation, forming techniques, pot firing and post-firing treatment. In the following pages, a detailed description of each technological tradition will be presented.

III.1 Pottery Tradition I

The spatial distribution of this technological tradition includes all the villages that were visited in northern Jordan. It was shared by all the potters in the study area. The following is a detailed description of this tradition with the production of water jars as an example.

III.1.1 Selecting raw materials

The first decision of the potter is to choose an appropriate clay and temper to make the desired vessel. The observed potters made no correlation between clay type and the desired class of pot. The gathered clay is employed in making both cooking pots and non-cooking ware.

However, the chosen clay is defined according to the potters by the one which stand the forming technique. The clay should not collapse during the forming technique, and also should not dry quickly.

All potters associate these properties with clay colour. They try to mine clay chunk that has a greenish-blue colour. During clay mining, therefore, potters separate from the clay the chunks that do not match their chosen colour.

The potters then mix the clay with temper. Grog, locally *ghouf*, is the main shared temper used to produce non-cooking wares. The use of this material is widespread among all observed potters in the Ajlun region.

III.1.2 Preparing the materials: clay and temper

After selecting the appropriate materials comes the preparation stage. Clay preparation involves drying, crushing, grinding and sieving.

The gathered clay lumps are first dried. They are dumped from the sacks in which they were collected onto a clean surface in the courtyard. Once dried, the clay lumps are subjected to crushing and grinding. Usually a hand-sized stone is used to break the clay chunks into smaller pieces. The potters then subject the dried clay to grinding with a cylindrical stone. Generally, it is a roughly symmetrical stone measuring 30 x 35-40 cm. Some of the dried clay is then spread onto a clean hard surface, usually a cement one. The potter starts rolling the stone over the clay backwards and forwards. This process is continued until the clay becomes a fine texture, appropriate for passing through a sieve – a *girbal* – which usually has a 2-2,5 mm aperture.

The activity area where grinding is performed is first cleaned in preparation for tempering. The pottery sherds are soaked in water before grinding and are left overnight in water. The aim is to loosen the texture of the temper in order to facilitate the grinding process. The same method used to grind the clay is applied to the temper. The grounded pottery sherds are then sieved with a fine aperture sieve – a *munhul*. It has a 1,5-2 mm mesh and is smaller in size than the clay sieve.

III.1.3 Preparing the clay body

Clay body preparation involves four main stages: measuring the volume of clay to temper, dry mixing the clay and temper, wetting the mixture, and finally aging. The most common method of clay and temper measuring involves the use of a cylindrical container with a capacity of 2 kg. The proportion of clay to grog is 1:1. It should be noted, however, that this percentage is not absolute. Most often potters add a handful of temper to the mixture.

The mixing of clay and temper is first performed by measuring the needed amount of clay and organizing it in a pile. The same amount of temper is then added and placed at the centre of the pile and on its sides. The mixing of raw material consists of two stages: first, the quantities are mixed without adding water to ensure as much as possible a systemic distribution of both clay and temper. The second stage is performed by adding water to the mixture, but only to the point where it is wet. In both cases, kneading is performed by hand. It is done by kicking down material from the top to blend it with that at the bottom. This process is repeated until a consistent wetting of the clay body is achieved. At the end of the kneading process, the clay body is wrapped with textile and left overnight for aging. This process is called *tahmir*. Potters make a correlation between the degree of aging of the clay and a greater workability of the clay body.

The clay body will not be suitable for forming at this stage; further kneading therefore will be conducted just before forming. It is performed in sub-stages. A handful of clay is periodically cut from the clay body, each time adding to it a sufficient volume of water while kneading it continually with the hands. During this stage it is trampled with the hands fist. The finished lumps of clay are left on a piece of textile or a wide plate. When an adequate quantity is finished, more kneading is conducted on the clay mass as a whole.

III.1.4 Forming methods and techniques

Shaping a water jar involves the following phases: forming the base, the body and the rim (**Fig. 1**).

III.1.4.1 Forming of the base

The base of the water jar is formed from a ball of clay. A handful of clay is shaped into a ball by rolling it between the palms. Potters use a flat-face supporting tool, made either of wood or iron, and sprinkled with ashes which function as an isolating agent. The ball of clay is first subjected to thinning by flattening it between the palms. At the end, the ball assumes a roughly rounded shape and thickness. It is then placed on the supporting tool which has already been sprinkled with ashes. Potters then modify the shape and thickness of the base by smearing knots of clay at uneven points. Shaping is performed with wet palms moved horizontally to even the face and smooth it.

III.1.4.2 Forming of the body

The body of the water jar is shaped using a *segmental coiling* technique. This technique refers to the way in which the body of the jar is formed; several coils are applied until the entire circumference of the vessel is covered. Potters form the coil from a handful of clay rolled between the palms using a vertical motion. The coil is then placed against the inner side of the base. More coils are added until the entire circumference of the base is covered. The coils are then *joined* with the base and with each other. This is done by scratching and smearing the clay from the coils vertically against the base and horizontally against other coils.

The next stage of body fashioning involves the thinning of the coils. This stage is conducted by applying pressure with the index finger and thumb: a) along the internal face using a horizontal and diagonal motion, and with the other hand supporting from the opposite side, and b) along the external face, using a vertical motion near the base and a diagonal one along the upper part.

The pot walls are then subjected to shaping operation. This is done by applying horizontal pressure with the fingers and/or the side of a lunar-scraper or of a broken spoon against the internal face while supporting the external face with the other hand. This, in turn, is shaped by applying pressure with the fingers and/or straight side of the scraper, using horizontal movements. The uppermost part of the worked-on area is evened by a process of folding and smearing – the uneven is folded and smeared downward with the thumb.

The shaped part – course – of the pot is then subjected to smoothing. This is done using wet palms against the internal and external faces in a horizontal movement. The finished part of the pot will then be left to dry in a semi-shadow area until it takes on a leather hard stage.

The same technique, segmental coiling, is used to build the next courses of the pot – that is, to extend the body of the pot upward. The number of coils increases with the circumference of the body. The coils are joined with the previously formed course in two ways: a) by grooving one side of the coil through applying pressure with the index finger or b) by abutting the coils to the previously formed course. The thinning and shaping of the coils follow the same method as with the previously formed course, though the pattern of movement is, on both faces, more horizontal.

Before starting to shape the neck, two or/and four loop-handles are attached to the body of the pot. These may be placed either vertically or horizontally against the body.

III.1.4.3 Forming the neck and rim

The same previously mentioned methods and techniques are used in forming the neck of the jar. More coils are added and joined against the lower part. The coils are then

a) joining and thinning the coils with the base

b) shaping the wall of the pot

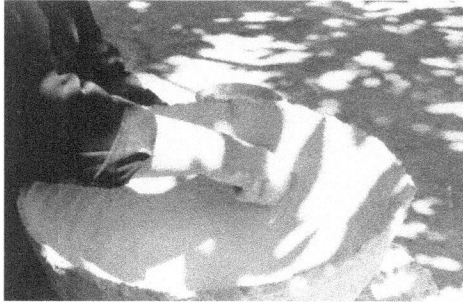

c) shaping the wall of the pot

d) thinning and joining the coils

e) shaping operation

f) joining the neck with the body

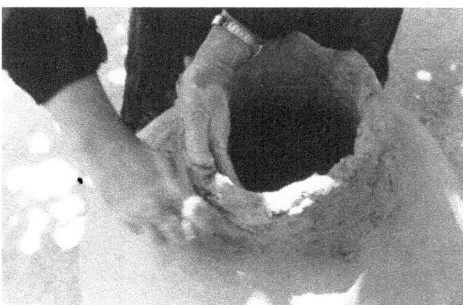

g) thinning the coils of the neck

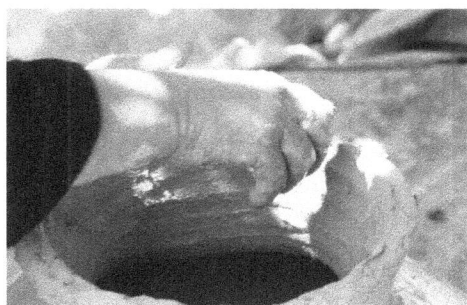

h) shaping the neck

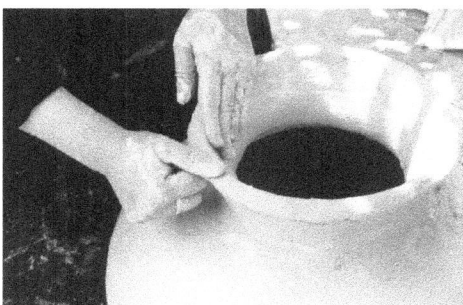

i) shaping the rim of the pot

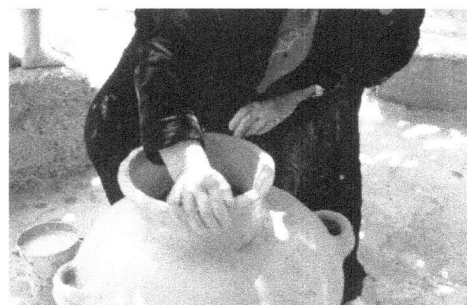

j) finishing the rim

Fig. 1: Fashioning water jar (Tradition I)

subjected to thinning with the index finger and thumb in a vertical motion. Shaping of the coils is performed by applying vertical pressure with a scraper and/or fingers against both faces. The lunate side of the scraper is applied to the internal face whereas the straight side is applied to the external face. The uppermost part is evened by folding and smearing the clay with the thumb.

The rim is formed either by smearing clay knobs onto the plastic upper part of the neck or through continuous forming from the clay of the neck. It is then shaped by applying pressure with the thumb horizontally at the rim while giving support with the other hand. Both faces are then smoothed with fingers, using a horizontal motion.

III.1.5 Finishing

Surface finishing refers to the potter's actions applied to the faces of the pot that do not change its profile. No new material is added. Smoothing of the leather hard clay with moistened hands is a common technique of surface finishing among observed potters in Jordan. Smoothing may also be conducted using a hard tool, especially those which present a very smooth face, such as a broken spoon. The spoon is dipped in water and used to smooth the pot face while it is in a leather-hard state.

III.1.6 Methods of decoration

Generally potters use two different decorative methods. The first one entails the application of plastic decoration while the second involves the application of organic or inorganic, slip, or painting. Plastic decoration is applied by rolling a small clay rope and then applying it against the external face of the pot. Usually it is attached to its shoulder. Several thumb impressions are then pressed against the rope at various intervals.

The second method to decorate a pot uses inorganic

Fig. 2: Decoration patterns applied at pots external surfaces, examples from different villages in northern Jordan (a: Ballas, b and c: Arjan, d and e: Kufranjeh, f: Ammyria)

material, which is applied before firing. These materials are rich in iron oxide or magnesium. They are first suspended in water and then applied to the face of the pot in one of two ways: they are either painted as a pattern (for instance, as a zigzag pattern) (**Fig. 2**) or as a slip that covers the whole external face. Organic matter is also used which is applied after the pot has been fired. The raw materials used are derived from plant sources, especially oak. In this case, only the roots of the tree are collected. The roots are boiled in water and, after cooling, are used to cover either the whole face of the pot or part of it, through slipping.

III.1.7 Firing

Pots tempered with grog are fired in pits, using cow dung as the main fuel. The pit is roughly 30-40 cm in depth and 2 m in diameter. It is first filled with animal dung cakes. The dried pots are then placed directly over the dung and some of dung is placed inside the pots (**Fig. 3 a**). Next the

Fig. 3: Firing technique related to Tradition I:
a) furnishing the pit with animal dung-cakes, b) covering the pots with fuel in dome shape

pots are covered with more animal dung cakes, usually arranged in a dome shape. Finally, fast fuel – e.g. dry wood branches – is placed on top facing the wind. The firing lasts for a few hours (ca. 2-3 hours). After much of the fuel is spent, a large iron plate is placed on top, facing the wind's direction. The duration of firing is defined by the changing colour of the pots. During firing, potters usually distinguish two main colours: black, indicating that the pot is in the smoking stage, and red when the pot is completely fired. After the fire has died down, the pots are removed.

III.2 Pottery Tradition II

This technological tradition was found in all villages visited except Arjan. It is mainly associated with the production of cooking pots.

III.2.1 Raw material selection: clay and temper

Generally, potters use the same type of clay in making cooking pots as employed in making other categories of pot. Clay type, therefore, is independent of the category. A different temper, however, is used in making cooking pots: calcite is the main temper. In addition to calcite, some potters use *terra rossa* as a secondary temper.

III.2.2 Preparing the materials: clay and tempers

When selected and gathered, the preparation starts. Clay is subjected to the same preparation method as mentioned above. Calcite, generally collected in chunks, is prepared using two ways. First, the calcite chunks are soaked in water over-night. The next day, they are crushed into small pieces using hand-sized stones. The small pieces are, then, ground with the same method as the one used for grinding clay and grog. Where *terra rossa* is used as a temper, given its soft texture compared to calcite, it is only ground.

After the grinding stage, both clay and temper are sieved, using for clay either a coarse sieve of 2-2,5 mm mesh or a fine-mesh sieve (1,5-2 mm).While a fine-mesh is used for tempers.

III.2.3 Preparing the clay body

The main difference between water jars and cooking pots is in the ratio of clay to tempers. Some potters use calcite as a main temper. In this case the proportion of clay to calcite is 1:1. The clay needed is measured the same way as in the case of grog and clay. The proportions change when potters use *terra rossa* as temper in addition to calcite. The mixture of clay and tempers is 2 (clay): 1 (calcite) and 1 (*terra rossa*).

III.2.4 Forming methods and techniques

Unlike the description we gave of the various phases of shaping Tradition I (i.e. base, body and rim), cooking pots are defined on the basis of the methods and techniques employed and the shaping steps of the pot. Cooking pots are formed using two techniques: moulding and segmental coiling. The following is a description of these two techniques and the phases of shaping (**Fig. 4**).

III.2.4.1 Moulding technique

During the first phase a moulding technique is used. First potters prepare the supporting tool, which very often is a convex-shaped object, either a medium-sized basketry object or an aluminium bowl. An old or partly broken cooking pot might also be used as a supporting tool. As an isolating agent, textile or plastic sheets are employed. The operation begins with the forming of a ball of clay. The clay ball is then flattened by applying pressure with one palm while using he other palm for support. The shaped clay has an irregular-rounded shape and thickness. The disc-shaped clay is then placed over the mould by applying pressure with hand. More clay discs are added till the mold is covered.

The second stage of forming is thinning. Thinning is conducted by first wetting the clay with a wet palm, and then slightly smoothing it. The joining area between clay discs are next smeared against each other using the fingers. Thinning and shaping the clay is accomplished with a wooden scraper, during which regular thickness is achieved. While scraping the clay, the potter dips her index finger into the clay to measure body thickness at different points. Thicker areas are scraped and the excess clay is smeared at thinner ones. After a partial drying – less than 10 minutes – the formed part of the pot is subjected to finishing. This is performed mainly by applying wet palms against the body of the pot, using a horizontal motion, for the most part at the base and a diagonal one at other parts. After that, the end of the pot is wrapped with textile to keep moist, and it is left to dry until it achieves a leather hard state. By the end of these forming stages, almost three-quarters of the pot has been shaped.

III.2.4.2 Segmental coiling technique

Once achieving a leather hard stage, the pot is removed from its mold and turned upside down. The pot is placed on a supporting tool, which is concave in shape. It might be a deep plastic bowl or a flat iron sheet. As isolating agent, the potter inserts textile or plastic sheets between the pot and the supporting tool. More textiles are then wrapped around the pot to hold it stable. Usually the potter will place the supporting tool on a raised object so that the pot will be at waist-level while sitting.

a) covering the mould with a textile sheet

b) covering the mould with clay sheet

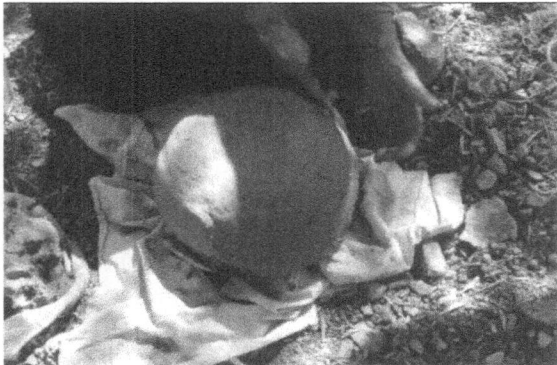
c) smoothing the moulded part of the pot

d) leaving the shaped part to leather-hard drying

e) turning the shaped part up-side-down
inside a supporting object

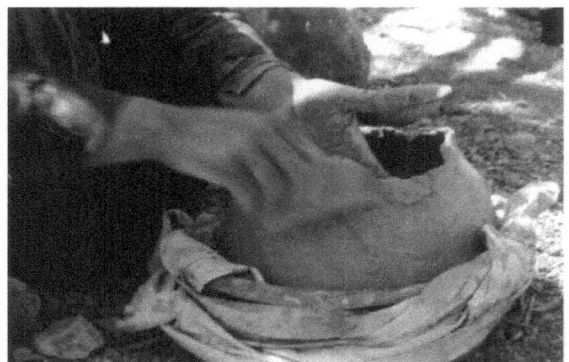
f) re-shaping the upper part of the moulded pot

g) thinning the coils

h) shaping the rim

Fig. 4: Fashioning cooking pot (Tradition II)

Once removed from the mould, the internal face of the pot is subjected to scraping with a scraper in order to regulate the shape of the pot. Small coils are wrapped around the circumference of the pot. These coils are shaped by rolling a handful of clay between the palms while being held in a vertical position. These are placed abutting uppermost part of the pots. Scratching part the clay of the coils against the pot body on both surfaces with the fingers modifies the joining area between the coils and the lower part. The coils are then subjected to thinning, the fingers scraping in both a diagonal, vertical, and horizontal directions.

The thinned part is then subjected to shaping. This is performed using a wooden scraper and/or an aluminium spoon. The convex side of the scraper is used to shape the inside surface while the straight side is used outside. Shaping is done primarily with a horizontal motion on the external face and a diagonal motion on the internal one.

Finishing is performed by applying a wet palm on both faces using a horizontal movement.

Rim forming is done either by smearing small clay coils against the plastic lower part, or by forming it directly from the previous clay course. When coils are used to form the rim, they are formed from small clay balls rolled vertically between the palms. These are applied directly to the plastic clay by smearing. They are then subjected to thinning using the thumb and index finger. Finally, a wooden scraper, moved horizontally against the faces, is employed to shape the clay. The uppermost end of the clay is evened by folding and smearing clay from higher part to the lower one. The lip is then smoothed by applying a wet palm in a horizontal motion, followed by the application of a slight pressure by the thumb in a sloppy pattern, the index finger meanwhile supporting the external face. This produces a clay edge along the external surface, which is then shaped by smoothing with the wet thumb. The lip likewise is smoothed using the wet thumb.

Two vertical loop handles are attached to the external face of the pot. They usually extend from just under the rim to the middle-section of the pot.

III.2.5 Finishing

Usually, cooking pots are partially smoothed. Potters usually spend less time smoothing the external face of the pot. This is done using the wet hand.

III.2.6 Firing

The firing technique associated with cooking pots differs from the above-mentioned technique, both in the firing feature and in the fuel type. A pile of wood is piled direct-

ly on the ground (**Fig. 5 a**). The pots are, then, placed on the wood bed, usually at a height of ca. 40 cm. More wood is added in equal amount like that placed initially (**Fig. 5 b**). The wood is then ignited. During firing, the pots are rotated using a long wooden branch to ensure systematic roasting. At the same time, more fuel is added until the pots are uniformly fired. In most cases, the pots are removed from fire when they have a dark grey colour.

Fig. 5: Firing technique related to Tradition II:
a) placing the cooking pots on a wood bed,
b) covering the pots with wooden branches

III.2.7 Post-firing treatment

The pots are usually removed from the firing location while they are still hot. Directly after that operation a certain amount of yoghurt is immediately poured into the hot pots. This stage is locally known as *ta'ashin*.

The two described technological traditions in Jordan can be summarized geographically in Table 4.

IV. Finished products

The variability in pottery as observed among potters in Jordan will be described. The aim is to classify the produced pottery assemblage on the basis of formal-functional

Potter	Village	Pot class	Temper	Forming technique	Firing technique
Potter 1 Potter 2 Potter 3	Arjan	Water jars & cooking pots	Grog & goat hair	Segmental coiling	Open fire pit Fuel: animal dung
Potter 1	Anjarah	Water jars	Grog & goat hair	Segmental coiling	Open fire pit Fuel: animal dung
		Cooking pots	Calcite	Moulding & coiling	Bone fire Fuel: wood
Potter 1 Potter 2	Ammyria	Water jars	Grog & goat hair	Segmental coiling	Open fire pit Fuel: animal dung
		Cooking pots	Calcite	Moulding & segmental coiling	Bone fire Fuel: wood
Potter 1 Potter 2	Kufranjeh	Water jars	Grog & goat hair	Segmental coiling	Open fire pit Fuel: animal dung
		Coking pots	Calcite	Moulding & segmental coiling	Bone fire Fuel: wood
Potter 1 Potter 2	Ballas	Cooking pots	Calcite & *terra rossa*	Moulding & segmental coiling	Bone fire Fuel: wood
Potter 1*	Safsafa	Cooking pots	Calcite & *terra rossa*	Moulding & coiling	Bone fire Fuel: wood
Potter 1*	Kufr Khall	Water jars & others	Grog & goat-hair	Segmental coiling	Open fire pit

Table 4: The geographical distribution of potters and variability in forming techniques
Note: * indicates that information was gathered from potters who had at that point stopped producing pottery

types. Pottery functional types have a direct relation to the production and socio-economical context of the activity (Deal 1998: 51). It helps to understand the pottery variability and the functional requirements of the community. These requirements in turn reflect the socio-economical needs of the society. Moreover, potters, as mediating agents between the environment and the social and cultural systems, produce pottery forms that fulfil these requirements.

The functional classification of the pottery repertoire in Jordan explains the relationship between pot form and the kind of activities performed by the society. This repertoire includes four formal-functional types. These are water jars, bowls, platters, and cooking pots. Nonetheless, these types are part of a larger assemblage including the ones that potters have ceased to make (see below). The production level or frequency of each type varies. As an average, each season, potters produce between 10-15 water jars. Next comes cooking pots and platters which ranged between 3-5 per season. Bowls are the least frequently pro-

duced object and some potters do not even produce them at all. When produced, they number from 1-2 per season. The causes of this variation are economical. The change of the consumption-locus from the household to the market has been a major factor (see pottery consumption and distribution below).

Below I will address the function of these four categories and after that list the functional forms that were previously produced.

IV.1 Water jars

The water jar is the most commonly produced pottery form (**Fig. 6**). Locally, it is called *habia*. The principle function is to preserve drinking water. The use-life of a water jar is dependent on its performance in preserving cold water. This in turn is determined by the ware's porosity. Therefore, the use-life of a water jar usually does not exceed two years. Water jars which are no longer used for storing water can be used for storing either liquids like oil,

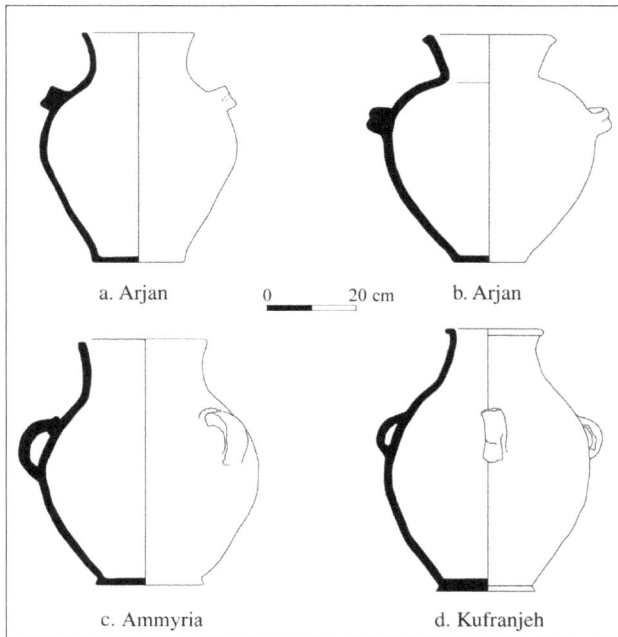

Fig. 6: Various types of water jars produced in northern Jordan

or solid products like wheat.

IV.2 Bowls

Bowls are known locally as *duggiya or zubdia*. It functions as a food-serving pot, either for yogurt or for cooked food with sauce.

IV.3 Platters

These are large and relatively deep. Three functional subtypes can be distinguished on the basis of size. Locally, they are known as *suhfia, karmia,* and *ma'gane*.
a) The *suhfia*, functions as food-serving pot. It is mainly used to serve rice. This pot ranges from 25-30 cm in diameter.
b) The *karmia* is used to dissolve dried yoghurt in water (Mershen 1985: 77). It is almost 35 cm in diameter.
c) The *ma'gane* is the main vessel associated with bread preparation. It is almost 40 cm in diameter.

IV.4 Cooking pots

Cooking pot – or *tashtoush* – is the main type of pottery employed in food preparation. It varies in size depending on household size, and the type of food they are intended for (**Fig. 7**). It ranges in size between 16x19 or 16x12 cm. Cooking pots are used for both vegetable and meat preparation.

In addition to the above observed domestic pottery objects, oral information was gathered on other functional objects which are no longer produced. Since they are the

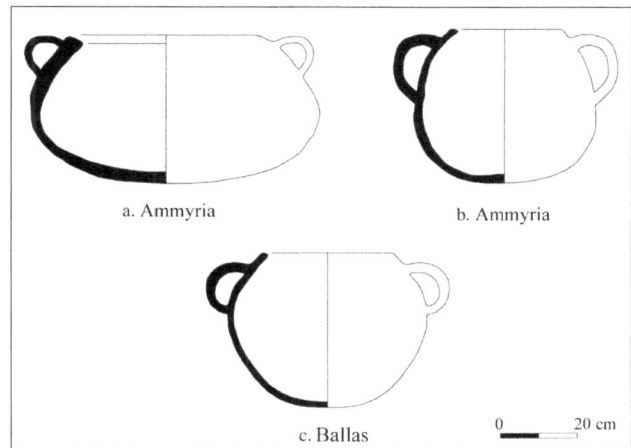

Fig. 7: Various types of cooking pots produced in northern Jordan

main interface between society and both the natural and cultural environment, potters were the main source of data in listing concerning these other functional categories. Potters see a correlation between these categories and the subsistence strategies and functional requirements of the household. They reported several objects, which directly corresponded to certain domestic needs (**Table 5**). These included pots which are directly related to animal husbandry – milk pots, for instance, which are known locally as *bouksa* – and also pots used for transporting food to workers in the field, known as *Shawayia*. Other pot forms included water carrying jars and jugs.

Pot etic name	Pot emic name
1. Water carrying jars	*jara*
2. Water storage jars	*habia*
3. Olive-oil storage pots	*sfal*
4. Milk pots	*bouksa*
5. Cooking pots	*tashtoush*
6. Food transporting pots	*shawayia*
7. Food serving pots	*suhfia*
8. Bread preparing pots	*ma'gane*
9. Jugs for drinking without spout	*kouz*
10. Jugs with a spout for washing before praying	*ibriq*
11. Bread-mould	*galib*

Table 5: Pots functional – type variety, emic and etic names

The household inventory includes other objects that have a ritual function. Here we refer mainly to those ceramic objects which were used directly in ritual practices. Arnold (1993: 124) describes these ceramics as a "channel of mythological and ritual information which flows between members of a society". Two ceramic objects in particular are associated with Islamic ritual. These are the jug – *ibriq* – and the bread-mould. The former is used for ritual washing. Its shape is suitable for the motor pattern of use. It is almost 20 cm in height, has a spout at one side, one vertical-loop handle attached at the neck and shoulder, and a bow neck to prevent water from flowing while being used.

The bread-mould – *galib* or *gusmat* – is used to produce special decorated bread. This bread is often baked during the two main Islamic feasts (Mershen 1985: 78).

V. Scale of production and pottery distribution

In the previous parts, an attempt was made to define the identity of potters, the means of pottery production, its schedule and variability, and its socio-economic significance. These aspects of pottery production are significant for understanding its level of production as well as for whom the pottery is made – that is pottery distribution.

Several studies have proposed typological schema for defining the modes of pottery production (Balfet 1965; van der Leeuw 1977; Peacok 1982; Costin 1991). The aim of such studies is to differentiate between different types of specialization. Parameters such as scale and intensity of production are used to define the typological schema. In Jordan, the intensity and level of specialization depends largely on the level of demand. The scale of pottery production in the villages studied can be described as elementary specialization (Balfet 1965) or household industry (van der Leeuw 1977; Peacok 1982). Pottery is produced to meet requirements beyond the household level, either at the community or regional level. Women, as elementary specialists, produce pottery to aid the income of the household, or for their own personal economic benefit. The former case is more evident among potters of low economic rank. Usually, they are not landowners and have limited economic resources. Potters who are landowners, on the other hand, find in pottery production, a means of economic independence. For example, they can buy other household objects.

The frequency of pottery production is seasonal. It is a part-time activity, conducted between June and September. The intensity of production varies from one season to the next, depending largely on the level of demand. Pots are produced mainly for market, accounting for more than 90% of production. Only a small portion is consumed at the village scale. For example, Potter 1 at Arjan produced during one season 10 water jars and three cooking pots. The next season, however, the number of water jars produced dropped to two.

The number of pots consumed and the nature of storage facility utilized correspond with seasonal fluctuation in production. One potter defined this relationship when she was asked why her production was low this season. Most potters do not have special facilities for storing unsold products; they may be stored in the living room; if so the average number of pots produced the following season will be reduced. Other potters – such as Potter 1 at Arjan and Potter 2 at Kufranjeh – have storage facilities for unsold products. Such a facility may be a shelter or the basement of the house.

Considering pottery production and the types of pots produced, marketing demands also play a selective mechanism. This is one of the main external economic factors that influences the limited number of pot types produced. Thus, most of the potters in Jordan now produce mainly water jars as these are the pot types that are most in demand.

Seasonal fluctuation with respect to pot types produced is related to other factors, like potter's age. Old potters – over 55 years of age – like Potter 3 at Arjan, and Potter 1 at Ammyria prefer making small and/or medium size pots. These include platters, cooking pots, and medium size storage jars. Such choices are influenced mainly by the level of energy input required in raw material preparation and the method of forming. With respect to the water jar for example – which are almost 55 cm in height – potters must work while standing and therefore must bend over in order to form the upper courses of the pot. This is physically tiring for the potter. It is therefore preferable to produce small or medium-sized pots that enable the potter to work while sitting.

Potters in Jordan were deriving more economic benefits previously than recently. The demand was both at the intra-village and inter-village ones. At Arjan, for example, between 1955 and 1970, there were almost 10-15 potters. The village was a regular production centre. Pots were produced to be consumed locally, and by nearby villages. People would come from nearby villages, such as Rasun, Rihaba, Judeita, Zubya, Ausarah, Deir es-Smadiyah, and el-Hashmiya to get pots from Arjan (**Map 4**).

At Kufr Khall, there were 5 potters: they produced pottery either for village consumption or external exchange. Pottery was distributed to villages like Qafqafa, Suf, el-Mshierfa and Balila. The nature of the economic system at these villages affected the type of pots exchanged. The settlers of Qafqafa were originally pastoral-nomads (Beduins). They were looking for specific types of pottery, such as milk-pots, platters for dry yoghurt working, and jugs. These pastoral-nomads acquired the pots in exchange of milk-products (milk and dry yoghurt), or sometimes agriculture products, like wheat.

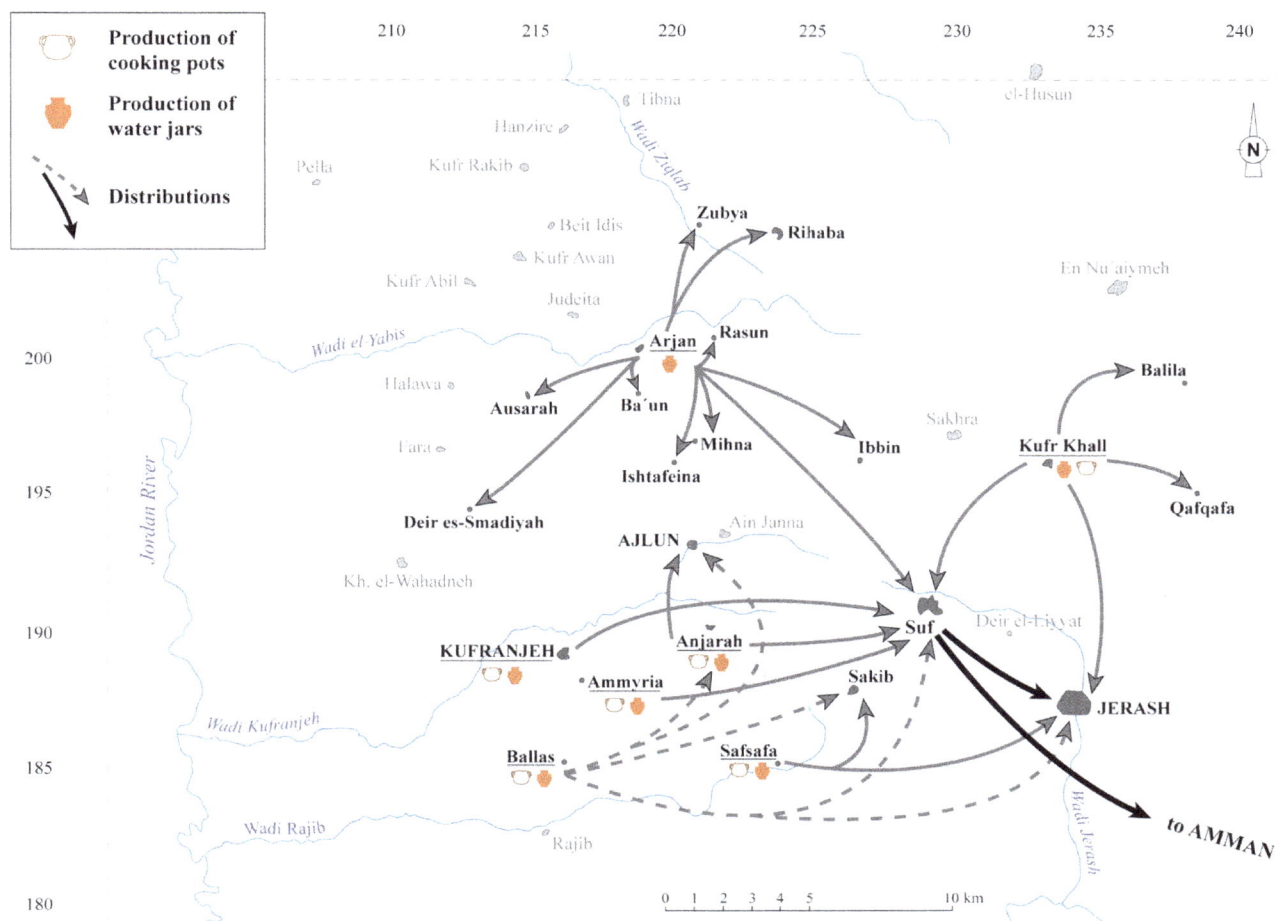

Map 4: The distribution pattern of pottery production in northern Jordan

Transactions for pottery were conducted usually on a barter system involving crops. Potters exchanged pots and different types of crops. The weight of exchange was equivalent to the amount of grog used for making a pot. The grog used was weighed and the same weight in wheat or lentil was given to the potter. Nowadays, many potters no longer practice this profession. They abandoned this craft because of the small income yielded compared with the level of energy needed. Moreover, new technological innovations led to the replacement of pottery vessels by other materials.

These new technological innovations influence not only the intensity of pottery production but also its consumption locus. Pottery vessels are distributed to two kinds of consumers: the local ones and outsiders. The reason for this general categorization is the difference in the mechanism of distribution. In all cases, the potter constitutes a production centre to which most of the consumers move. The inhabitants of the village usually ask directly the potter the pot shape they want (e.g. a water jar or a cooking pots). Such consumers are often the potter's relatives or neighbours. Distribution of pots to this group is seconda-

ry, and is based on socio-technological demand. In most cases, only 5-10% of pots are consumed this way. The mechanism of distribution is the movement of the consumer to the potter's household where he/she purchases the finished product. Nowadays, the transactions for pottery are only in cash.

Another form of pot distribution is also evident. The inhabitants of nearby villages may come to buy crops and occasionally pots from potters who are settled in adjacent orchards, as in the case of Potters 2 at Arjan or Potter 1 at Anjarah. As noted above, these potters practice pottery-making in the field, and pots can therefore be purchased directly. These buyers include city inhabitants who come to the orchards and purchase pottery as well.

The majority of pottery products are distributed to intermediaries or middlemen. This group forms the main mechanism of distribution and consumes almost 90% of pottery products. In many ways, it is this mechanism which is responsible for the craft's survival. Middlemen come from three main sites: Suf, Jerash and Amman. In large part, they determine where pottery is still produced.

They buy new vessels such as water jars, and used vessels such as cooking pots as well. These middlemen sell the pottery products to traders, who in turn sell them as curiosity for tourists or other city inhabitants.

These changes in consumption locus influence the mode of transaction for pottery. Instead of exchanging pottery with crop products, transactions are made now only in cash. Thus, for example one water jar usually costs 10-13 JD. Small objects, like platters and cooking pots, usually go for 3-5 JD.

Chapter Three: Recognition of the technological patterns of the studied pottery in northern Jordan

In the previous chapter, the main concern was to describe the dynamic context of pottery production within the potter population in northern Jordan. In this context, behavioural patterns with respect to the operational sequences of pottery-making were described. For archaeological purposes, the presentation of the dynamic context of production is just one aspect of the technological study of pottery. To be archaeologically useful, correlations should be made between behavioural patterns and their materialization in the finished product (pottery). This is one of the problematic issues in archaeological studies of pottery fashioning techniques. It involves the difficulties to recognize the fashioning methods and techniques as examined on pot's surface features. Hence, the task in this chapter is to define the technical attributes that can aid recognition of the pottery technological traditions observed in northern Jordan that we just described.

I. Methodological considerations

The study of pottery-forming techniques involves the observation of macro-traces left behind by the potter on the final product (Rye 1981). The identification of the macro-features on the surfaces of the pot is just one step in the study of fashioning techniques. The interpretation of these features is the difficult task. Usually, two sources of reference are used to achieve this aim: ethno-archaeological and experimental pottery studies (ex. Franken and Kalsbeck 1983; Longacre 1991; Roux 1994; Rye 1981; Vitelli 1984). These two sources determine references by which then archaeologists are able to establish a correlation between the potter's behaviour and the materialization of this behaviour in the final product.

Pottery ethnoarchaeology, as a source of reference, is a methodological framework within which both behaviour and its output can be observed. It enables one to observe the methods and techniques of pot forming and the physical attributes or macro-traces associated with each of them (Rye 1981: 58). An additional objective of ethnoarchaeological research is to establish a reference by which explanations might be provided based on cross-cultural studies. Nonetheless, one main problem regarding some of pottery ethnoarchaeological studies is the little emphasis put on the description of the technological attributes associated with given forming techniques or methods. Few researches have been made on this aspect of pottery production in comparison with the economic aspects or the mechanism of pottery distribution. In consequence, experimental pottery studies, as a supplementary methodological approach, are often utilized in archaeological pottery

research (Roux 1994; Roux and Courty 1998; Vitteli 1984; Schiffer *et al.* 1994).

Both methodological approaches have their objectives. In this study, the reference base is derived from ethnoarchaeological pottery sampling. This is justified by the assumption that the accumulative know-how or skill of individual potters is constructed differently. Therefore, it provides a large sample of objective, different outputs than subjective experimental study. Therefore, ethnographic observation is the main means in this study for providing the technological data-sets derived from the two pottery traditions mentioned above.

II. The ethnographic observations

The ethnographic observations have been conducted in five different villages in northern Jordan. The pottery products of 8 potters in these villages have been studied. In each case, the operational sequences of pot forming have been documented. The macro-traces or diagnostic features related to each fashioning stage has been described and illustrated. This included the methods and techniques employed in thinning, shaping and finishing operations. The focus was on defining the surface features observed on the bases, bodies and rims, and their spatial and temporal distribution.

The surface features of each forming tradition have been defined and grouped. The following is the result of the technical analysis of each tradition and their associated surface features.

II.1 Defining the surface-features associated with the two pottery traditions

As we have seen, the pottery repertoire in northern Jordan has been produced with two technological traditions: coiling and moulding. The analysis of these two traditions enables to define criteria that help the identification of the fashioning methods and techniques. For each tradition these have been organized according to the base, the body and the rim.

II.1.1 Identification of the base forming and shaping technique

1- Moulding
The base is made while forming the body, and there are no traces of sequence-separation between them (**Fig. 8**). On the outside the face of the base keeps the impression of

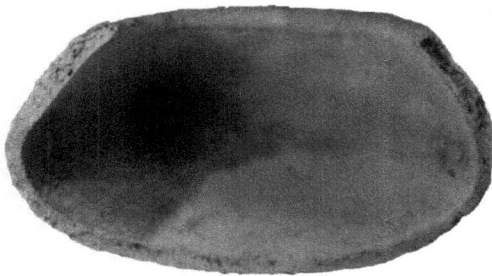

Fig. 8: The continuous profile between the base and the body indicates the use of moulding technique

Fig. 9: The exterior of the base shows the impression of a textile, which has been used as an isolating and supporting material to fix the pot

Fig. 10: The technical feature that reveals the use of moulding: a) the uneven part showing the use of coiling in shaping; b) the even part on the mould side

textile (**Fig. 9**).

2- Coiling
The base is flat and takes the shape of the supporting tool. It is made separately from the body, as marked by the presence of an undercut between the base and body.

II.1.2 Identification of the body forming technique

1- Moulding
The use of a mould in pot forming:
a) Vertical cracks due to dissecting and tensile stress.
b) A regular and continuous profile between base and body.
c) A wall profile that is more regular.
d) Relative regular wall thickness.
e) An even part on the mould side (the inner surface which is in contact with the mould) and usuallu has no traces of mould impression (**Fig. 10**).
f) A bumpy external face, with an irregular recess with no specific pattern, i.e., not following any horizontal pattern – some of the bumps are due to handling of the pot when being removed from the mould.
g) No visible junction between base and body.

2- Coiling
a) Undercut between the base and the body.
b) Binding marks are evident (**Fig. 11**).

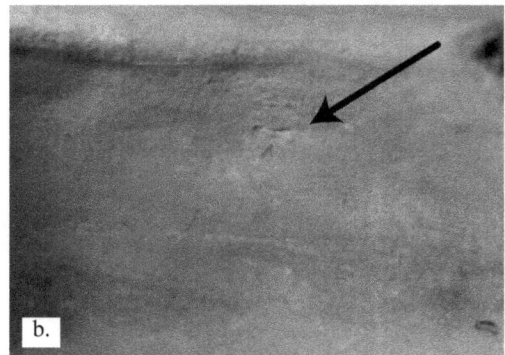

Fig. 11: Binding marks between coils represented by horizontal voids

Fig. 12: Horizontal corrugation between the coils

c) Corrugations between the coils (**Fig. 12**).

d) Smearing of the plastic clay evident against the leather hard clay at the binding areas.

e) Irregular wall thickness at regular intervals at the binding areas.

f) Presence of a recess on the inside and outside, and a horizontal pattern following the binding area.

II.1.3 Identification of the body forming and shaping operation

1- Moulding
No trace features indicative of the shaping operation, they are obliterated by the finishing operation of the external face.

2- Coiling
a) Evident coarse texture striations that are horizontal on the body of the pot.

b) Finger width scraping pattern (**Fig. 13 a**)

c) Ridges (L: 3-3,5 cm; deep to shallow) left by the scra-

ping tools (**Fig. 13 b**).

d) Even and soft area at the binding areas, due to the shaping operation when a scraper has been used.

II.1.4 Identification of the finishing operation

1- Finishing with a wet hand / palm on humid clay
A very fine set of striations.

2- Finishing with a tool on humid clay
Drag-marks are evident; striations have a deep and raised edge, and a coarse texture

3- Finishing with a wet hand on leather-hard clay
Striations sets are very fine and shallow; drag marks have been obliterated, seemingly filled with fine clay (**Fig. 14 a**). The surface has a very soft face, slipped-like (**Fig. 14 b**).

4- Finishing with a tool on leather hard clay
Very even and soft facets (**Fig. 15 b, c**); or spots of burnished like face (**Fig. 15 a, d**).

a.

b.

a.

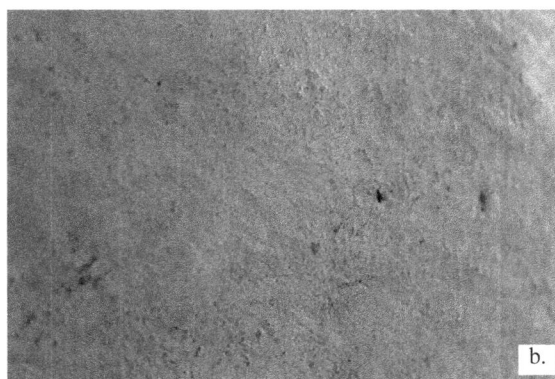

b.

Fig. 13: Technical features of hand and tool shaping:
a) hand-shaping features on the wall of the pot;
b) ridge left by a scraping tool used in wall shaping

Fig. 14: Technical feature of the surface of the pot that finished with wet hand smoothing

a. Finishing with wooden tool

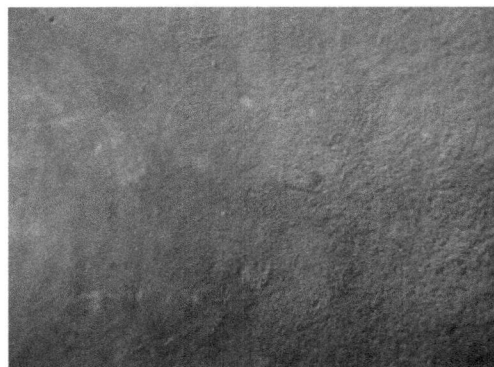

b. Finishing with hard and smoothed metal tool

c. Finishing with wooden tool

d. Finishing with smoothed metal tool

Fig. 15: The different technical features associated with using hard tools in finishing the surface of the pot

II.2 Technological classification

Depending on the technological-comparative description of pottery production in northern Jordan, the two *chaînes opératoires* can be differentiated (**Fig. 16**). They differ in their structural operational sequences with respect to the making of cooking pots. These differentiations can be summarized as follows (see **Table 6**):

1- Clay body preparation: in Tradition I, only grog is mixed as temper with clay. Meanwhile, in Tradition II, the clay body is prepared by mixing the clay with calcite as the main temper.

2- The base supporting tool: the two pottery traditions are distinguished in terms of the shape of the supporting tool. In Tradition I, potters use a flat supporting tool, whereas in Tradition II, a convex supporting tool is used.

3- Forming techniques of the body: segmental coiling is the only technique used in Tradition I. In Tradition II, potters use a moulding technique to form part of the pot body.

4- Clay-thinning operation: in Tradition I, both surfaces of the clay coils are subjected to thinning. In tradition II, only the exposed surface (not attached to the mould) has been thinned.

5- Application of decorative elements: only pots of Tradition I are occasionally subjected to painting decoration.

6- Type of fuel: Tradition I only uses animal dung; Tradition II only makes use of wood.

7- Methods of firing: in Tradition I, pots are fired in a pit; in Tradition II they are fired in a bonfire.

8- Firing duration: in Tradition I, not less than 90 minutes; in Tradition II, more or less 40 minutes.

Preparing the clay body for shaping

Without RKE*

Fashioning the roughout

Discontinued pressure on assembled elements: **_forming and thinning the coils._**

Discontinued pressure on mass of clay-molding: **_shaping and thinning the clay sheet_.**

The roughout

Fashioning the preform

Discontinued **_scraping_**: shaping with fingers

Discontinued **_scraping_**: shaping with hard tool

The preform

Finishing

Hand, hard tool
Smoothing

Finished body

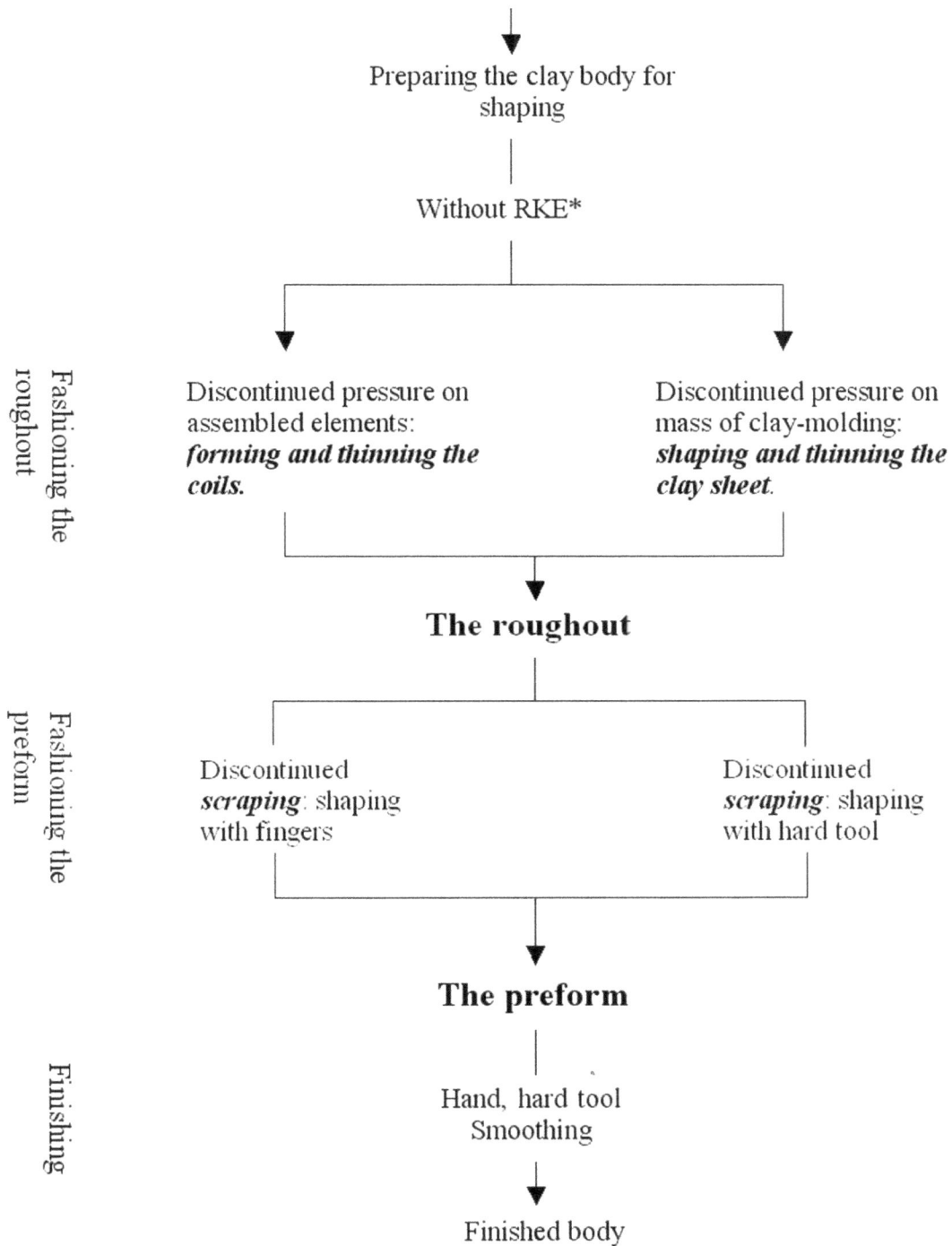

Fig. 16: Diagram showing the fashioning techniques of pottery observed in northern Jordan
* refers to rotative kinetic energy (RKE)

Chaîne opératoire	Tradition I	Tradition II
Clay body	Grog	Calcite
Supporting tool	Flat surface	Convex surface
Base forming	Handful of clay, turned into ball shape by rolling it between palms (clay ball flattened between palms, forming a roughly rounded shape disc, placed on a supporting tool covered with ash). Thinning the clay with palm pressure, cutting off the irregular clay at the edge of the base and smearing it on uneven parts, shaping with wooden scraper	Ball of clay, flattened by hands to obtain a disc with an irregular rounded shape and thickness. Placing the disc over the convex mould, which is covered either with textile or plastic bags; pressure applied with hand; addition of other clay discs till the total covered the mould
Body forming	Segmental coils: small size coils, around the circumference of the pot. Thinning conducted with finger scraping. Shaping conducted either with lunate shape scraper or by finger scraping	Part of the body is formed from the same clay discs used in base forming. Joining and thinning the clay performed with finger scraping. Shaping obtained with a scraper
Rim forming	Segmental coiling: the same operation of body forming is anew	Segmental coiling: the same operation as tradition I
Surface treatment	Hand-smoothing	Hand-smoothing
Decoration	Red-painting, red-slip	None
Fuel for firing	Animal dung	Wood
Firing feature	Pit	Bonfire
Firing duration	90 minutes	40 minutes

Table 6: Comparison of the two *chaînes opératoires* identified in northern part of Jordan

40

Chapter Four: **Variations in pottery production in northern Jordan**

In the previous chapter, our attempt has been dedicated to the identification of the macro-features that are associated with the two pottery technological traditions observed in northern Jordan. Each tradition has been differentiated according to significant features. These traditions revealed variations either among or between the potters we observed. Therefore, this chapter is devoted to measure these variations as they are reflected in the final products.

I. Background

Usually, at a given site, any pottery assemblage reveals variations. These include technical (e.g., method and technique of manufacture), formal (e.g., shape and size) or stylistic ones (e.g., decoration type, slipping, burnishing, etc.) (Costin and Hagstrum 1995; Deal 1998: 32-33; Rice 1996).

Stylistic variation has been addressed in ethnoarchaeological and archaeological studies (Deetz 1968; Longacre 1991; Graves 1991; Skibo, Schiffer and Kowalski 1989). Such studies focus on the structural elements of decoration as an indicator for social organization. Variation in decoration style has been explained as being caused either by age-cohort, learning sources or personal knowledge and skill (cf. Hardin 1977).

Parameters, either metric or morphological, have been emphasized as a means of measuring uniformity in pottery production. These are employed in pottery studies so as to distinguish the output of various craftsmen and/or their motor habits. To put it in another way, such studies aim to identify the appropriate parameters that can be archaeologically significant in defining the degree of standardization (to define the finished products of different production units or micro-styles / traditions) (Deal 1998; Longacre 1981, 1999). Several morphological parameters have been chosen to meet such an aim. These include the body shape of the pot, the base and rim shapes, and appendices. Metric parameters have been identified to include as well pot aperture, maximum circumference and height. The metric measures have then been subjected to statistical analysis, such as the coefficient of variation, to confirm the correlation between the producers and their finished product (Kvamme, Stark and Longacre 1996; Longacre 1999).

Technological parameters were mostly derived from compositional analysis of clay as a means of classification and/or measuring variation as functional ends. Such parameters have been re-evaluated as a means of measuring standardization and/or uniformity in pottery production (Arnold and Nieves 1992). They suggested that uniformity in production should be measured in relation to the effect of manufacturing technique, market demand and the potter's ideas concerning shape and dimension.

Technological parameters, especially those associated with shaping operations, are less often evaluated with an eye looking for the causes of such variation on the basis of the learning environment and/or the motor habits of the potters. In this part, I will focus the attention on the two types of pottery variations – technological and formal – in order to evaluate the kind of parameters that can help to identify such a correlation. Stylistic variation is of less significance as a parameter of analysing the pottery assemblage from the northern part of Jordan. Two main reasons justify this assessment. In the villages visited, the production is a small-scale one and decoration cannot be considered as a factor, as members other than potters participate to the decoration. Moreover, decoration is determined by external factors, such as consumer preference, which makes it less a *constructed* parameter that can be directly correlated with the motor habits of the maker.

II. Methodological consideration

Here, pottery production in northern Jordan has been evaluated considering three criteria: morphological, metric and technological parameters. The morphological and metric indexes will be encountered under the formal parameters. The technological index will be described separately which will include a comparison of the processes embedded in object becoming. The data base is derived from two villages in northern Jordan. These are Arjan and Kufranjeh. In these two villages, however, the output of four potters has been studied. The seasonal fluctuation in pottery production played a main reason for this sampling limitation. The rate of production for the observed potters does not exceed 15 water jars a year.

This study will focus on one pot functional class which is most frequently produced in the villages visited: the water jars. The data set for each potter is varied from other sources which depend largely on the rate of production for each season. However, a total sample of 44 water jars have been analysed (**Table 7**), and represented by the product of four potters operating at two villages.

Village name	Potter n°	Number of sampled pots
Arjan	Potter 1	14
	Potter 2	10
Kufranjeh	Potter 1	10
	Potter 2	10

Table 7: Number of sampled water jars according to village and potters

III. Formal variations in the pottery assemblages

Both morphological and metric indexes are used to monitor variation in water jar assemblages. The measurements have been made on intact water jars: their aperture, base diameter, height and maximum circumference. In the following, these indexes will be used to describe and analyse the water jar assemblages at the village scale. Then, a comparison of these variations will be addressed at the intervillage scale. The data set includes the pottery products of two villages, Arjan and Kufranjeh, and for each village, the formal characteristics of a pot related to two potters is looked at.

III.1 Formal variations in water jar production at the intra-village scale

III.1.1 The potters at Arjan

III.1.1.1 Morphological variation

Water jar assemblages at Arjan share a similarity in terms of shape. The jar has an ovoid body shape with two horizontal loop handles. Potter 1 produces a neck which is sharply carinated and with a wide mouth or opening. It has an inward junction with the lower part of the body. The rim is everted and bevelled (**Fig. 17**).

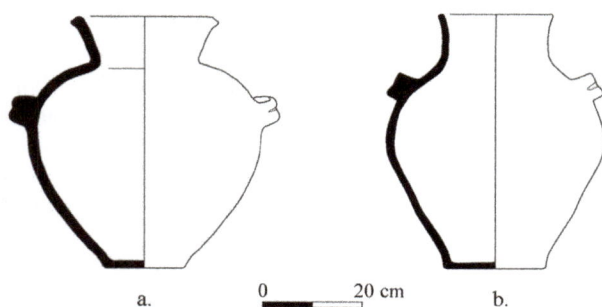

Fig. 17: The morphological characteristics of water jars at Arjan: a) product of potter 1, b) product of potter 2

Potter 2 at Arjan makes ovoid body-shaped water jars with two applied loop handles that are most often horizontal ones, but some are vertical. The neck, in most cases, has a straight profile and ends with a simple rounded rim.

A comparison between these potters' products shows that they mainly differ in neck and rim shape. The necks shape of the jars produced by potter 2 has straight profile, whereas the ones of potter 1 have outward profile. Of potter 2, the rim of the jar persists to have either a straight or bow profile, whereas the one of potter 1 has an everted levelled shape.

III.1.1.2 Metric measures

The products of the two potters at Arjan show few metric similarities. The results of coefficient of variation show that the minimum range of difference between the products of the two potters is to be found in the base and height of the pot (**Table 8; Fig. 18**). However, the products of the two Arjan potters seem to be differentiated based on the results of the coefficient of variation taken for the aperture and maximum circumference of the pot (**Fig. 18**). The range of difference of these two variables is high which makes them distinctive measures of variations.

The other parameter measured for variation was the thickness. The water jars produced by Potter 1 have a median of 1,5 cm thickness, whereas Potter 2's ones have a median thickness of 1 cm.

At the intra-individual scale, the measures of the products of the two Arjan potters show a high rate of coefficient of variation (**Table 8**). This can be seen for Potter 1 in terms of height and maximum circumference of the pot. Meanwhile in the products of Potter 2 this is clear in terms of the height and aperture of the pots.

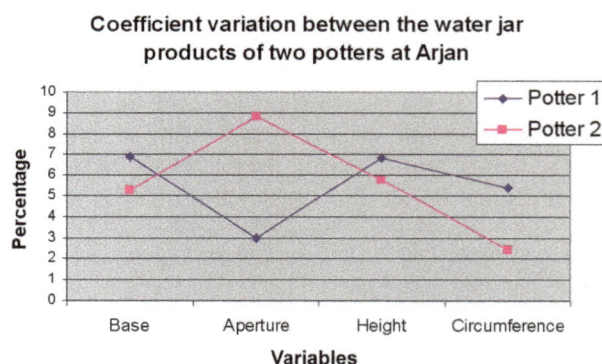

Fig. 18: Coefficient variation of the water jars produced by the two potters at Arjan

III.1.2 The potters at Kufranjeh

III.1.2.1 Morphological variation

The water jars produced at Kufranjeh share several morphological similarities, which is not surprising given that they are the product of a teacher and apprentice. Unfortunately, it was not possible to observe the products of other potters of the same village who got a different learning source. Both potters at Kufranjeh make water jars with an ovaloid body and four vertical loop handles. These handles are attached on the maximum circumference of the body (**Fig. 19**). The two water jar assemblages share similarities in their base shape, in the part of the base left untrimmed, and in the rim shape which has a flattened, everted profile.

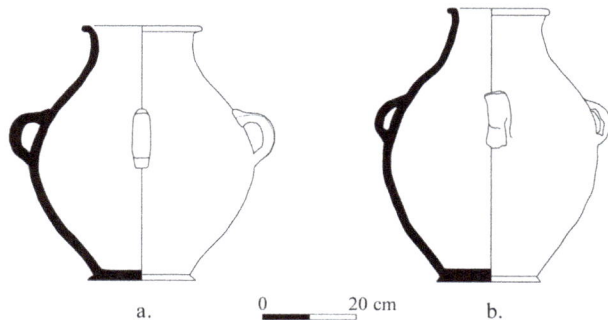

Fig. 19: The morphological characteristics of water jars at Kufranjeh: a) potter 2 product, b) potter 1 product

Morphological variations, however, are found in the neck profile. Water jars produced by Potter 2 have a neck profile which tends to slope inward. Those produced by Potter 1, by contrast, tend to slope outward.

III.1.2.2 Metric measures

At the inter-individual level, the coefficient of variation between the products of the two potters at Kufranjeh is minimal (**Table 8**). This ranges between 0,10 to 1,76%. The highest measures of variation, in terms of the coefficient of variation, are to be found in the pots' height and maximum circumference (**Fig. 20**). On the contrary, the minimum coefficient of variation is clear in pots' aperture and base which does not exceed 1,06%.

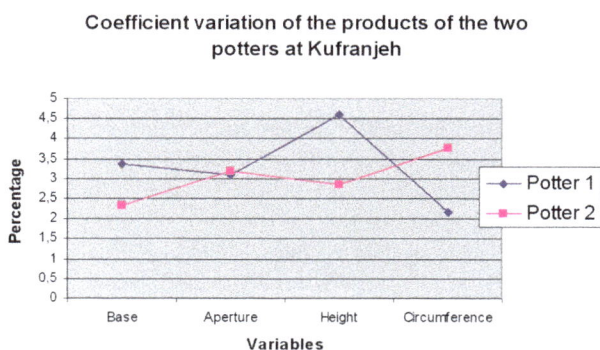

Fig. 20: Coefficient variation of the products of the two Kufranjeh potters

Variable	Mean	S.D	C.V
Arjan			
Potter 1, n°14			
Base	19,5	1,34	6,88
Aperture	26,75	0,79	2,98
Height	52	3,55	6,84
Circumference	145,5	7,84	5,39
Potter 2, n°10			
Base	22	1,16	5,28
Aperture	23,25	2,04	8,79
Height	52,25	3,00	5,74
Circumference	145	3,51	2,42
Kufranjeh			
Potter 1, n°10			
Base	24	0,81	3,37
Aperture	22,85	0,70	3,07
Height	60,25	2,77	4,59
Circumference	138,5	2,99	2,16
Potter 2, n°10			
Base	23,85	0,55	2,31
Aperture	24,1	0,76	3,17
Height	55,25	1,56	2,83
Circumference	152	5,73	3,77

Table 8: Metric evidence for measuring variation of water jars measurements: intra-individual scale

At the intra-individual scale, the results of coefficient of variation show that the products of each potter show moderate variation. In the case of Potter 1 the minimum variation percentage is to be found in the maximum circumference of the pot, whereas in that of Potter 2 this is clear in the base and height of the pot (**Table 8**).

The other metric measure taken is the wall thickness of the pots. The median thickness of water jars produced by Potter 1, at Kufranjeh, is 11,3 mm; whereas that produced by Potter 2, is 8,6 mm.

III.2 Formal variations in water jar production at the inter-village scale

III.2.1 Morphological variation

The water jar assemblages from the two villages differ either in their general or partial morphological features. At Arjan, the dominant water jar body-shape is globular. At Kufranjeh, the ovaloid body-shape prevails. This particular variation produces other smaller sub-variations (**Table 9**). For instance, this results in two different neck profiles. The first is produced at Kufranjeh and is characterized by a profile that appears continuous with the body itself, whereas that produced at Arjan, appears more detached from the body of the pot. The other resulting morphological variation concerns the rim profile. At Kufranjeh, the dominant rim profile is flattened and horizontal-everted, while at Arjan, it is either simple-rounded or bevelled. The other morphological variation between the two villages is related to handle. Water jars produced at Kufranjeh have four vertical loop handles. This is a feature distinctive of water jars produced at Kufranjeh. At Arjan, water jars generally have only two loop handles, in most cases, applied horizontally on the shoulder. Only in a few cases are vertical loop handles applied.

	Arjan	**Kufranjeh**
Body shape	*Globular*	*Ovaloid*
Rim profile	*Simple rounded or bevelled-everted*	*Flattened horizontal-everted*
Neck shape	*Detached from body*	*Sloppy with the body*
Handles	*Two handles*	*Four handles*

Table 9: Comparison of morphological characteristics of water jars at inter-village scale, northern Jordan

III.2.2 Metric measures

The second index of measuring variation for water jars assemblages at the inter-village scale is the metric analysis. Here, the coefficient of variation is used to describe and evaluate the degree of similarities and/or variability in vessel dimensions. In this case, variability will be expressed in the form of a percentage. The comparison of the coefficient of variation (C.V.) results (**Table 10**) shows that the two water jar assemblages, from Arjan and Kufranjeh, are distinguishable. The assemblage produced at Arjan has higher percentage variability compared to the one made at Kufranjeh. The higher range of C.V. variability is to be found in the base and aperture of the pots (**Fig. 21**), and lower in the maximum circumference of the pot. The low C.V. range percentage – 0,76% – has been observed in the height of the pot.

Variable	Mean	S.D	C.V
Arjan : n°24			
Base	20,5	1,67	8,19
Aperture	26	2,24	8,62
Height	52,25	3,32	6,36
Circumference	145	6,49	4,47
Kufranjeh : n°20			
Base	24	0,71	2,96
Aperture	23,5	0,94	4,00
Height	56,75	3,18	5,60
Circumference	143	7,97	5,57

Table 10: Metric evidence for measuring variation of water jars measurements: inter-village scale

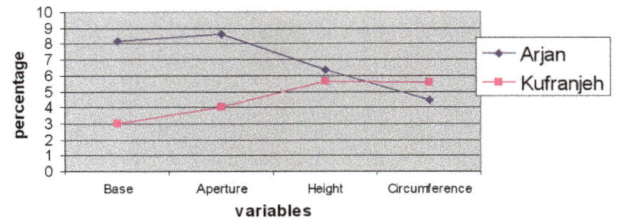

Coefficient of variation of water jar production between two villages

Fig. 21: Coefficient of variation of water jar production between the potters at an inter-village scale

In short, the metric data from the two villages show a level of variability that enables us to distinguish them as two different pottery assemblages.

IV. Technological parameters

This is the third index of measuring variation in water jar assemblages from the two villages chosen for this study. In this section, the focus will be drawn on the materialization of technical actions, undertaken by potters and reflected in their final products. We will use a set of technical features to measure the variability between the potters (different units of pottery production), instead of using decorative criteria, to identify micro-style or traditions.

The data set for evaluating technological parameters as a means of measuring variation is based on detailed description of three potters' work – two from Arjan (Potters 1 and 2), one potter from Kufranjeh (Potter 2) – and their finished products. These potters employed the same technique (coiling) in forming a specific pot shape (water jar). The invariant or strategic components of this technique have already been described (see chapter 2: III.1). However, the following is a description of the variant components of the technique that are reflected in the potters' final products. These variants have been identified after the following technical parameters.

IV.1 Coil size

This parameter has been reflected in the pot thickness. At the village scale, differences exist between potters. For example, in Arjan, there is a clear difference in the size of coils used by different potters (**Table 11**). Potter 1 uses larger coils compared to the ones of Potter 2. The product of the former, therefore, has a median thickness of 1,5 cm while that of Potter 2 has a median thickness of 1 cm. Such a correlation is also clear at Kufranjeh. The potters use smaller coils in pot forming which resulted in their final products. In this village the pot median thickness of Potter 2 is 8,6 mm.

Forming the body / stages	Potter 1 (Arjan)		Potter 2 (Arjan)		Potter 2 (Kufranjeh)	
	Coils N.	Coils size	Coils N.	Coils size	Coils N.	Coils size
1	2	19 x 5,5 x 5,5	2	24 x 8 x 3	Substage 1: 3 Substage 2: 4 Substage 3: 4	23 x 5,5 x 5 10 x 2 x 2 15 x 2 x 2,5
2	3	26 x 5,5 x 5,5 + 8 x 5 x 5,5	4	24 x 7,5 x 2,5	5	17 x 3 x 2
3	4	24 x 6 x 6	4	34 x 7 x 2	6	18 x 3 x 2
4	5	22 x 5 x 5,5	5	24 x 6 x 2,5	5	30 x 5 x 2
5	3	20 x 5 x 5	3	20 x 4 x 2	4	29 x 5 x 2,5
Forming neck + rim	3	10 x 5,5 x 5,5	3	20 x 5 x 2,5	3	28 x 6 x 3

Table 11: Correlation between the pot segment being formed and coil sizes

IV.2 Coils joining pattern

At Arjan one end of each coil is grooved and this increases the thickness of the joined parts. At the same time, the joining area is characterized by the presence of elongated voids. By contrast, joining coils by using abut methods, which at Kufranjeh is the choice of the potters, result either in a constant thickness with the previous finished course or in a relative decrease of the thickness.

IV.3 Segmentation of the pot body

This technological parameter is relatively consistent between the two potters in Arjan. In their products, the corrugations between coils appear in a relatively equal distance along the body (**Table 12**). At Kufranjeh, body-forming courses differ in size (21,5 cm, 21,5+4 cm, 25,5+9,5 cm, 35+9 cm and 44+5 cm). It is only at a height of 21 cm that the first corrugation of coils can be identified (**Fig. 22 b**). This is in contrast with the products of the potters at Arjan where this can be identified at a height of 14 cm (**Fig. 22 a**).

Course	Potter 2 (Arjan)		Potter 2 (Kufranjeh)	
	Height (cm)	Diameter (cm)	Height (cm)	Diameter (cm)
1	14	37	21,5	40,5
2	24	45	25,5	45,5
3	35	42	35	45
4	44	34	44	37.5
5	46	24	49	24
6	54	24	60	25

Table 12: A comparison between the height of worked segments of pots made by potters from Arjan and Kufranjeh

IV.4 Evenness

This parameter reflects the *degree* of evenness acquired by the pot face during the shaping operation. At Arjan, Potter 1 produces pot faces with less recesses or dent

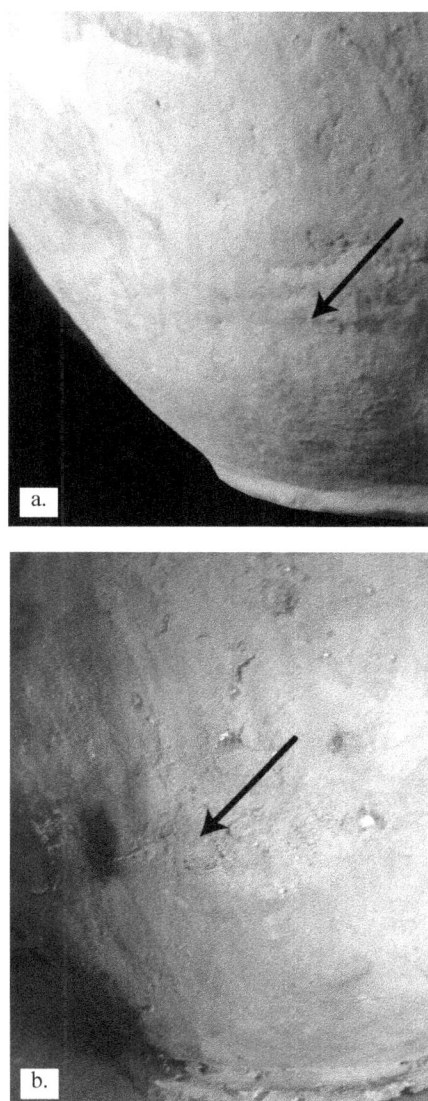

Fig. 22: The technical features associated with using different coils sizes in building the lower part of the water jar: a) the potter at Arjan, b) the potter at Kufranjeh

along the face of the pot. The case differs with the vessels of Potter 2 (**Fig. 23 a**). Here the pots are characterized by a domination of relative recesses that are distributed along the face of the pot. The pattern and the recesses are clearer in the coils joining areas. At Kufranjeh, the products of Potter 2 are characterized by a relative evenness of the faces with less dominance of recesses along the pot's external face (**Fig. 23 b**). Meanwhile, the product of Potter 1 is characterized by overlapped clay layers which result in a micro-relief surface (**Fig. 23 b**).

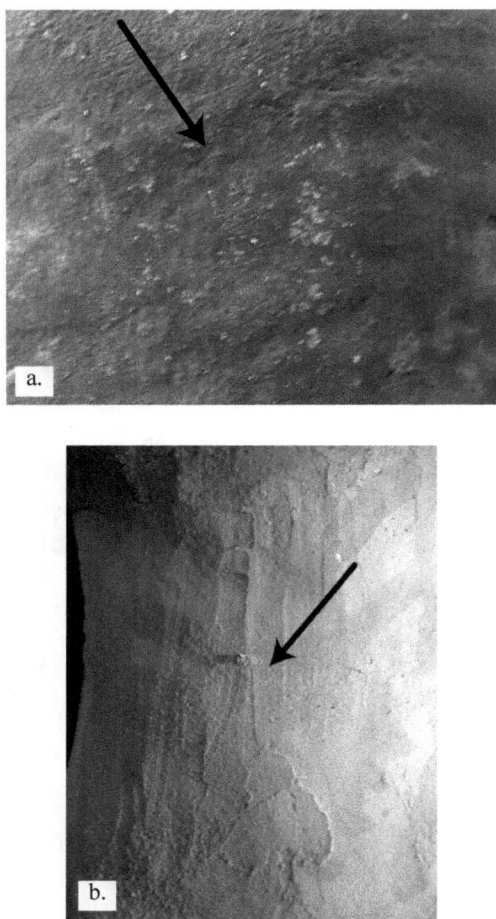

Fig. 23: A comparison of the degree of pot surface evenness among the potters in northern Jordan: a) a product of Potter 2 at Arjan showing the recesses along the surface of the pot; b) a product of Potter 1 at Kufranjeh showing the overlapped clay layers in a micro-relief pattern

IV.5 Finishing

At Arjan, the products of Potter 1 are often characterized by self-slip faces whereas the water jars produced by Potter 2 show outside faces characterized by a random distribution of burnished like-spots / areas. At Kufranjeh,

the product of Potter 2 reveals the same pattern and also entails a self-slip face beside the burnished like-one.

V. Discussion

Measuring pottery variation aims at correlating the human behavioural pattern with the structural organization of production units. Variables such as paste variability, technology, and skill have been evaluated to identify such a correlation (Arnold 2000; Costin 2000; Longacre 1999). Moreover, the emphasis on multi-variables to measure the structural organization of production units has been recommended (Gosselain 2000). For example, the combination of paste variability and operational sequence of production have been used to identify the production units (Gosselain 2000). The multi-variables based inferences are significant when potters are operating within the same environmental and geological conditions such as are the ones in northern Jordan. Under these production conditions it is significant "to see if there are other ways besides general composition … to distinguish among the products of different potters or work group" (Costin 2000: 389).

In the above study, three criteria have been chosen to measure variation in northern Jordan between the production of the potters. These are morphological, metric and technical features. Morphological variation, in terms of rim profile, and body shape, show a significance in defining the production units either at the village level or among villages. Such a set of parameters were significant in segregating the products of the two villages in two formal distinctive groups (**Table 10**). These are also of significance in defining pottery micro-style. For example, water jars at Arjan can be classified into two groups based on the rim profile. These groups, however, represent the output of two potters who are differentiated in thier source of learning.

Metric measurement is significant because it can be employed to infer the degree of potter's skill (Deal 1998; Longacre 1999). The metric analysis of the four potters' products shows that the most skilful potter produces an object with higher coefficient of variation, when the less skilled potters produce lower C.V.

Identifying micro-styles has been based on the technological features, especially the one related to shaping and finishing operations. The potters we observed share the same *chaîne opératoire* but they participate in this *chaîne* knowledge differently. Their products can be grouped mainly according to the degree of pot evenness and the method of face finishing. The products of the two potters at Arjan, for example, can be clearly classified into two technical groups based on the degree of evenness and finishing of the outside surface of the pots.

To sum up, the analysis of the pottery corpus from northern Jordan revealed that the identification of micro-styles in pottery production can be achieved based on two interrelated variables. These are formal variables such as morphological and metric ones that are supported with technological analysis in terms of the operation sequences.

Chapter Five: **Explaining pottery variation between potters in northern Jordan**

In the previous chapter, an attempt was made to identify the parameters that can help in defining variation for one functional pot type – the water jar. Two main indexes have been analysed: a formal and a technological one. In this chapter, the focus will be on establishing valid explanatory framework for understanding pottery variation in the northern part of Jordan.

Several studies on pottery variation have been conducted, stressing on the social, political and economic dimensions underlying its cause. These include, among others, the degree of social interaction and the learning framework, the age at which the craft is learned, factors related to potter decision-making, and individual motor performance or habits and skill (Arnold 1989; Hill 1977; Longacre 1999; van der Leeuw 1991, 1994; Deal 1998; Hardin 1991; Graves 1991). The significance of these studies is that they tackle different dimensions underlying pottery variation. They show also the difficulty in emphasizing one aspect or dimension over others, and the difficulty in proposing one explanatory model that encompasses all the dimensions underlying pottery variation (van der Leeuw 1991).

In the following pages, the causes of pottery variation in Jordan are addressed with respect to the social and economical dimensions. These are organized chronologically according to the processes that are enhanced in artefact becoming.

I. Social interaction and learning

The social dimension, as represented by the source of learning, has been evaluated as a main cause of pottery variation, both with respect to style and techno-form (Arnold 1993; Hayden and Cannon 1984; Graves 1991). In this context, the products of potters who share the same source of learning will exhibit more similarities which can be materialized in the final products as micro-style / tradition. The source of learning has been assumed to be closely related with the residence pattern within a community.

The correlation between the residence pattern and the source of learning has been positively attested with respect to Jordanian potters. This has been manifested in the technical as well as the formal (metric and morphological) characteristics of pottery repertoire at the village scale. At the inter-individual scale, it has been noticed that concerning the potters who share the same source of learning, the product will reveal little differences in terms of the morphological, metric (coefficient of variation) and

technical characteristics of the pot. The study of water jar assemblages at Kufranjeh shows such a correlation. In contrast, at Arjan various sources of learning have been reflected, within the potter population, by the morphological parameters of their products and supported as well by technological ones in terms of shaping operation as it is obvious in the evenness and finishing of the pots. The range of coefficient of variation is a good tool to support such a difference.

So, it can be supposed that social organization within a community corresponds spatially to household distribution patterns. Potters who are socially and spatially close to each other might well develop a pottery micro-tradition at the community level, often defined by a shared source of pottery learning. Each micro-style or tradition can be well identified based on morphological, coefficient of variation and technological indexes.

II. The conceptualisation of water jar

The conceptual scheme of the shape of a pot is considered here as a second factor in explaining variation in pottery. The main reason is that the conceptual scheme requires less time to acquire compared with the operational sequence of pot shaping (Arnold 1993). The term concept refers to the general mental representation and abstraction of an object (Petit Robert 1993: 429). It implies a general representation of typical entities rather than specific definitions (Thagard 1996). The reason for employing such an analysis stems from the idea that artefacts or objects encode the artisan's thoughts and intentions (Renfrew 1994). Consequently, actions undertaken by the maker are considered as being preceded by a mental scheme (Karlin and Julien 1994; Schlanger 1994; van der Leeuw 1994), which guides her/him through the different steps of object manufacture.

In pottery studies, it has been postulated that the conceptual scheme can be explained by analysing the shape of the pot. By reconstructing and defining the *chaîne opératoire* of pottery-making, van der Leeuw (1994) proposes three conceptual components related to pot-shaping: a) *topology*, b) *partonomy* and c) *sequence*.

a) Topology: examination of the shape: whether it is horizontal or vertical; whether its shape was transformed by stretching or compressing, whether anything distinguishes the internal or external face.
b) Partonomy: the conceptual division of the pot into parts; i.e., the basic components out of which the pot is made – for example, the number of coils.

c) Sequence: the sequence of pot forming – for instance, whether it was formed from bottom to top or top to bottom.

In analysing the forming sequences of Tradition I in Jordan, we consider these three conceptual components. A detailed analysis of the *chaîne opératoire* will not be repeated here, as it was discussed previously. Only the main points will be presented to illustrate the conceptual components of pot shaping. The discussion will focus on the shaping of the water jar. Here, we examine the output of two potters at Arjan and one potter at Kufranjeh. The related forming sequence passes through three phases: forming the base, the body, and the neck-rim-lip.

The three potters follow the same sequence. The base is formed first, then the body and finally the neck-rim-lip. The same conceptual scheme is shared with respect to base orientation and forming method. The base is transformed from a ball of clay, flattened between the palms, and then placed on a flat supporting tool.

The pot body may be seen as being composed of several continuous horizontal partitions, and each transformation of segmental coiling – as a basic entity. Each horizontal partition is chronologically separated from the next by a drying interval, but together they are conceived as a continuous conception of shape. Cases differ, however, between villages. The conception of the lower part of the pot's body at Kufranjeh is different from that at Arjan. At Kufranjeh, potters conceptualised the lower part of the body as composing three sub-phases, and without any leather hard drying interval (**Fig. 24 a**). The potters conceptualise this part as one unit. At Arjan, by contrast, the size of the lower part is symmetrical, and there is a drying interval (**Fig. 24 b**). The causes of such variation is related to the conceptualised form of the water jar. At Kufranjeh, potters tended to produce larger water jars. This corresponded to an increased diameter of the lower part of the pot.

Within this tradition, there is also a similarity in the shaping of the neck-rim-lip part. This is reflected in the segmentation of the pot and the volume of clay used in shaping this part.

III. The motor habit

Habit is defined as "a thing that a person does often and almost without thinking". This is inclusive of the motor pattern involved in exploiting the environment and the mechanism of behaviour learning (Bril *et al.* 1996; cited in Gelbert 2000: 160). Motor habit has generally been characterized as being unconscious, i.e. learned through the medium of one's culture and thus difficult to change (Arnold 1993: 121; Hill 1977: 56). The stability of motor

habit reflects the long time needed to learn complex gestures and related practices (Karlin and Julien 1994). As such, it has been assumed that variation in material culture, e.g. pottery, can be correlated to the maker's motor habit, and the individual variation (Muller 1977: 27).

At the methodological level, the task is to define those attributes that can be of use in measuring potters' motor habit. The characteristic of these attributes should be the ones that do not relate to pots functional requirements (Costin and Hagstrum 1995). One of the methods to measure potter's motor habit has been the coefficient of variation (C.V.) (Roux: personal communication). This statistical analysis seeks to define the range of variation that can be identified in the final products of a given potter. The data set of such an analysis is the proportional dimensions of the pottery assemblage.

The role of motor habit as a cause of pottery variation has been attested with respect to the water jar assemblage produced by the four potters in northern Jordan. The result of C.V. of the two potters at Arjan showed that they are clearly differentiated in terms of the proportional dimensions of their products. It seems that each potter is accustomed to produce water jars with a definite proportional dimension that differs from the other. This has been attested with the high range of percentage of C.V. between their products. In contrast, the potters at Kufranjeh seem to have more similarities in their motor habit concerning the proportional dimensions of the water jars. This has been attested with respect to the low range of C.V. difference of their product.

IV. The different levels of know-how

Above, we have seen that potters at the village scale share the same conceptual scheme of pot-shaping with respect to pot operation sequence, the manner of partition and the spatial conception of shape. Moreover, we have examined the role of motor habit as a cause of pottery variation. In this part, the aim is to define the different levels of know-how, skill of pot shaping as a variable that can be correlated with pottery variation as they have been identified in the water jar assemblage from northern Jordan.

The basis of asserting this variable is the proposition that "the variations in a technical production depend... on the difference between levels of technical skill, that is the degree of proficiency in acquiring both knowledge and a more or less advanced know-how" (Karlin and Julien 1994: 156). At the out-set, it is of value to define what skill is. Skill is assumed to reflect "the craft-person's experience, proficiency, and talent and is recognized and appreciated by artisans and consumers alike" (Costin and Hagstrum 1995: 623). However, measuring the level of skill is a subjective matter and it is a difficult behaviour to

WATER JAR

Kufranjeh

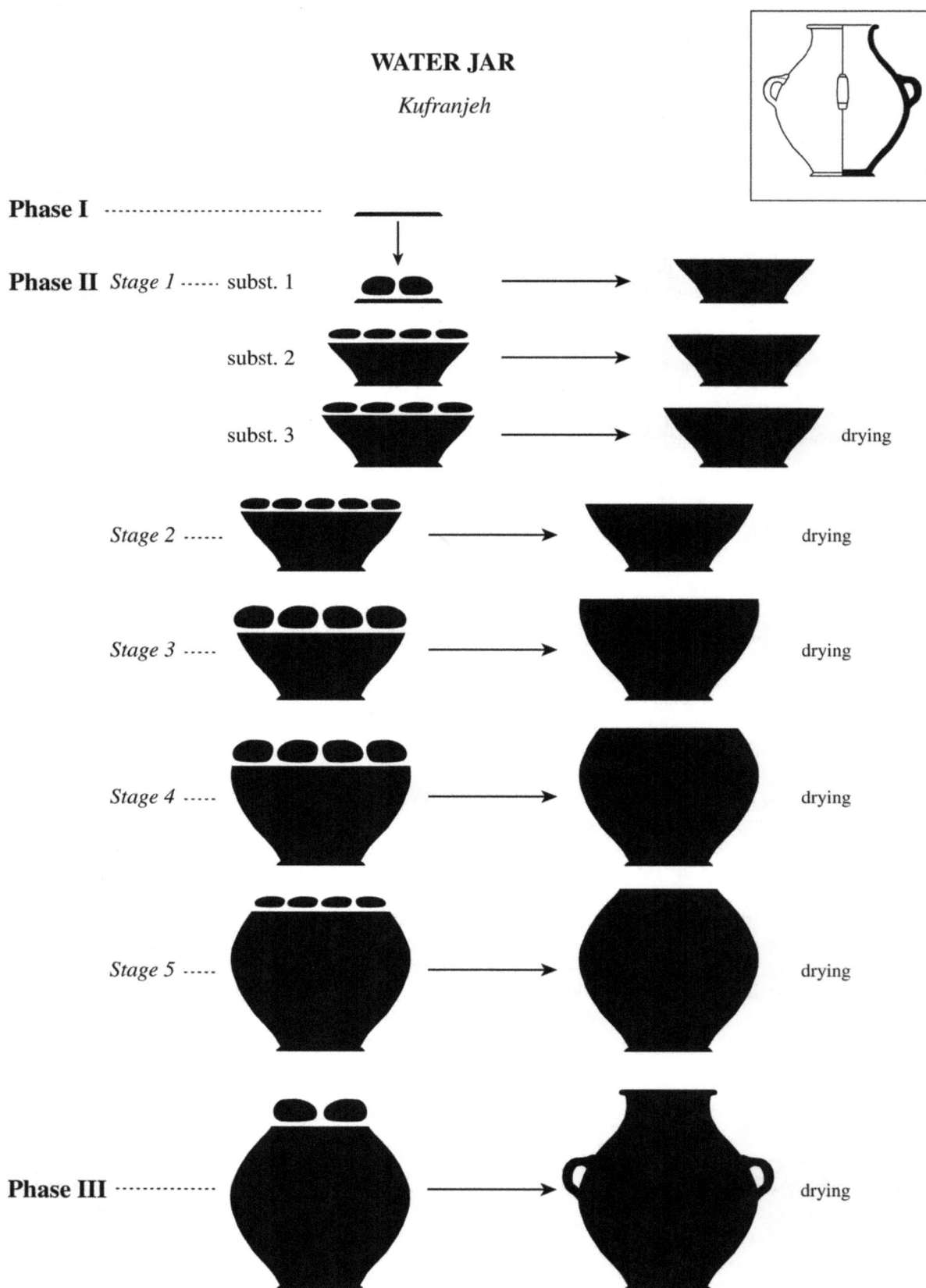

Phase I ....

Phase II *Stage 1* ...... subst. 1 .... →

subst. 2 .... →

subst. 3 .... → drying

Stage 2 .... → drying

Stage 3 .... → drying

Stage 4 .... → drying

Stage 5 .... → drying

Phase III .... → drying

Fig. 24 a: The partition of water jar form – Kufranjeh

WATER JAR

Arjan

Phase I ················

Phase II *Stage 1* ····   drying

Stage 2 ····   drying

Stage 3 ····   drying

Stage 4 ····   drying

Stage 5 ····   drying

Phase III ···············   drying

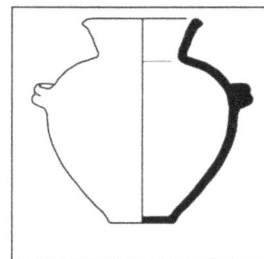

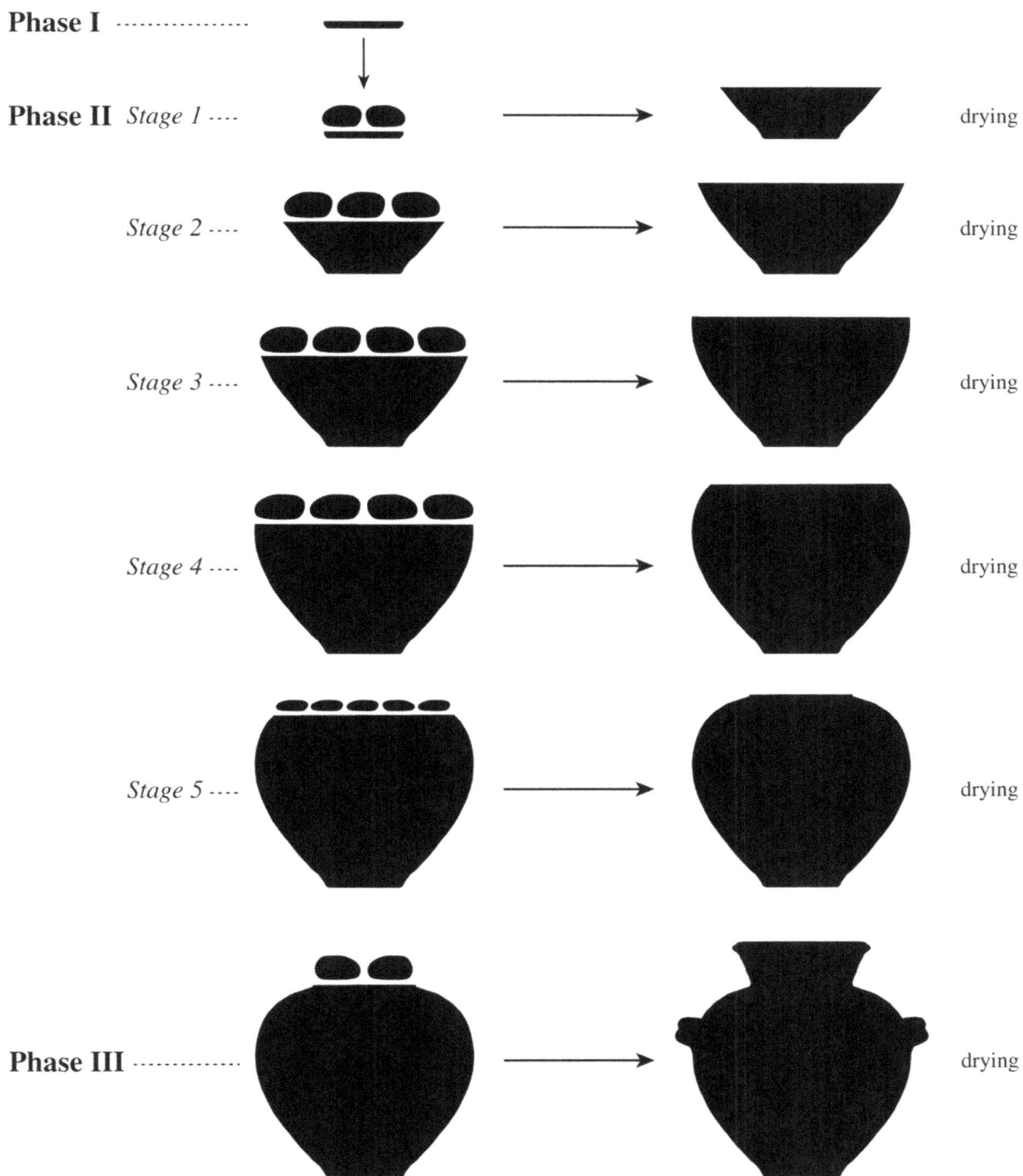

Fig. 24 b: The partition of water jar form – Arjan

be measured either in the actual studies or in the archaeological ones. This difficulty laid, in identifying and quantifying those material culture attributes that can be of use in measuring the level of skill. Therefore, for some ethnoarchaeologists, like Rice (1996), skill can not be measured on material culture. Whereas for others, like Longacre (1999), Costin and Hagstrum (1995), they postulate the possibility of measuring the different levels of skill.

Two kinds of criteria have been postulated for measuring the level of skill in pottery production: the proportional dimensions of the pot and their technology. The former is based on the metric analysis of the assemblage. In this regard, it is assumed that the degree of standardization in pottery production, as measured by the coefficient of variation, can be correlated with the potter's level of skill. Hence, skilled potters would make standardized pots which would have low C.V., as marking standardized objects (Longacre 1999). Such a correlation between the degree of standardization and the level of potter skill has been assumed to be related to the intensity of production (Costin and Hagstrum 1995; Longacre 1999). In this case, the products of full-time specialists are assumed to be more skilfully made in comparison with those of part-time potters.

In the previous chapter, we have seen that there is a remarkable difference in the results of C.V. among the potters in northern Jordan. Whether these variations of C.V. are related to the level of a potter's skill is questionable. Pottery production in northern Jordan is a part-time activity, and the rate of production does not exceed 15 water jars per year. The different level of skill among the observed potters in Jordan has been evaluated against the age at which they learn the craft, their age and the community consensus. The correlation between the level of skill of these potters and the C.V. of their products is noticeable. At Arjan, the products of the most experienced skilled potter (Potter 1) are characterized by high C.V. This result was contrary to the expected ones that the products of this potter will exhibit high degree of standardization. Potter 2, at the same village, has a moderate skill and the C.V. is consistent with her level of skill. At the inter-village scale, the two Kufranjeh potters have a moderate skill, in regard to the criteria mentioned above. But the C.V. result of their products is lower compared with the one of the Arjan Potter 1, whose high skill is deemed. This difference in C.V. can be explained not in terms of potter's skill but in terms of technological attributes (see below).

The second index that can be used to measure skill is the technological attributes. For most of them, they should be the ones that have no functional requirements, and could then be an indication of the regularity and consistency in technique (Costin and Hagstrum 1995: 623; Karlin and

Julien 1994).

Here, the technical attributes that are related to operation process of pottery shaping is evaluated as a means of measuring variation and consequently the level of skill. The level of technical skill is evaluated by a comparison between the final product and the extent to which the whole operative process of manufacture is actually performed. The operative process embedded in the manufacture of an object can be defined by a fine analysis of the gestures involved and their chronological succession. Not all objects will reflect the same pattern. Some of them will either reflect the whole operational sequences of manufacture or will miss a few steps. Hence, technical skill can provide a measure of the quality of production compared to the ideal (i.e., the intended final product) by taking into account the operational sequences or technical scheme. In this regard, the artisan's level of experience could play a role in improving the manufacturing of the intended object by incorporating more complex technical scheme. Experience plays a role in the way an artisan evaluates technical problems that can emerge during the manufacture of an object. During the early stage of this ethnographic research, an attempt has been made to replicate the manufacturing of a very large storage jar (1,6 m height x 1,13 m in diameter) found in the upper levels of the Abu Hamid settlement and dating to the early fourth millenium BC (Ali 1998). Three potters were asked to make the same jar. Two of the potters were from Arjan, (Potters 1 and 2), and the third from Ammyria (Potter 2). Only Potter 1 from Arjan accepted the challenge to replicate the storage jar. She evaluated the problems linked to the possibility of collapse of the body due to the relation between its flaring profile and its thickness (4-5 cm). Potter 2 from the same village failed to solve these problems. She had learnt the craft later in her life, when she was over 30 years old. Moreover, it seems that she was restricted with respect to the motor know-how she acquired during her learning. Her case differed for Potter 1's one, who acquired the technical knowledge early in her life. This potter was used to a relatively intense level of production compared with other potters of the village.

At Arjan, the difference in the degree of skill between these two potters has been manifested in their water jar production. The products of Potter 1 differ from that of other potters in the same village in terms of the technical proficiency. The bodies of the water jars show a high-level of symmetry indicating a greater control during the shaping operation at pot's different spatial distance. Additionally, the surfaces of the pot were subjected to a greater degree of evenness. In the same village, the second potter's skill can be measured in the degree of control during shaping operation; despite the fact that she utilized the whole technical scheme of shaping, she exhibited less ability to produce a symmetrical body profile. One half of the profile was dented showing a rip in the body. Moreover, the pot bodies were marked by shallow micro-reliefs and recesses.

The degree of skill with respect to the complexity of technical scheme of pot shaping has been attested against the products of Potter 3 at the same village, Arjan. The products of Potter 3 are characterized by one step missing in the shaping sequence: the evenness operation, to obtain a smooth outside surface. The product is characterized by the dominance of recess and a micro-relief surface (made up of overlapped micro-layers of clay). The degree of skill is also evident in the way the plasticity of the clay has been controlled when the pot was shaped in order to prevent any collapse. Potter 3 at Arjan achieved this by an intense use of goat hair. The goat hair, in this case, strengthens the body of the pot during the shaping operation. However, the possibility of collapse resulted from the technical scheme used by the potter, the stage of roughing-out and preform, usually moves from one stage to the next without allowing enough time in between for the clay to rest, *yartah*, before further shaping. This is an important step in preventing the part of the pot, which was worked on from quick collapsing.

Discussing the different levels of know-how in the manufacture of pots, one can conclude that technical skill can be measured by identifying the potter's operative ideational know-how. This can be measured through close observation of the various successive gestures performed during the time the pot is shaped. This has an application to the analysis of pottery coming from archaeological sites where usually few complete vessels are found.

V. The economical dimension

In Jordan the potters' motivation to go on pottery production has an economic dimension. As stated above, most of the pots produced by potters are made for the market. This factor affects largely the diversity of the pottery. The constraint of market has a clear manifestation considering the way the surface of the pot is finished and sometimes decorated. Three kinds of decoration have been identified on water jars: application of organic slip, inorganic slip and painting. As usual each potter uses one of those, but it happens that a potter utilizes the three. Variation in the decoration of water jars is related to the demand of middle-men. Because the market's demand is more in favour of decorated vessels than of plain ones, potters use these modes of decoration to increase the opportunity for selling their products.

From a technical point of view, the effect of demand on pottery-shaping is manifested in the finishing methods applied. Potters usually make a correlation between the smoothness of the surface and increased sale opportunities. Potter 2 at Arjan, therefore, spent additional time in ensuring that the surface of a pot is smooth – a supplement aesthetic factor perceived as indicating good product quality. The same was observed in the production of Ballas Potter 2. She likewise sees a correlation between the smoothness of the surface as well as the thickness of the body and increased sale opportunities.

To sum up this chapter, it is important to address the many dimensions involved in studying pottery variation. It has been noted that focusing on one dimension will not co-operate with the multi-factors that can play a role in explaining this variation. On the other hand, it should be emphasized that factors of explaining variation among potters who operated in a small-scale production may be addressed differently.

PART II:

FROM STATIC TO DYNAMIC CONTEXT OF ARCHAEOLOGICAL POTTERY PRODUCTION AT *ABU HAMID*: LATE 6TH – 5TH MILLENNIUM BC

Chapter Six: **The archaeological context of Abu Hamid**

The main aims of this chapter are to define the location-setting of the archaeological site of Abu Hamid, a history of the research is done at the site, a description of the spatio-temporal context and finally a description of its archaeological context.

I. Site setting

The archaeological site of Abu Hamid (32° 19` N, 35° 32` E) is located in the Jordan Valley, at an equal distance from Tiberias Lake in the north and the Dead Sea in the south (**Map 5**). The settlement, almost 20 km north of the Zarqa River, is situated at an elevation of 240 m below sea level (Dollfus and Kafafi 1986: 91). On its northern and southern sides, it is bordered by two small *wadis*, and to the west by the Jordan River, which flows nowadays almost ½ km to the west of the site (**Fig. 25**, see next page).

In addition to the Jordan River, two other main water resources are located near the site. These are the Abu Hamid Spring to the north, and Umm el Ghuzllan to the south-east (Dollfus *et al.* 1988: 571).

Abu Hamid falls in the central Jordan Valley which extends from about 50 km north of the Dead Sea to the northern shore of Lake Tiberias. The area is a depression, bordered on the east by the Ajlun Mountains which reach an altitude of approximately 1200 m above sea level, and on the west by the Nablus Mountains. The Jordan Valley, as well as the region of Abu Hamid, is characterized by four main zones. From east to west these are:

1. The piedmont: located about 4 km east of the site. It is a steep fault, and is intersected by a number of wadis. Three of them have an impact on the region of Abu Hamid. From north to south these are Wadi Subeirra, Wadi el-Laman (Suleikhat), and Wadi Sarar.

2. The Ghor, which slopes gently from east to west at an angle of about 2, 5 %. It is 3, 9 km wide, and is covered by a layer of brown-reddish clay. From north to south in this zone runs an artificial canal. Both sides of the canal are cultivated with a variety of fruits and vegetables. However, cultivation on the east side of the canal, and at the piedmont, is concentrated on seasonal crops, such as cereals.

3. Al-Qatarat (the Bad Lands), the site where Abu Hamid is located is a zone ranging in width up to about 500 m. This is a gulleyed area, consisting of alluvial heaps, some of which are covered by a residue of dark-red clay.

4. Al-Zor, where the Jordan River flows. It is situated about 300 m below sea-level. This area varies in width from 0,5–2 km; it is situated about 0,5 km west of Abu Hamid, and ca. 60 m lower than the level of the site (Hourani 2002: 49, 87-89).

II. The climate conditions in the Jordan Valley

The site of Abu Hamid, as part of the central Jordan Valley, is located within Irano-Turanian region, which characterized by poor soil types, poor vegetation, low rainfall precipitation and high temperature (Al-Eisawi 1985: 46). The

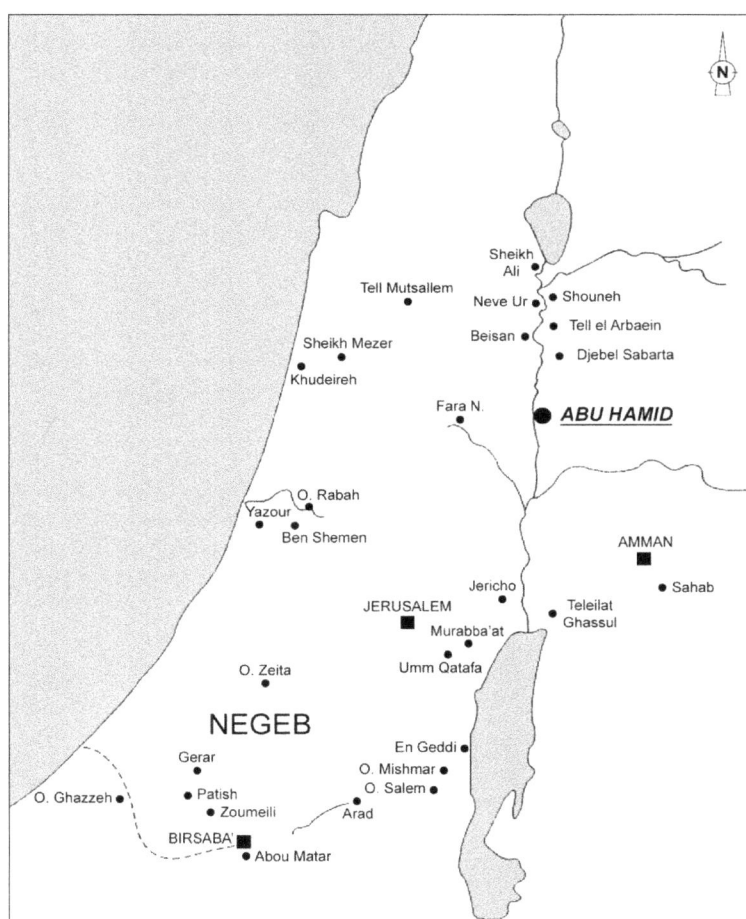

Map 5: Location of Abu Hamid (after Dollfus *et al.*, 1988)

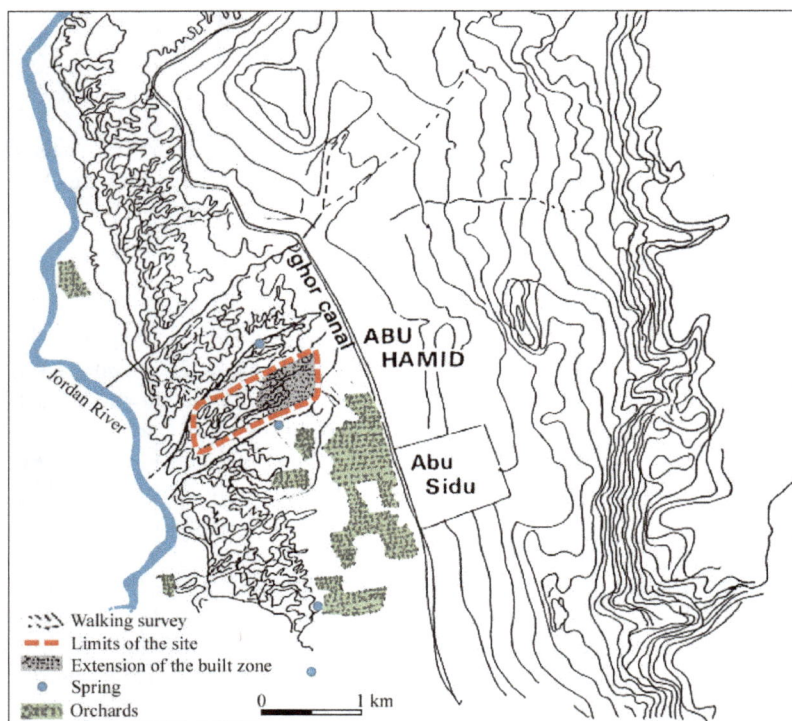

Fig. 25: The topographical features around the site of Abu Hamid
(after Dollfus *et al.*, 1988)

and considered for this period as one of the most important sites in the Valley. In his survey of Neolithic sites in the Jordan Valley, Kafafi re-visited the site and also dated it to the Neolithic / Chalcolithic period (1982).

On the suggestion of Prof. Dr. M. Ibrahim, a joint jordano-french project was launched in 1986 under the direction of Dr. Z. Kafafi (Yarmouk University) and Dr. G. Dollfus (CNRS). Since then 5 field seasons- survey and excavations-followed by analytical one, were made (Dollfus and Kafafi *et al.,* 1986, 1988; Dollfus and Kafafi 1988b). The early 4th millennium settlement has been evaluated to cover 6 ha where the extension of the earlier occupation are still unknown. 2000 m² of the Upper Levels have been exposed whereas 1500 m² for the Middle Levels. The Basal Levels were reached on 200 m² in two long perpendicular trenches (N-S 60x2 m and E-W 30x2 m that were dug to the virgin soil (Dollfus and Kafafi 1993, 2001).

valley and the piedmont are located in warm steppe climate region which is characterized by high temperature in summer and moderate one in winter. The mean minimum temperature, in the coldest month, January, ranges between 1°C and 11°C. Meanwhile the maximum temperature in the hottest month in August ranges from 28°C and 39°C (Al-Eisawi 1985: 50; Shehadeh 1985: 35). The annual rainfall in most of the Jordan Valley is less than 200mm. In particular, the annual rainfall at Abu Hamid ranges between 200-250 mm.

Recent Paleo-environmental studies in the Jordan Valley showed that three morpho-climatical phases can be identified that covered the early to mi-Holocene (Hourani 2002; Hourani and Courty 1997). The first phase, between 10500-8000 BP, is characterized by warm and humid climate condition. At the beginning of the second phase (8000-6500 BP) the climate condition was instable which is characterized by erosion and torrential flows. This, however, has been followed by a period of stability, cold, and humidity conditions. The last climate phase is characterized by semi-arid conditions.

III. History of research at the site

Abu Hamid was first identified in 1975 during a general archaeological survey of the Jordan Valley (Ibrahim, Yassine and Sauer 1976: 50). Based on pottery readings, the site was dated to the Neolithic / Chalcolithic period,

IV. The stratigraphy and sequence of occupation

IV.1 Stratigraphy (**Fig. 26**)

The excavations in Area A showed that the archaeological deposits at Abu Hamid from top to bottom consist of:

1) A very disturbed surface layer: 30-60 cm, greyish and powdery sediment with red patches of clay, in some areas traces of plough furrows.

2) Thin layers of grey very powdery sediment: 50-70 cm. In some areas these grey layers directly overlay a thick (ca. 1,8 m) red and sterile clay deposit whereas in other zones, they cover a fine red-pinkish sediment with thin horizontal ashy layers. A series of levels (1-2c) have been recognized:
a) Levels 1a-c: very clumsy remains of walls; occupation floors; hearths; series of small shallow pits.
b) Levels 2b-c: houses with either mud-bricks walls or mud brick ones laid on stone foundations

3) Pinkish-greenish loamy layers: 50-100cm.
Levels 3a-c: mud-brick pluricellular houses; hearths and cooking pits outside the habitations

4) Pinkish-reddish and green marly clay: 80-120cm.
This includes Levels 4-5b:
a) Level 4: 60-80 cm pinkish and greenish sediments with

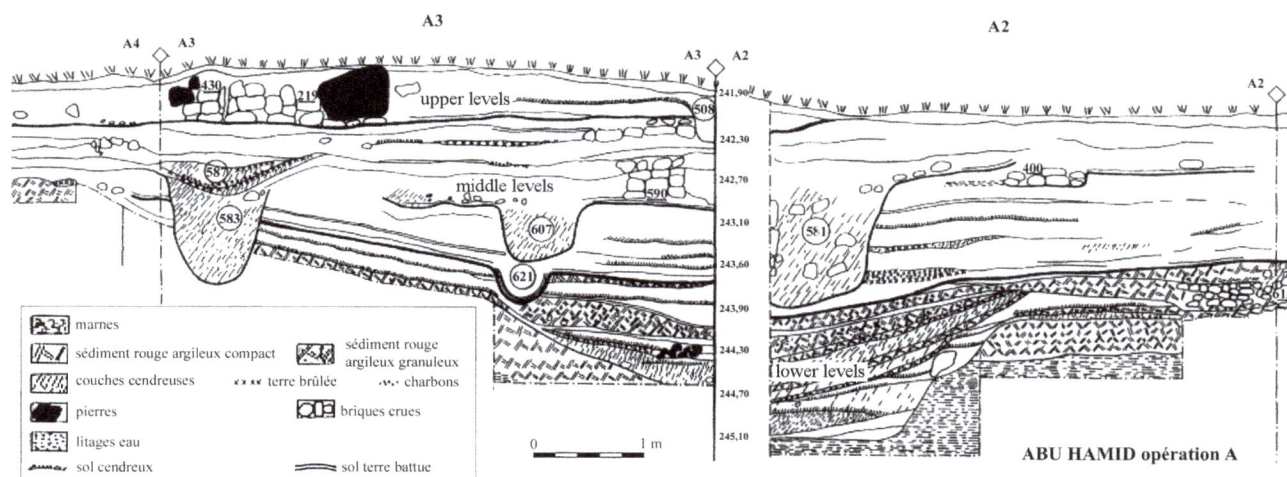

Fig. 26: Section-drawing showing the stratigraphy of Area A at Abu Hamid (after Lovell *et al.*, 1997: Fig. 1)

a series of thin ashy layers: traces of non permanent occupations

b) Level 5a-b: dark-red compact clay that covers the surface of the marls of the Lisan.

Remains of dwellings. 5a circular -oval semi-subterranean house. 5b dwelling pits (170-180 cm deep) cut into the clay sediment and the top of the marls (Dollfus and Kafafi 1993: 242-243).

IV.2 Sequence of occupation (**Fig. 27**)

According to the stratigraphy and the analysis of the material culture, it has been possible to divide the sequence of occupation in three main cultural phases:

1) Lower Levels

This includes Levels 5-4. At its beginning (Level 5b), Abu Hamid settlement was formed by a series of "dwelling pits" which could be either natural depressions, the side of which being re-cut and the floor levelled by humans – the fill of at least one of them shows that they have been used as a dwelling (Hourani 2002) – or totally artificial excavated ones. The hearths are on the outside ground.

In Level 5a, a circular-oval house (living floor 40cm beneath the ground) has been excavated. A hearth was inside.

In Level 4, a series of layers of ashes as well as numerous post holes, hearths; fire pits and basins show clearly that, at least in this area, the site was occupied by non sedentary groups.

These Levels can be related to what is called Late Neolithic by (Kafafi 1988). According to the ceramic typology in the Jordan Valley the pottery shows ties with

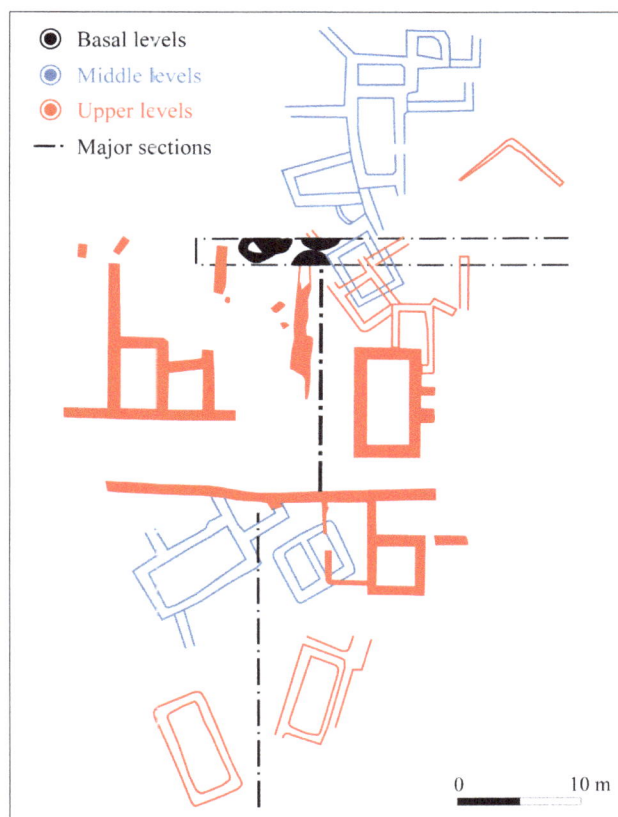

Fig. 27: Ground plan showing the 3 main levels at Abu Hamid (after Lovell *et al.* 2004: Fig. 3)

Ghrubba material (Mellaart 1956), and if we consider the painted decoration to Jericho IX and to the Munhata phase defined by Perrot (1964, 1968). It is clearly post "classical Yarmoukian" (for "classical Yarmoukian" cf. among others Stekelis 1950-51, 1972; Perrot 1964; Garfinkel 1992). A slight change in the pottery appears in Level 4 (cf. Lovell, in preparation). The relative chronology of these Levels places them at the late eight millennium BP.

2) Middle Levels

In these layers (3c-a) were excavated rectangular mud-brick buildings forming large multicellular complexes of habitation: living rooms with domestic structures like platforms, smaller storage rooms, courtyard or outside areas where cooking and other domestic activities were taking place. There, fired pits, clay or plaster-lined basins, very deep conical or cylindrical large pits are found.

These levels have to be related to the Wadi Rabah chronological Horizon (Kaplan 1958, 1972). Even if some forms characteristic of the Wadi Rabah pottery such as carinated bowls and bow rimmed jars are in a smaller amount than in the eponym assemblage or even lacking, the decorated pottery and the very rare(1-2% of the Abu Hamid assemblage) highly burnished ware (DFBW, RFBW) show very clearly that Abu Hamid Levels 3 should be tied to this horizon.

The Wadi Rabah horizon is related to what is generally called "early Chalcolithic" because the type of settlements as well as the cultural material is much more linked to what is known of their future than their past. These Levels have been dated to the late seventh millennium ^{14}C BP.

3) Upper Levels

Almost 2200 m^2 of this phase has been excavated and revealed:

Levels 2c-a: large rectangular structures built of mud bricks for some of them and with walls on stone foundations for others. To the main rooms that can be subjected to modifications, smaller rooms might be added. The habitations are separated one from the other by large and well-organized open space areas.

Levels 1c-a: these levels close to the surface are very disturbed. Occupation floors with material on it. The remains of walls, preserved only as traces (at the most one or two layers of bricks), the large cylindrical pits as well as areas with numerous small diameter (ca. 30-50 cm) make very difficult to understand the plan of the settlement in Area A. However, in Area B (50 m east, a zone separated from the Area A by a deep erosion gulley) were found rectangular rooms linked one to the other; in one of them was a very large storage jar.

The settlement pattern, the material culture are related to what is known in the Jordan Valley north of Abu Hamid for example at Neve Ur (Perrot and Zory 1967), south of Abu Hamid as Ghassul (Hennessy 1982) and further south

and west in the Negev (Gilead 1987, 1990). Now this cultural phase is most often called "late Chalcolithic". The dating of these Levels places them in the early 6th millennium ^{14}C BP.

V. Cultural development and the site-life history

Few sites, either in the Jordan Valley or in other regions in Jordan, have yielded such a comprehensive cultural history running from the late sixth to the fourth millennium BC, as does Abu Hamid. During this time-span a large number of occupational levels have been recognized. They have been grouped in their major cultural phases designated as the Lower, Middle and Upper Levels. The study of these levels sheds light on the various ways of occupation and their evolution through time. At first (Lower Levels), the human groups were occupying large and deep pits. Some of them were natural depressions, others were natural depressions but the side was re-cut by humans (Hourani 1997, 2002). The organization of these pits is not yet totally clear but two of them are very close one to the other. These pits seem not to have been occupied at the same time. Trampled floors have been identified in pits' fill. At least one had been re-used and its sides re-dug (Hourani 1997). The excavators think that at this period, late sixth and early fifth millennium, the occupation was a seasonal one.

After the "pit-dwelling" has been abandoned, in the part that has been excavated only post-holes, pits, basins, and hearths are present. It seems that the groups coming to the site were more mobile previously, and most probably living under tenets (Dollfus and Kafafi 1993, 2001).

After this transitional period, begins a totally different mode of occupation at the settlement. It is during this period that permanent architecture appears. The architectural complexes have a multi-cellular plan, consisting of a large rectangular room adjoined by small rooms. It seems that the large room is for living while the smaller ones were kept for storage. Additionally, several domestic features outside these rooms were exposed, and this may be an indication that domestic activities were carried out in open space. These archaeological remains suggest that the mode of occupation at the site had shifted from the temporal, may be a seasonal occupation of a mobile group to a more permanent one as suggested by the architecture.

During the last period of occupation, the Upper Levels, a remarkable change is observed in the organization of space. Instead of constructing multi-cellular complexes, a uni-cellular complex dominates and adjoined with a courtyard. These houses which were not close to one another have been separated by large spaces, where eventually the sheep and goat herds could be kept.

Chapter Seven: Morpho-stylistic description of pottery assemblages at Abu Hamid

The main aim of this chapter is to present a morpho-stylistic description of the pottery assemblage collected at Abu Hamid. The focus is on the pottery repertoires that were recovered in the Lower and Middle Levels. This description does not seek to make a determination of a pottery seriation or type–varieties (see Lovell, Dollfus and Kafafi n.d), but to describe the Lower and Middle assemblages in terms of their general formal characteristics that we are going to deal with in the following pages.

I. Background

In the southern Levant, the period from the Late Neolithic to the end of the Chalcolithic is still subject to debate: a debate on its terminology and typo-chronology (Joffe and Dessel 1995; Kafafi 1998; Kerner 2001; Lovell 2001). The reason for this is that not a large number of radiocarbon dates are available; and discrepancies that are the result of environmental conditions. Very few sites related to these periods have yielded such dates; furthermore, it has proven difficult to correlate these dates with stratigraphic or occupational sequences. Another problem related to this debate is that there is noticeable regional variation throughout this period (Banning 2002). Thus there is disagreement as to how to correlate archaeological assemblages with the probable "cultures" belonging to these periods. At the terminological scale, the periodization of the Late Neolithic and Chalcolithic periods has been approached differently. The Late Neolithic has been divided into two general periods: 1 & 2, with their schematics related to specific "traditions" or "cultures" (Kafafi 1995, 1998). Others, like Kerner (2001) and Lovell (2001), periodize the over all period differently, preferring the term Late Neolithic (for what Kafafi calls LNI) and division of the Chalcolithic period into early, middle and late. This terminology contrasts with that postulated by Kafafi. What he designates the Late Neolithic 2, Kerner and Lovell designate as the Early Chalcolithic. This re-evaluation is based on pottery and architectural evidence, which they assume as sharing more in common with the Chalcolithic period in general rather than with the Neolithic one.

Disagreements are particularly pronounced in the ordering of pottery traditions related to the Late Neolithic and early Chalcolithic periods. The pottery's morpho-stylistic attributes have generated debate as to whether variations chronologically overlap or co-exist (Kafafi 1995). Radiocarbon dating has been less useful in this respect, and in several cases they have not helped at all in affirming a correlation with stratigraphic sequences.

Concerning the Late Neolithic period, for example, the Yarmoukian pottery style, which is characterized, among other characteristics, by incision decoration, has been assumed as being followed by Jericho PNA (of painting decoration). Regional variation has been documented, and in a few archaeological sites such as Ain Ghazal and Abu Thawwab, these two styles may have existed together (Kafafi 1995). At others sites, these styles are found separately, reflecting, it is assumed, regional or chronological variation. At other sites, dated to the Late Neolithic, neither the Jericho PNA nor the Yarmoukian styles were found. This has been well attested to the Lower Levels in Abu Hamid, where no "classical Yarmoukian has been found but only pottery similar to the Ghrubba one is found.

Concerning the so-called early Chalcolithic or Late Neolithic 2 period, a remarkable stylistic changes has been observed. Such changes are evident in both pottery decoration and form. Some pottery forms make their first appearance such as "churn" and footed/pedestal-bowls. Moreover, pottery surfaces were being subjected to various surface treatments, such as impressions or impressed and incised decorations and applied motifs bands, and for the first time applied motives like snake (Kafafi 1998:132). Other surface treatments include the red and dark faced burnished ware (RFBW & DFBW). However, regional stylistic variations existed. This is particularly evident in the morphological characteristics of the various pottery forms, such as the carinated bowl and the bow rim-jars which appear, for example, in some sites and not in others. The pottery repertoire dated to this phase, at Abu Hamid for example, lacks these two morphological attributes (Dollfus and Kafafi 1993), whereas they are found at other sites, such as Munhata 2a which is only 30 km from Abu Hamid (Garfinkel 1992).

II. The morpho-stylistic pottery assemblages at Abu Hamid

II.1 The Lower Levels: the A: 5 assemblage

The main objective here is not to establish a pottery seriation, but rather to give a quick glimpse of the morphological characteristics of the pottery so as to define the general functional-type categories of the vessels that have been collected in the Levels 5b-a at Abu Hamid. This will allow us to define, to some extent, the variability in pot forms that were made. Two main groups are present: closed or restricted (as it is sometimes called) shapes and open or unrestricted forms. Complete vessels are rare, so rims and handles were used to try to detremine to which group the sherds belonged. Forms were also identified, from a technological point of view, depending on surface shaping and finishing.

II.1.1 Closed shapes

In the Lower Levels at Abu Hamid, there is a restricted functional-type variability of closed forms. These are mainly hole-mouth jars and neck jars (**Fig. 28**, **Fig. 29**). The hole-mouth jars are characterized by simple-rounded and roughly bevelled rims. Other jar types include the simple tall-neck jars (Lovell *et al.* 1997: 366). The frequency of hole-mouth jars at the Lower Levels has been estimated as constituting 28% of total forms. By contrast, tall-neck jars represent only by 8%. These are having variation in their aperture (**Fig. 30**).

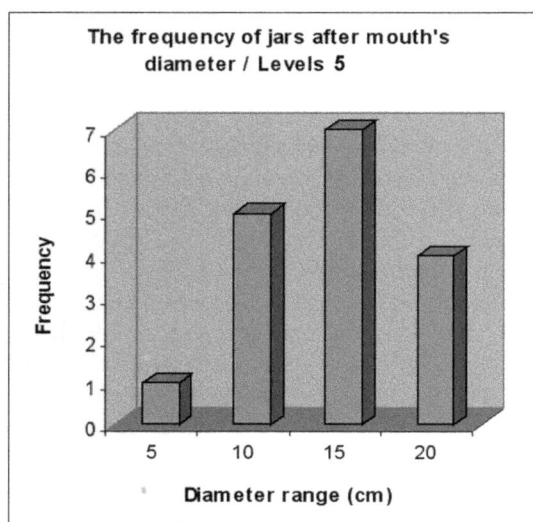

Fig. 30: Variation of jars on the basis of their mouth's diameter – Levels 5, N=17

Using the aperture as a criterion for classification, hole-mouth jars can be subdivided into three main categories: small (less than 10 cm in diameter), medium (between 10-20 cm in diameter) and large (more than 20 cm in diameter) (**Fig. 31**).

Regarding surface treatment, in terms of decoration, some of these forms were subjected to either painted decorations or incisions. The latter was generally performed at the junction of the body and neck. Hole-mouth jars, by contrast, were subjected only to painting decoration. Painting style generally took the form either of geometric patterns or spots (Lovell 1997: 366).

II.1.2 Open shapes

This general category is represented mainly by three

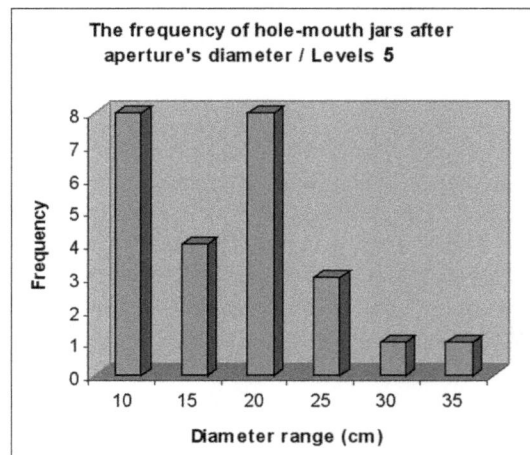

Fig. 31: The grouping of hole-mouth jars after mouth diameter – Levels 5, N=25

shapes: cups, bowls, and chalices. Bowls are the most dominant form that have been identified in the Lower Levels assemblage. They represent 68% of the assemblage. These include bowls with and without handles (Dollfus and Kafafi 1993: 246). They also vary in size: small, medium and large (**Fig. 32**, **Fig. 33**). Small bowls are defined as having a diameter of less than 10 cm; medium-size bowls as having a diameter ranging from 10-20 cm; and large bowls, with diameters of more than 20 cm.

Part of the bowls assemblage were decorated with painting of red-orange linear designs, lines of dots, zig-zags, and simple geometric patterns (Dollfus and Kafafi 1993; Lovell *et al.* 1997). Sometimes, decoration patterns were alternately applied to the inside or outside of the bowls surfaces.

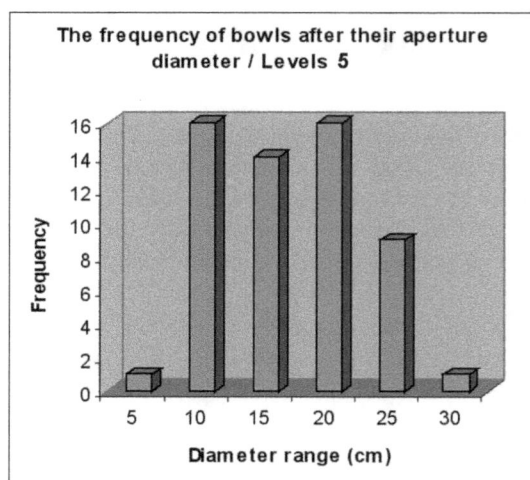

Fig. 32: The frequency of bowls after diameter range – Levels 5, N=57

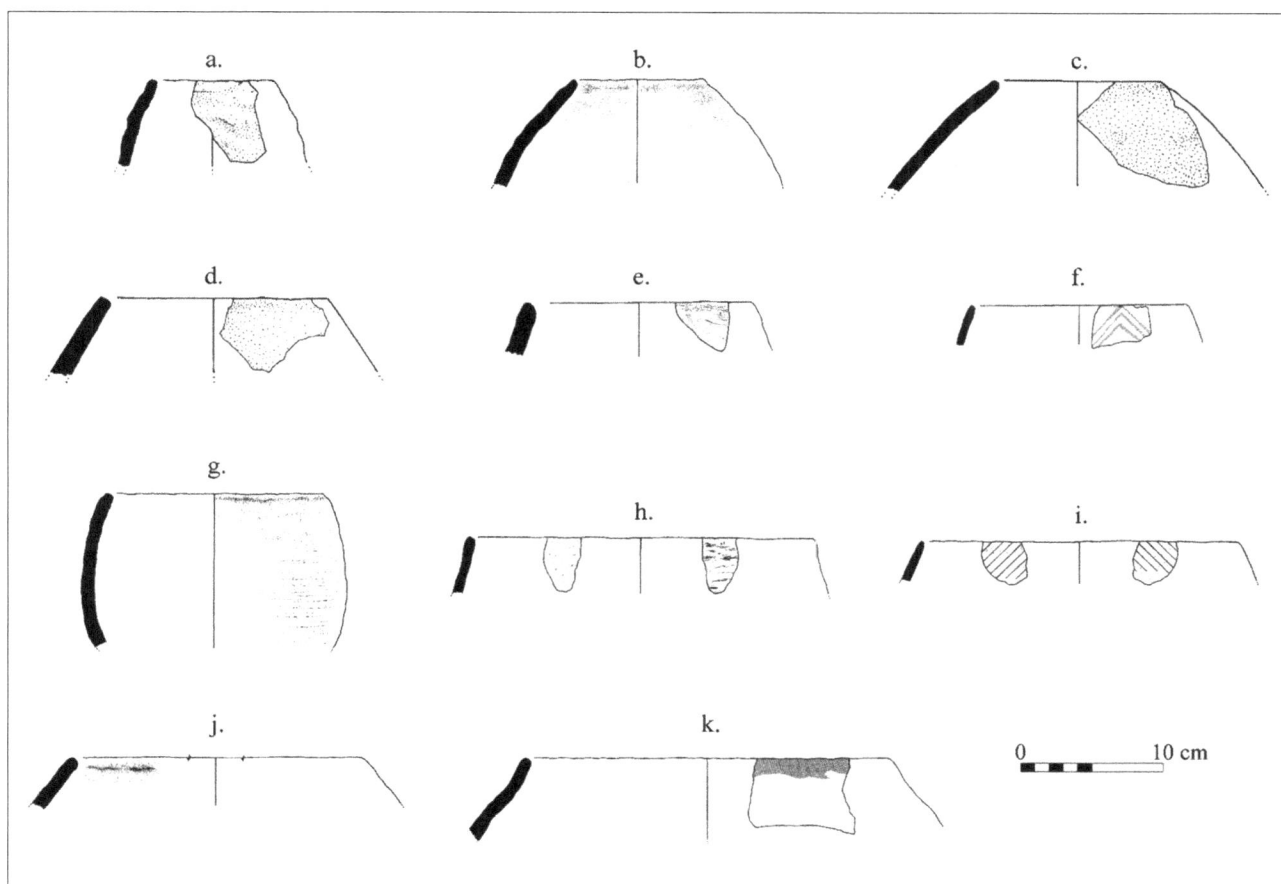

Fig. 28: Hole-mouth jars varieties – Levels 5

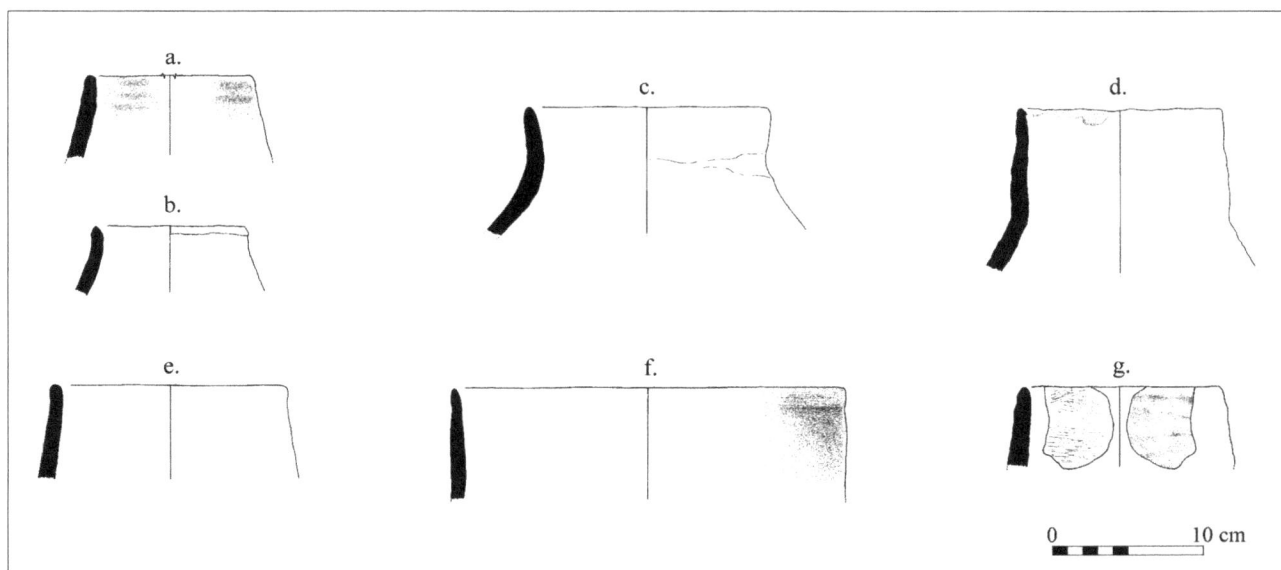

Fig. 29: Necked jars varieties – Levels 5

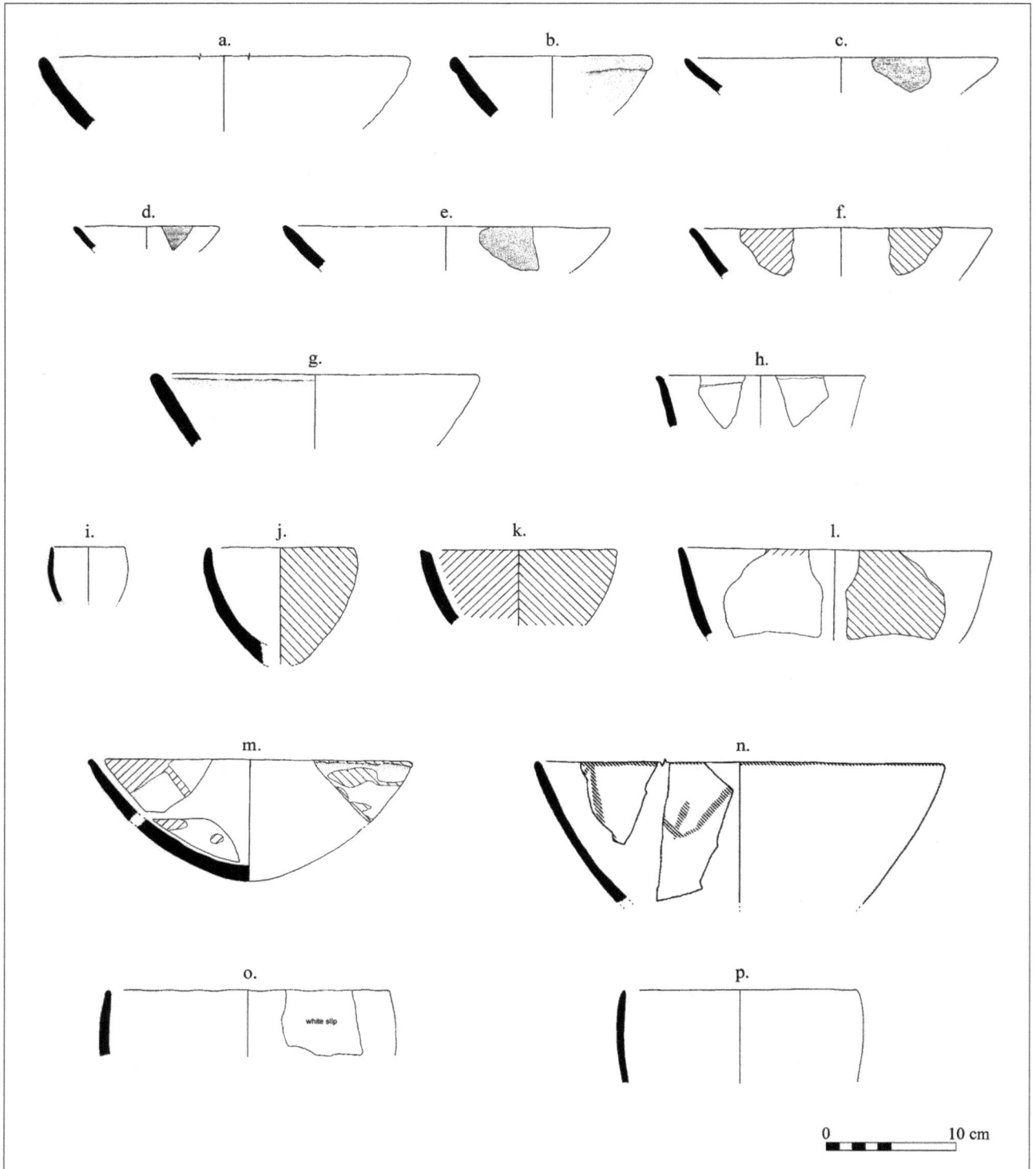

Fig. 33: Various types of bowls – Levels 5

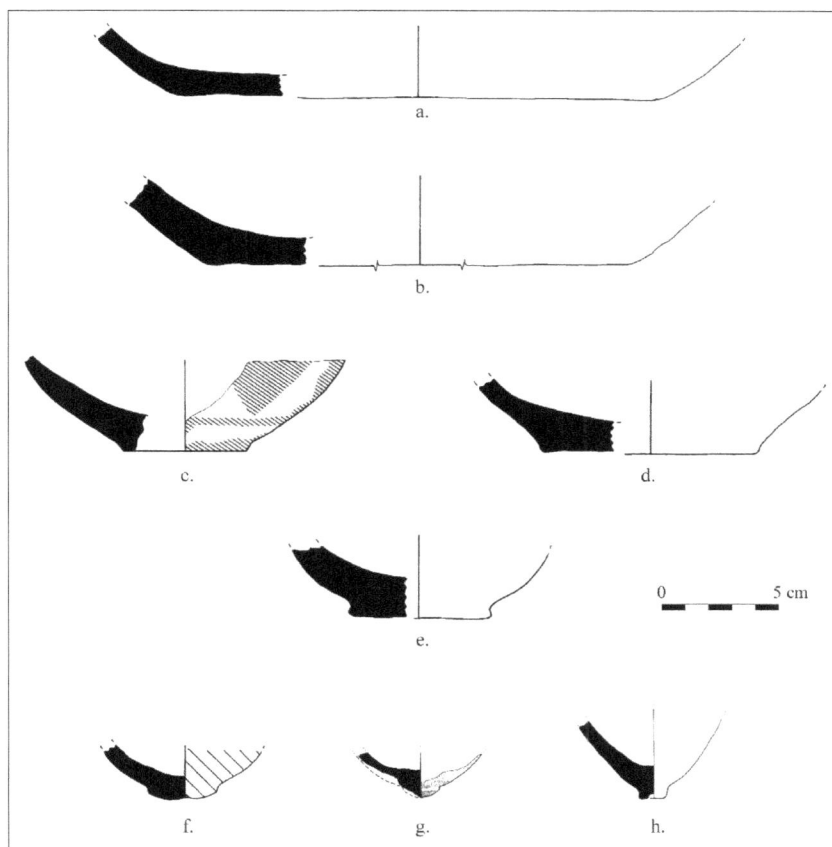

Fig. 34: Various base types – Levels 5

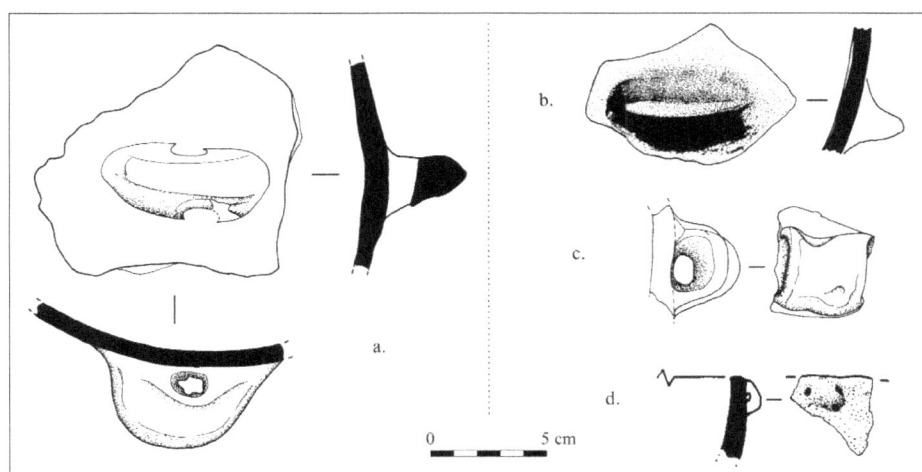

Fig. 35: Various handle types – Levels 5

II.1.3 Base shapes

The sherds related to bases in the Lower Levels at Abu Hamid can be classified into three groups (**Fig. 34**). These are a) flat base with sharp angles towards the wall of the pot (**Fig. 34 a, b**); b) disc bases with a curve angles towards the wall of the pot (**Fig. 34 c-e**), and c) button bases (**Fig. 34 f-h**).

II.1.4 Handles

In the Lower Levels, handles varieties include the following types: lug (**Fig. 35 a**), ledge (**Fig. 35 b**); strap (**Fig. 35 c**); and pierced knob (**Fig. 35 d**).

65

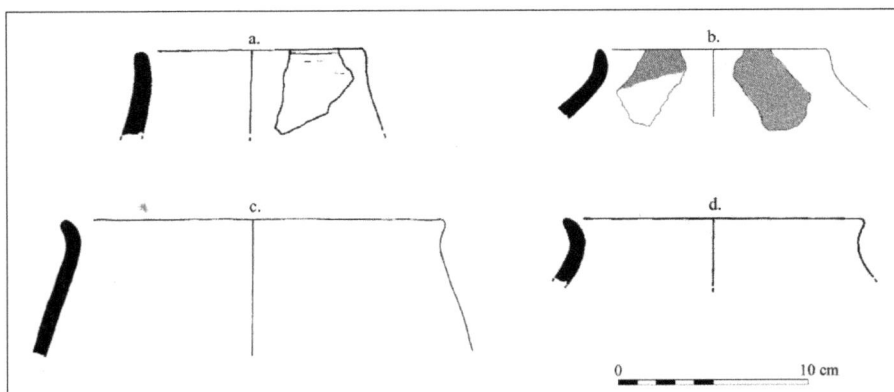

Fig. 36: Various types of necked jars – Level 4

II.2. *The Level 4 assemblage*

The same pottery categories described for A: 5 are present in Level 4. The first category is represented by the closed shapes: hole-mouth jars and jars. The second includes the unrestricted shapes: the bowls.

II.2.1 Closed shapes

This category includes hole-mouth jars and neck-jars. Considering the size of the necks they include one group with short and one with long necks (**Fig. 36**). However, these necks vary if we consider their mouth-size. Thus, three main groups can be identified: a) jars with a mouth diameter of less than 10 cm; b) jars with a 10-20 cm mouth diameter, whereas the last group is represented by jar of a mouth diameter which is more than 25 cm. Based

on that, it seems that the second group is more dominant compared with the other two groups.

The second functional-type is the hole-mouth jars (**Fig. 37**), which can be divided into three groups after their mouth diameter: 1) pots of mouth diameter less than 10 cm in size, 2) diameter between 10-20 cm, and the last is more than 25 cm in diameter.

II.2.2 Open shapes

Bowls are the main functional-type associated with this category. These can be described as either shallow or deep bowls (**Fig. 38**). Based on pot aperture diameter as a grouping factor, three bowl groups can be identified according to size: small, medium and large.

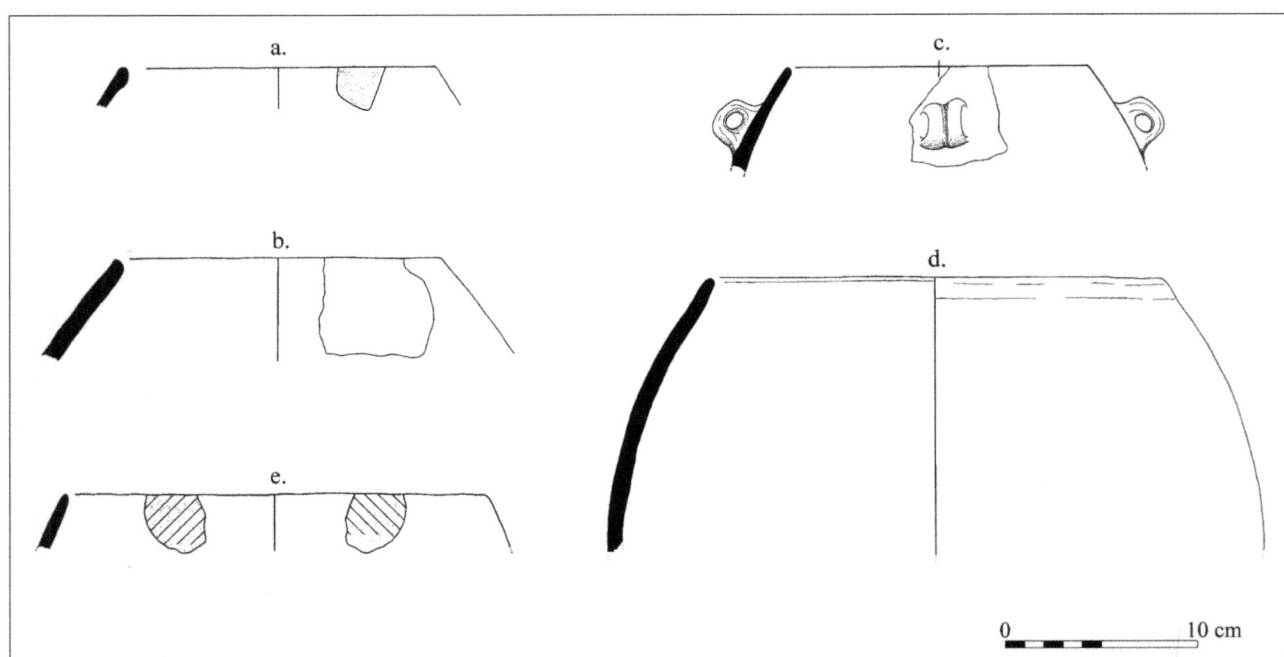

Fig. 37: Various types of hole-mouth jars – Level 4

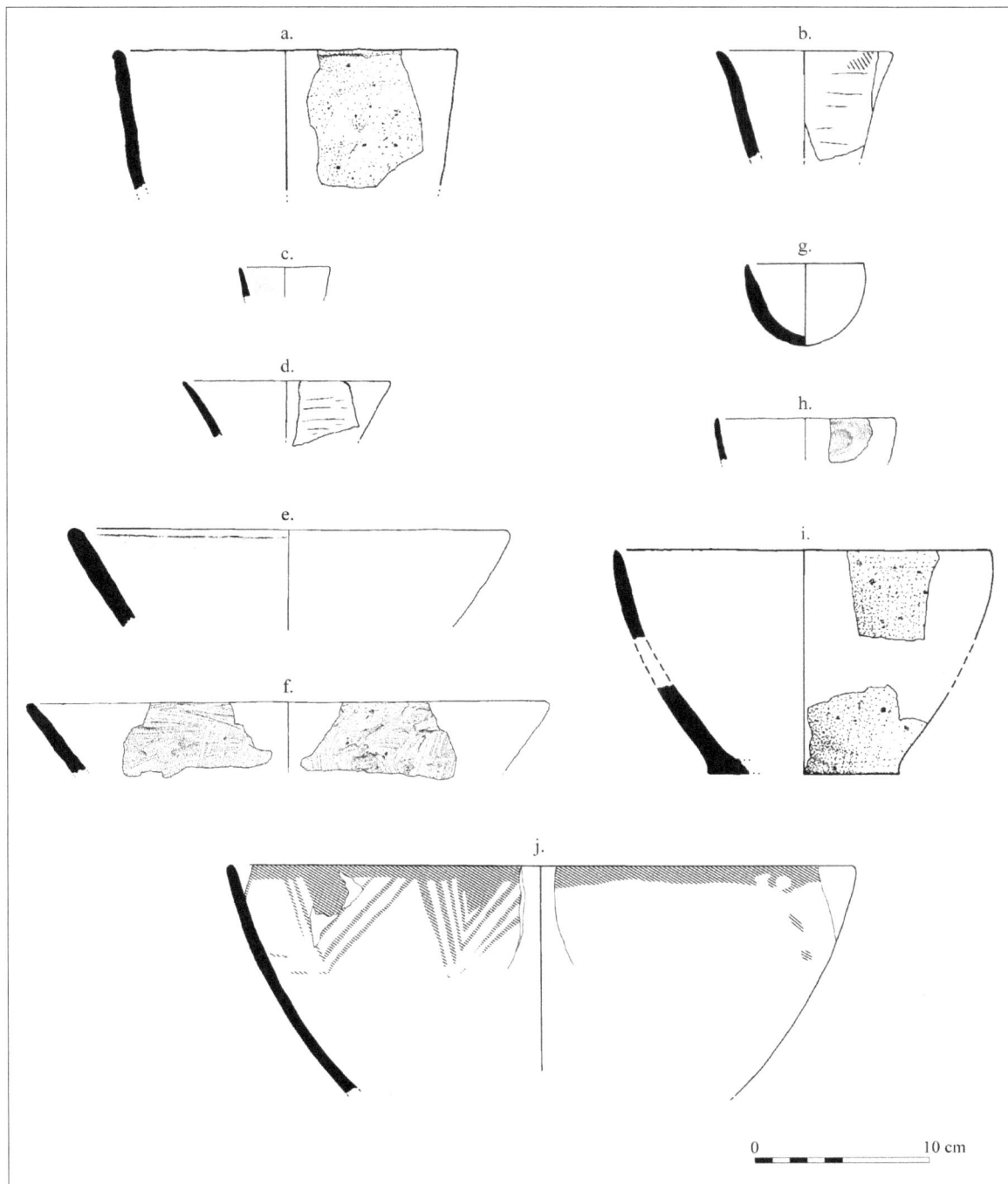

Fig. 38: Various types of bowls – Level 4

II.2.3 Base shapes

Despite the limitation of the samples from this pottery repertoire, sherds related to bases have been distinguished as having either, low disc bases (**Fig. 39 a, b**), flat shapes (**Fig. 39 c**), or round bases (**Fig. 39 d**).

II.2.4 Handles

The following types of handles have been distinguished in Level 4. These include lug (**Fig. 40 a**), ledge handles (**Fig. 40 b**), strap handles (**Fig. 40 c, d**), and loop handles (**Fig. 40 e**).

II.3 The Middle Levels: the A: 3 assemblage

The pottery from the Middle Levels show significant variability compared to that from the Lower Levels, both with respect to shape and decoration. The pottery repertoire of these Levels show significant continuity with older

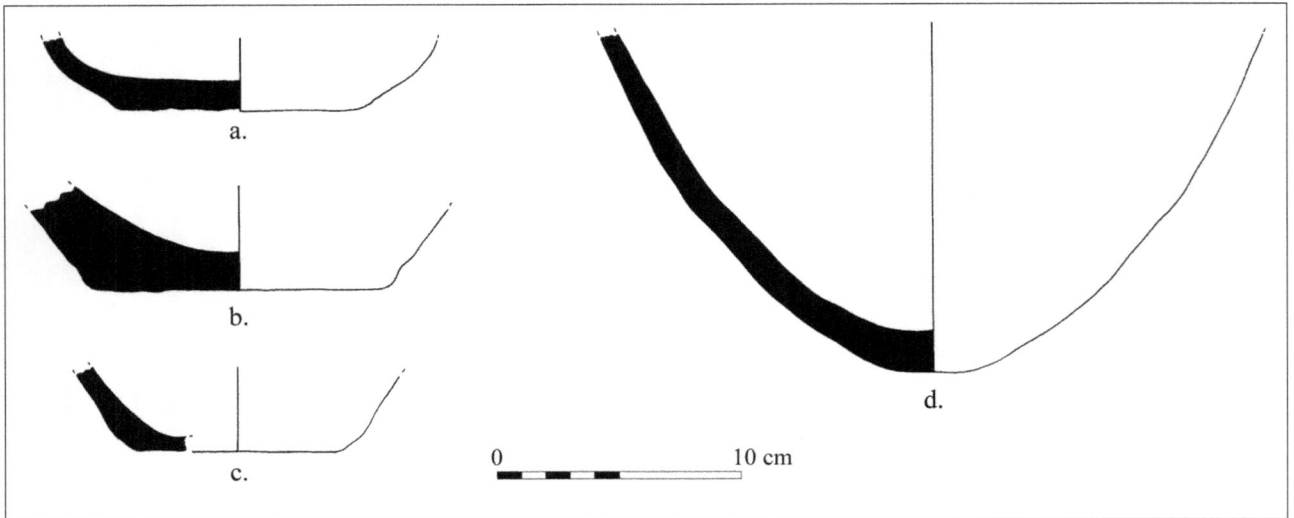

Fig. 39: Bases types' varieties – Level 4

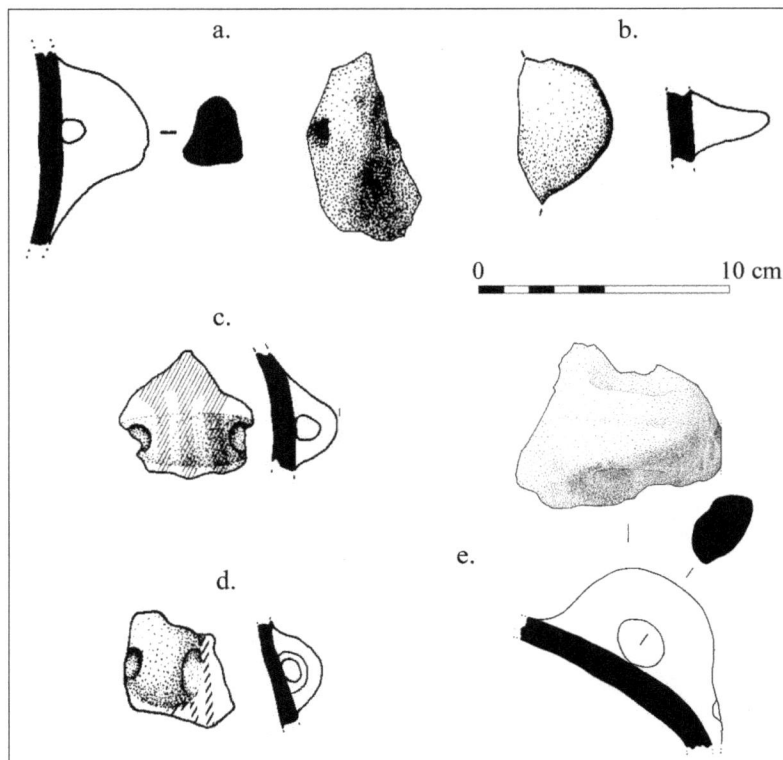

Fig. 40: Handle-types varieties – Level 4

forms as well as with the production of new ones such as *fusiform* vessels (found in literature as churn) and pedestal bowls. However, these can be classified under two main functional shape categories.

II.3.1 Closed shapes

Three main functional-types can be grouped under this category. These are hole-mouth jars, neck jars and churns.

1- Jars

These are characterized as having either short or high necks (**Fig. 41**). The latter group is characterized as having a limited variation in the mouth's diameter. They range between 9-15 cm in diameter. By contrast, the diameter of the short necked jars' mouth demonstrates greater variation (**Fig. 42**). The decoration styles consist of red-orange painting, incised, applied thumb impressions, and red slip.

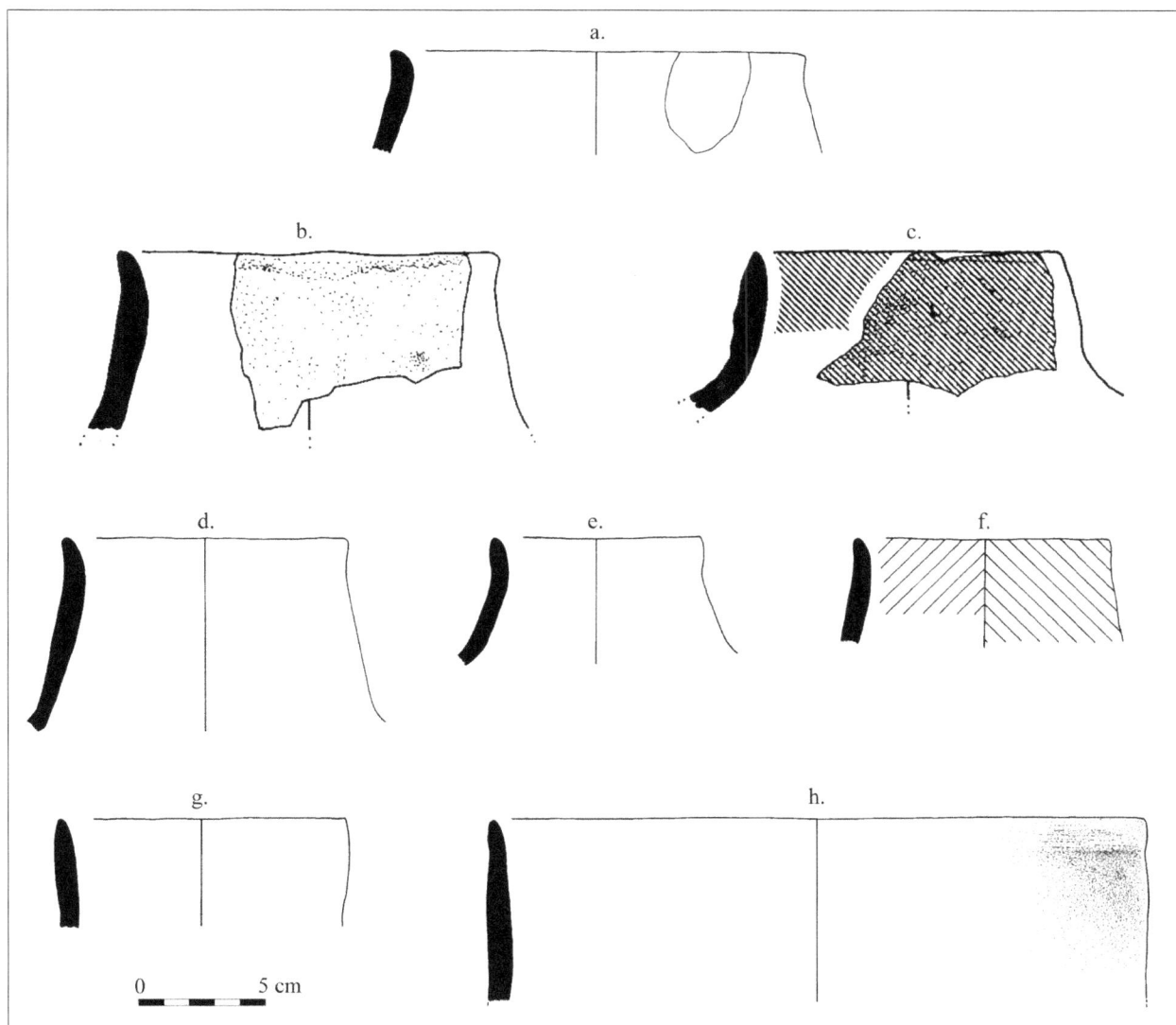

Fig. 41: Various types of necked jars – Middle Levels (A:3)

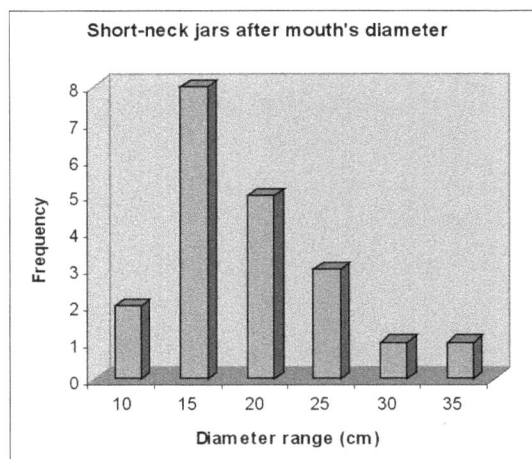

Fig. 42: The frequency of short-neck jars on the basis of mouth diameter – Middle Levels (A:3), N=20

This jar type is inclusive of storage jars, which are differentiated from other types by their diameter size. They range between 28-40 cm in diameter.

2- Hole-mouth jars

Variation in hole-mouth jars exists both in terms of size and decoration (**Fig. 43**). The latter includes incision, thumb impressions and red slip. Three groups can be differentiated on the basis of their diameters (**Fig. 44**). These include small, medium, and large hole-mouth jars.

3- "Churns"

They represent a new functional type-variety first manufactured in these Levels, but they are still very rare. The external faces were often subjected to red-slip.

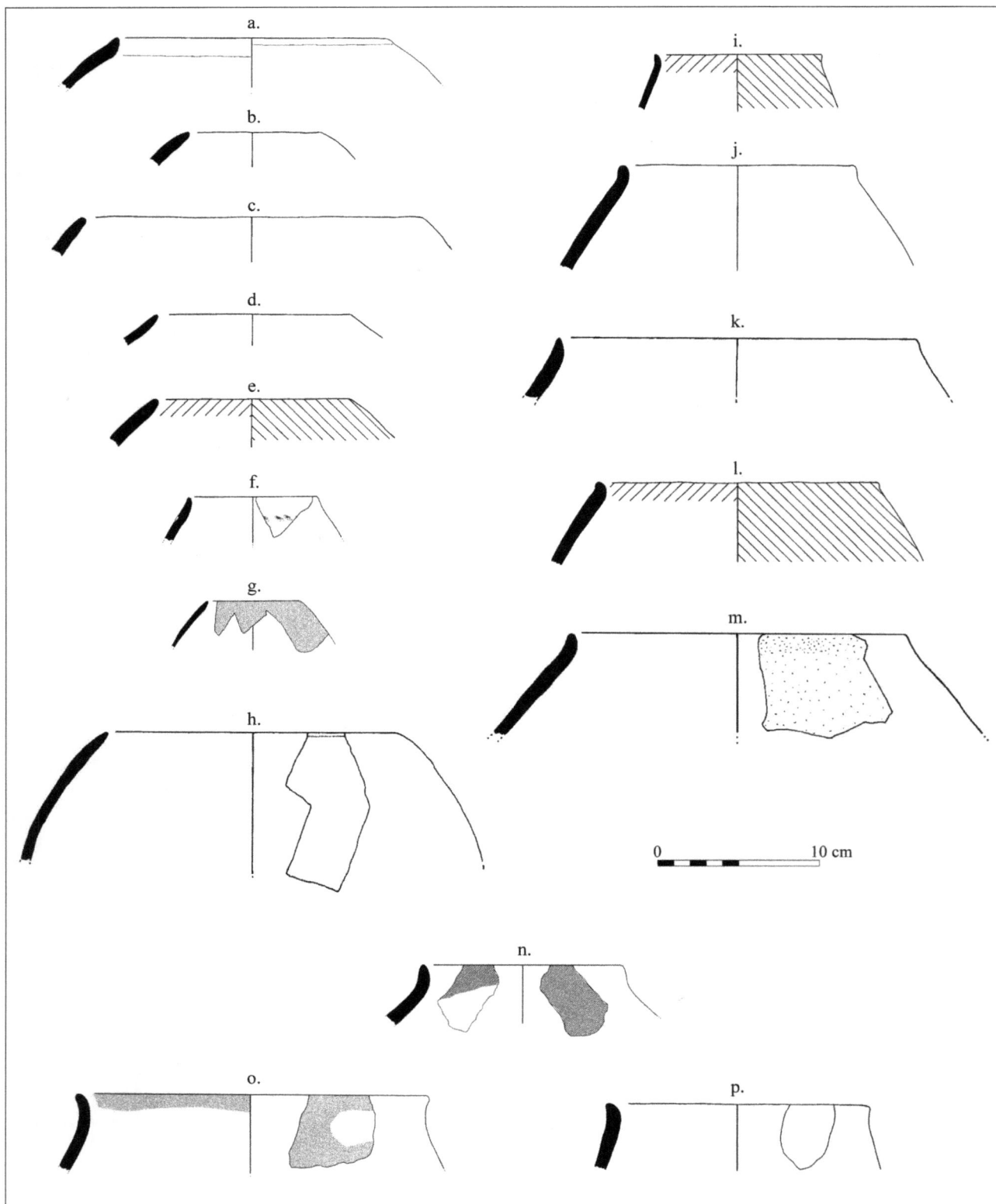

Fig. 43: Various types of hole-mouth jars – Middle Levels (A:3)

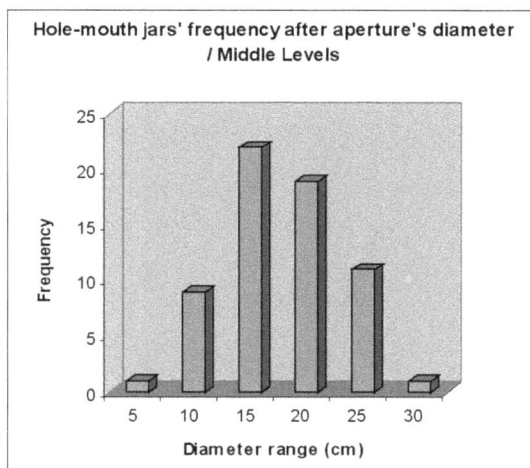

Fig. 44: The frequency of hole-mouth jars after aperture's diameter – Middle Levels, N=63

II.3.2 Open shapes

This category includes several vessel shapes – bowls, and basin (**Fig. 45**). Bowls show significant variation in diameter. They can be classified into three main groups (**Fig. 46**): 1) small bowls, with a diameter of less than 10 cm; 2) medium- sized bowls, with a diameter between 10-20 cm – this group can be further subdivided into two subgroups: a) including bowls between 10 to 15 cm in diameter; and b) between 15-20 cm in diameter; and group 3 large bowls, with a diameter of more than 20 cm.

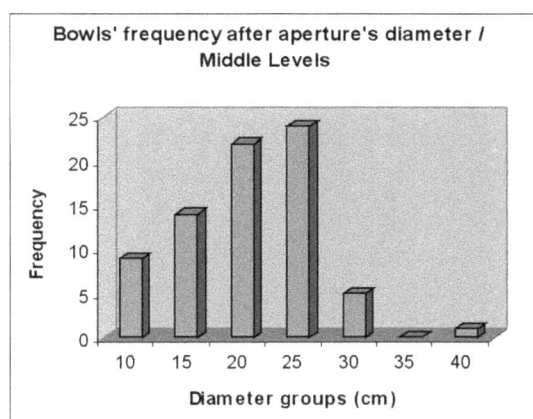

Fig. 46: The frequency of bowls after their aperture's diameter – Middle Levels, N=75

Bowls were subjected to different surface treatments, such as red-orange slip, and burnished red-slip. A characteristic is the red or black slipped vessels that are highly burnished (RFBW and DFBW). However, this style is assumed as being restricted to 2% of the overall assemblage (Lovell *et al.* 1997).

The second main functional type is the basin. Basins are characterized by a large diameter, ranging from 20 to 45 cm.

II.3.3 Base shapes

The most common base shapes in the Middle Levels at Abu Hamid were determined to include: a) flat bases (**Fig. 47 a-c**); disc bases (**Fig. 47 d-f**); and concave bases (**Fig. 47 g-i**).

II.3.4 Handles

The diagnostic handles that have been identified in the Middle Levels include the following types: lug handles (**Fig. 48 a, b**); strap handles (**Fig 48 c**); loop handles (**Fig. 48 d, e**); and pierced knob handles.

III. Summary and conclusion

The studied pottery assemblages at Abu Hamid have been mainly addressed under functional-types rather than type varieties. The main concern was to identify pottery variability and variation in terms of the produced shapes. Functional-type classification is of great concern since it sheds light on the pot categories that have been produced at each phase. This is of great significance as it can reveal the diversity of the activities that have been conducted at each phase. In the Lower Levels, variability in pot shape is restricted to three main functional types. These are bowls, hole-mouth jars and, less frequently, necked-jars. The frequency of bowls is estimated as outnumbering other functional shapes (at 64%). If we look diachronically to the production in the transition from the Lower to Middle Levels we obtain a different view in terms of the variability of produced pottery shapes or/and of their frequency. With the Middle Levels, new pot shapes were produced, such as "churn" and pedestal bowls. Moreover, there is a remarkable change in the frequency of previously produced shapes. Whereas bowls still dominate the assemblage, there is an increase in other shapes, such as neck jars (both short and tall neck) and hole-mouth jars. Percentages can be used to measure such changes. For example, neck jars increase in frequency from 8% for the Lower Levels to 22% for the Middle Levels. Likewise, the frequency of hole-mouth jars increases from 28% to 36%.

A question remains: are these changes in pottery variability and/or frequency relate to the modes of occupation and the hypothesis of greater mobility (Lower Levels) than in the sedentary permanent settlement where the whole group or part of it is living all around the year in the Middle Levels!

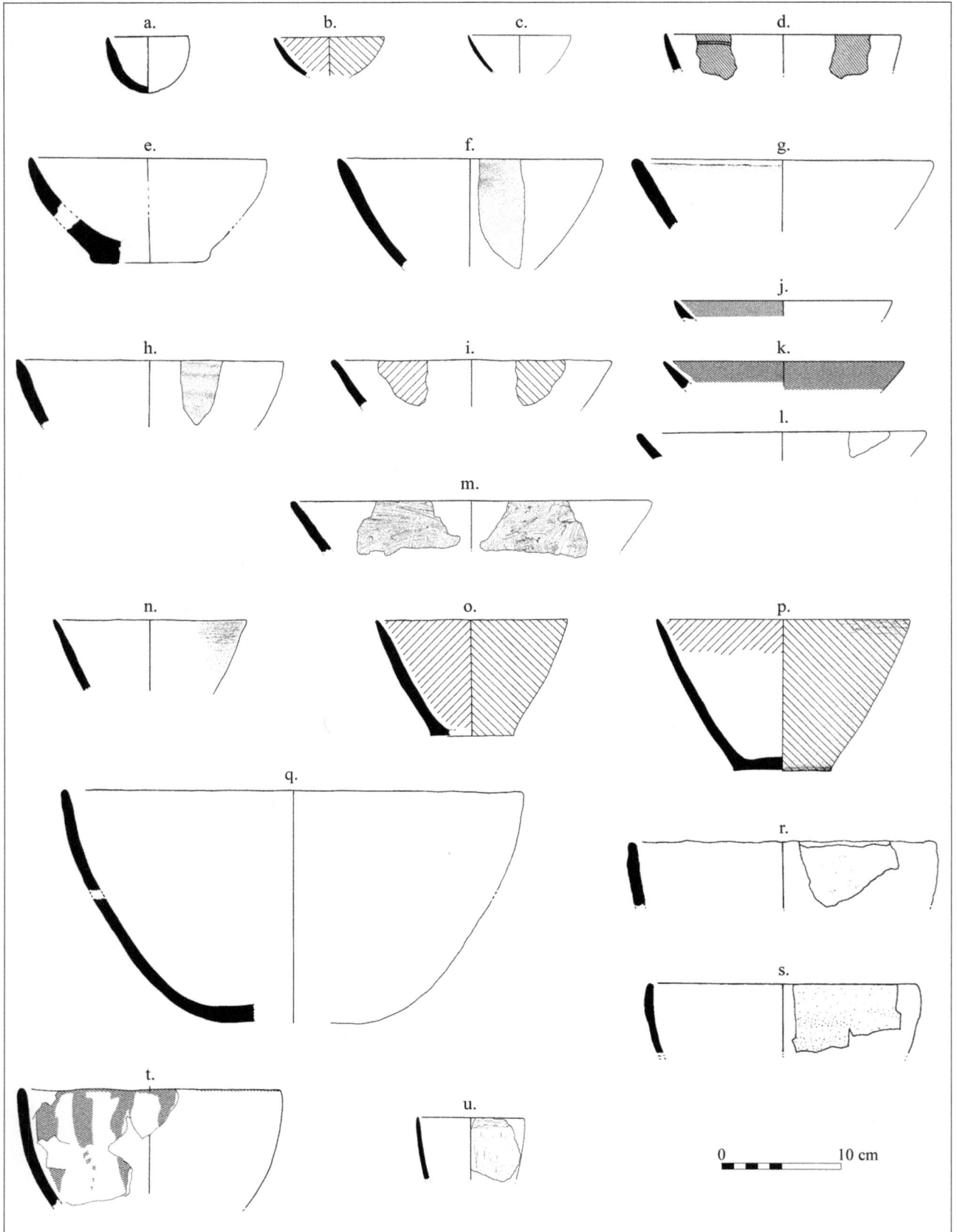

Fig. 45: Various types of bowls – Middle Levels

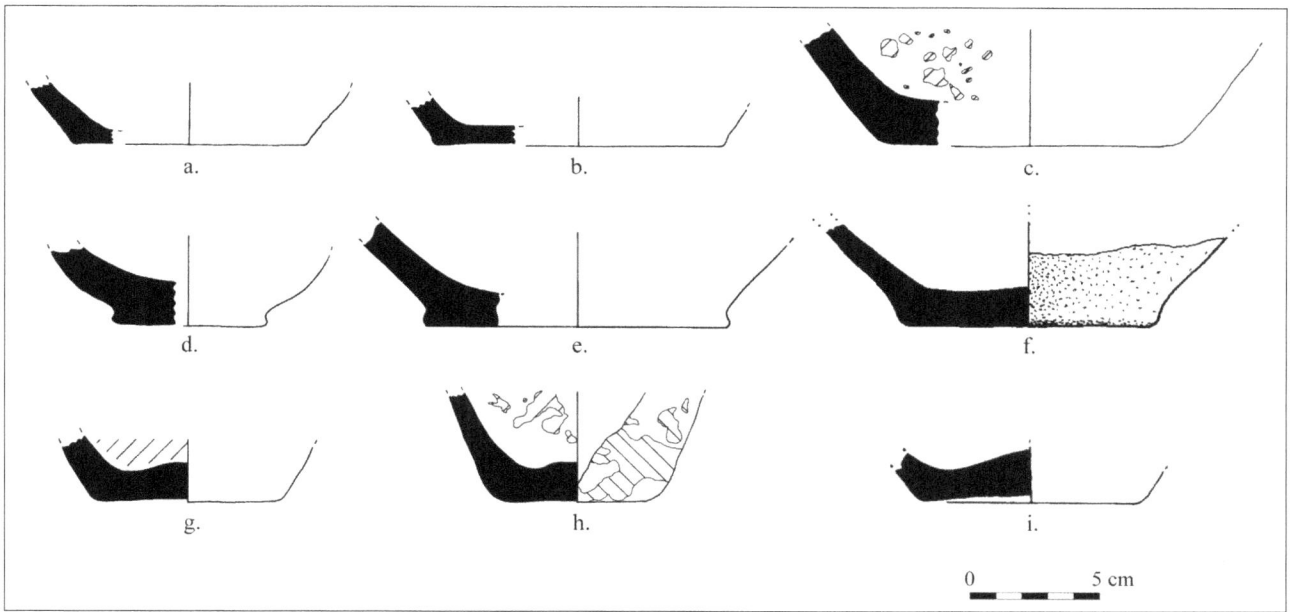

Fig. 47: Various types of bases – Middle Levels

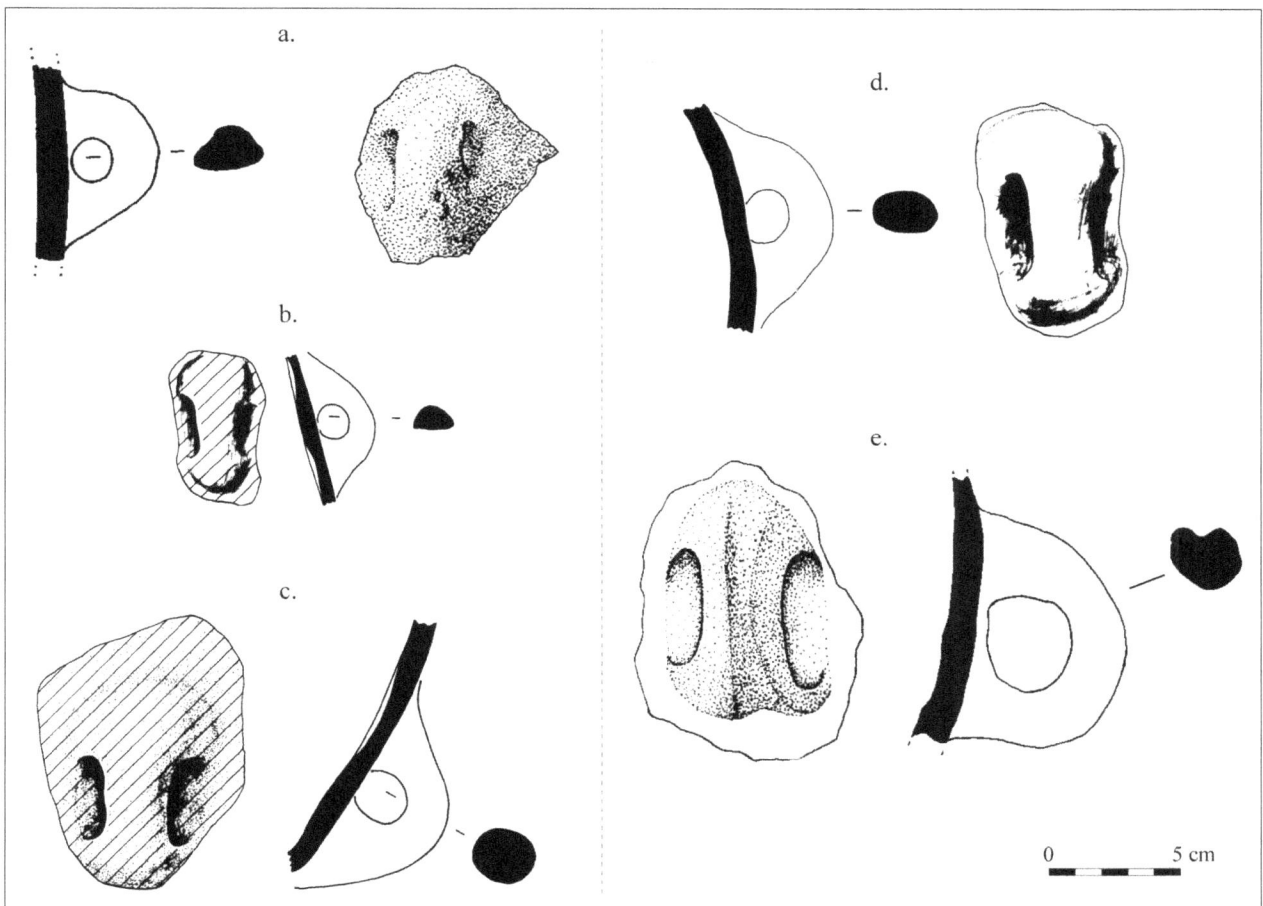

Fig. 48: Various types of handles – Middle Levels

Chapter Eight: Technological analysis of the pottery assemblages at Abu Hamid

In the previous chapters, the concern was to evaluate two main aspects related to the pottery production at Abu Hamid. The first attempt (chapter 6) mainly focuses on presenting the archaeological contexts of the studied pottery assemblages. This entails the identification of their spatio-temporal dimensions, on the one hand, and understanding the context from which each assemblage has been collected, on the other. The second attempt, of concern, is to determine the proper pot functional-types (chapter 7) that are related to each chronological phase at the site. This enables understanding of the type of pots used at each phase. These two aspects form the data base for approaching and defining the technological characteristics of the two pottery assemblages (in the Lower and Middle Levels) at Abu Hamid. The technological analysis involves mainly the identification of the methods and techniques that potters manipulated in transforming the clay body into a final product. But before starting this analysis, the conceptual method of approaching the methods and techniques of pot shaping will be addressed.

I. Methodological considerations

Pottery production is the output of a series of steps that potters undertake to achieve the intended object. These steps relate to the raw materials used, the forming operations, and firing (Rye 1981). The focus in this study will be put on the second of these components, the analysis of the forming techniques. A definition of the analytical framework for the study of ceramic technology, and the methods and techniques of analysis, will be given.

I.1 The analytical framework for the study of ceramic technology

The analysis of pottery forming techniques involves the identification of the kind of pressure that the potter applies on the clay (Rye 1981: 58): amount of pressure, part on which it is applied, and the state of the clay. This entails identifying the way by which the potter applies this pressure, whether it is with his or her fingers or with tools (Rye 1981: 58). Based on that, the reconstruction or studying pot forming involves the identification of a set of attributes that relate to three stages. These are the primary – forming technique (that does not represent the final form of the vessel, such as coiling, pinching), the secondary – forming technique (represented by techniques that enhance the final shape of the pot, such as scraping, and beating) and finally, surface modification. The latter is divided into: a) surface modification techniques such as burnishing, smoothing and incision that do not entail adding

materials, and b) decorative techniques employed on the pot surfaces using different materials such as pigment and painting.

Recently, a fine conceptual tool of analysing pot fashioning techniques has been evaluated through the concept of *chaîne opératoire* – operational sequences (Cresswel 1996 cited in Roux and Courty, *in press*; Dietler and Herbich 1998; Gosselain 1998; van der Leeuw 1993; Roux 1994). As we have seen supra (cf. chapter 3), this enables a systematic identification of the different sequences of pot forming , including the methods and techniques as well as the organization of the various steps and actions embedded in pot forming. This leads to the identification of *variants* and *invariants* of forming methods and techniques (van der Leeuw 1993: 240).

I.2 Reconstructing pottery forming technique

Archaeological pottery encodes the materialization of most of the potters actions and gestures. These are manifested on the surfaces of the pots in different kinds and states of attributes. The re-organization of these attributes, on the basis of their chronological performance, is an important step in reconstructing the sequence of pot forming. For that purpose two methods can be used: 1) surface-features examination, and 2) the use of x-radiography.

I.2.1 Surface features examination

This is one of the ways used by archaeologists to attempt to define pottery forming operations and techniques (Rye 1981; Franken 1974; Roux 1994; Shepard 1965: 53-7; Vandiver 1986, 1987). The analysis of surface attributes can be achieved with little or even no specialized tools or techniques (Rye 1981). The hand lens is the main tool used in the identification of macro-traces on pot surfaces . Such an examination aims at isolating those surfaces features and join patterns which, if they are found to be repetitive, help to reconstruct of the behavioural pattern employed in shaping the pots. Each forming technique is assumed to correlate with a set of surface features. When coils are used for pot shaping, such a technique can be identified from regular, horizontal corrugation at surfaces of the junctions (if not obliterated), horizontal voids at surface, increase or/and decrease in wall thickness especially at the coils' joining area. In some cases, on one surface the coils might not be obliterated by later shaping or/and finishing operation; this would be a good indication of the forming technique. Pots shaped by coiling would have an horizontal fracture pattern that follows the area of coils' joining (Balfet *et al.* 1989: 53).

Shaping operation can be identified based on different surface attributes as a forming technique. In the case of hand-shaping the surface of the pot might have finger-width shallow groove which intersects partly one on other (ethnographic observation in Jordan). If it has not been obliterated by further finishing operation, when a hard - tool has been used for shaping, at least one surface would show striations characterized by relative deep lines (Rye 1981: 86), when the clay was still plastic. In other cases, the tool's edge have left an impression on the pot surface (supra **Fig. 14 b**).

Moulding technique involves the pressing of plastic clay into or over a mould. The surface features or attributes used to identify this technique include the reproduction of mould surface on the pot one; the mould side has a uniform-textures surface with irregular recesses of clay pressing. The surface against which the clay is pressed would have recessed areas with tapered margins. Moreover, variation in pot thickness would appear more on the opposite surface of the moulded part (Rye 1981; Balfet *et al.* 1989).

Surface finishing can be identified according to the methods used on the pot surface. When hand finishing has been used when the clay was still leather hard, the pot surface would present a regular texture and a matte appearance. Such finishing method would leave fine striations randomly distributed. In case of using a hard-tool on a leather hard clay, the surface would show a combination of luster and matte appearance. This would be combined with regular sharp edge striations (Rye 1981: 89-90).

I.2.2 X-radiographic analysis

This technique has been applied in ceramics studies (Carr 1990, 1993; Braun 1982; Loney 1995; Rye 1977, 1981; Vandiver 1987). This effective method produces an image of the features of an object, differentiated on the basis of their composition, gravity and thickness, all of which are definable in their capacity to transmit x-rays. When applied to ceramic, the internal features of the part – such as temper particles, voids, voids between modelled segments that has been radiographed (coils or slabs), and fracture systems- can be observed (Carr 1993: 14).

These two analytical methods when combined, have produced significant results (Loney 1995; Rye 1977; Vandiver 1986, 1987). They allow a fine analysis of the size and the joint pattern of segments used in pot forming, which is particularly useful if the surface of the pot in question has been subjected to a high level of shaping and finishing.

The technological reconstruction of archaeological pottery should be correlated with a source of references, which are necessary to bridge the gap between the static traces observed on the archaeological sherds and the kind of behaviour that produced them. These source of references can be established either through experimental researches (Franken and Kalsbeek 1983; van As 1983; Vitelli 1984), ethnoarchaeology / ethnographic (van As and Jacobs 1986) or semi-experimental studies (Courty and Roux 1995, 1998; Roux 1994). Ethnoarchaeological pottery researches are an important source of reference especially when they are conducted in the same region where an archaeological site is excavated. They will make possible fine observations of the different stages of pot forming and the kind of traces they left.

II. The technological analysis of the archaeological pottery assemblages at Abu Hamid

The pottery assemblages of Abu Hamid that we have studied, have been subjected to surface features analysis (macroscopic), and x-radiographic analysis as ways to reconstruct the operational sequences of pot forming. For comparison, the source of reference that has been used is the ethnoarchaeological study we achieved in the Ajlun region (cf supra Part I). We chose this region because it is only 40-50km of Abu Hamid, even it is located in a different environment: Abu Hamid is a valley site whereas the Ajlun area is a mountainous area. However, it was the closest region to make observations and gather a reference close to the Jordan Valley. Moreover, Ajlun area was the only one that such observations on pottery production can be made.

These source of references provided information concerning the potters' actions associated with coiling and moulding techniques. Moreover, it provided the basis for making a correlation between the conceptual tool of investigation and its manifestation in the material product. In this way, it was possible to organize potters' actions on the basis of the stages of pot forming, and how potters materialized their technological knowledge in pots differently.

The following parameters have been used to aid reconstructing the pot fashioning methods and techniques. These have been evaluated to include:

1- form of the pot: either closed or open.
2- pot's fashioning phase: relating the pottery sherd to its phase of fashioning such as base, orifice or body.
3- surface regularity: based on measurement of the wall thickness.
4- fashioning technique: surface features of the inside and outside surfaces:
a- binding or joining marks; segment size
b- striation: type / shape / size / distribution / direction /

and state of performance at either leather hard or plastic clay.

In the following pages, the focus will be on defining the operational sequences – *chaînes opératoires* – of pot fashioning related to the three archaeological pottery repertoires at Abu Hamid.

II.1 Defining the pottery forming methods and techniques of Levels 5 and 4

The shaping technique involves the identification of three parameters: source of energy, type of pressure, and finally the clay mass on which the pressure was applied. The identification of this technique should be related to the forming methods in terms of phases and stages. That is to say, the identification of each forming phase such as the base, the body and the orifice, and the type of technique(s) performed in transforming its related forming stages: roughout, preform and finishing.

By examining the pottery sherds from Abu Hamid Levels 5 and 4 and A: 4 at Abu Hamid, it becomes clear that the potters at the site have participated in at least three techniques. These include a) *coiling* b) *pinching* and c) *moulding* to form pots

However, the structural organization of description for *each* forming technique is based on a) the identification of the mass of clay that has been subjected to pressure, b) the techniques employed in each forming stage, and c) the finishing technique. After that a presentation of the pot fashioning methods and operation will be followed.

II.1.1 The clay body

Depending on the radiographic images, the clay body of the pots can be characterized by the following technical features:
- low density of non-plastic inclusions.
- fine-medium size, and less larger non-plastic inclusions.
- the walls of the pot are characterized by medium / high degree of voids which are elongated and have an irregular shape.

II.1.2 Coiling technique

II.1.2.1 Surface features

The coiling technique has been identified based on:

1- horizontal corrugations between coils (**Fig. 49 a,b,c**)
2- horizontal voids on surfaces (**Fig. 50 a,b**)
3- voids in section.
4- irregular wall thickness at regular interval: at the binding places; the walls of the pot show either an increase or

Fig. 49: Horizontal corrugation along the surface of the pot as evidence of a coiling technique

Fig. 50: Voids along the surface of the pot, as an indication of the use of coiling

a decrease in their thickness.

5- presence of recesses which have a horizontal pattern on the inside and outside surfaces following the binding area (**Fig. 51**)

Fig. 51: Showing the horizontal finger recess on the surface of the pot according to the size of the coil

6- the fracture pattern of sherds: more straight horizontal fracture pattern where the coils were joined (**Fig. 52 a**).

7- coil preserved in section without thinning (**Fig. 52 b**).

a.

b.

Fig. 52: a) Horizontal fracture pattern along the coils' joining area, b) Coil preserved in section

II.1.2.2 X-radiographic features

On radiographic images coiling technique has been identified by:
- elongated voids between coils.
- horizontal concentration of non-plastic at the joining area. In some cases the coarse inclusions are aligned near the joining area.
- darker spots or areas in a regular horizontal pattern.

II.1.2.3 Identification of the body roughout technique

This stage refers to the technique employed in fashioning the roughout stage: type and source of pressure that is

applied when the coils are prepared. This forming stage has been performed with a discontinuous pressure made by the fingers on the surfaces of the coils in a downward direction. On the sherds this technique can be identified by the following diagnostic features:

1- vertical and/or diagonal shallow to medium finger-width intermittent grooves covering at least one of the surface of the pot (**Fig. 53**).

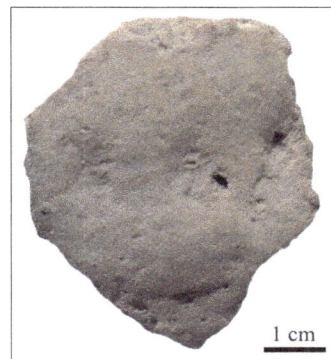

Fig. 53: Thinning the coils by vertical scraping with finger

2- irregular surfaces (internal or external) characterized by micro-relief morphology (**Fig. 54**).

Fig. 54: Thinning the wall of the pot which resulting in a micro-relief morphological surface

II.1.2.4 Identification of the body preforming technique (coiling)

This forming sequence refers to the technique of shaping the roughout. After the coils have been subjected to a thinning operation with discontinuous pressure pattern, the next forming stage is to shape the wall roughout. This is performed with discontinuous scraping either with a hand or a hard tool.

1- Shaping with hand
Shaping with discontinuous finger scraping has been identified according to the following diagnostic features:
a- medium-coarse striations that covered one of the surface of the pot when the clay was still humid. These have different directions either horizontal or diagonal / vertical (**Fig. 55 a**)

77

a.

b.

Fig. 55: Different patterns of shaping the pot surface with fingers

c.

d.

Fig. 56 c - d: Surface features left by the use of tool

b- shallow to medium discontinuous grooves of finger width; they are sometimes overlap and covering the whole face. The result is a medium size striation limited by two relatively raised ridges which is similar to ethnographic pattern observed in Jordan (**Fig. 13 a**).

2- Shaping with a tool
Discontinuous hard tool scraping has been identified by the following diagnostic features:
a- fine to medium striations taking place between two coarse lines (sometime ca. 15 mm wide), left on humid clay; cover one of the surfaces. These striations are either horizontal or vertical-diagonal (**Fig. 56 a,b**).
b- the use of a tool in the shaping operation erases partly the recess caused by the thinning and joining operations. The result is less recesses on the surface (s) (**Fig. 56 c**).

II.1.2.5 Identification of the body finishing technique

1- Hand finishing
This has been identified according to the following surface features:
a- matte appearance face (**Fig. 57 a, b**)
b- fine-medium set of shallow striations (**Fig. 57 b**).

a.

b.

Fig. 57: Hand-smoothing at leather hard clay

a.

b.

Fig. 56 a - b: Surface features left by the use of tool

c- self-slip surface with fine, shallow and random striations (**Fig. 58 a,b**). They are similar to the ethnographic example observed in the Ajlun area (Jordan).

a.

b.

Fig. 58: Surface characteristics of self-slip smoothing

2- Tool finishing
a- soft and relatively shiny facets (**Fig. 59 a**)
b- relatively shallow and sharp edges striations left when the clay was leather hard (**Fig. 59 b**)

a.

b.

Fig. 59: Finishing operation with the use of a hard-tool on leather hard clay

II.1.2.6 Forming methods and operations

After identifying the various forming techniques involved in pot forming stages, we will identify the sequence of the pot fashioning. This sequence includes pot phases, forming stages and operations.

II.1.2.6.1 Identification of the base forming and shaping operations

1- A piece of clay was flattened by hands or on a supporting tool. The base becomes flat and takes the shape of the supporting tool which can be made of matt.
Diagnostic features:
a- a flat or slightly curved base
b- matt impression on the outside surface of the base (**Fig. 60**).

Fig. 60: The use of mat as supporting tool

2- shaping the base internal face with hand smoothing.

3- the external face of the base is subjected to:
a- evenness with clay smearing,
b- scraping with a hard tool (**Fig. 61**).
c- shaping by adding a clay layer to the external surface. This action produces a stamped base.

Fig. 61: The external junction between the base and the lower part of the pot has been scraped with hard tool

4- the base–body junction area is subjected to:
a- levelling: by clay smearing which delimits the undercut (base-body) area (**Fig. 62**).
b- trimming with hard tool, which causes a rounded profile between the base and body (**Fig. 61**). Such an action has similarities to the ethnographic observation made in northern Jordan.

Fig. 62: Smearing clay at the base-body junction area

II.1.2.6.2 Identification of the body forming and shaping operations

In the previous pages, we have identified the type of clay mass and the type of pressure applied on the clay to perform the different forming stages. In this part, the concern is to identify the forming methods of pot shaping. The pot's forming sequences have been recognized to include five stages. These are:

1- Shaping the coils: a ball of clay is rolled between the palms. The common size of the segment used in shaping either closed or open forms ranges between 10-15 mm (**Fig. 63**).

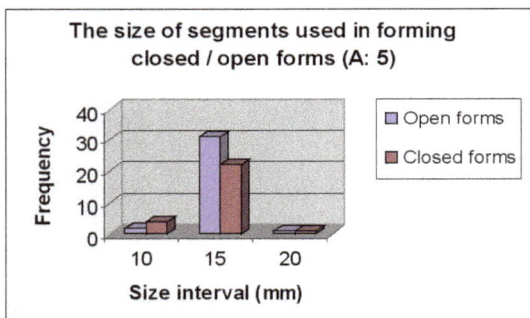

Fig. 63: The size of the segments used in forming closed / open forms of Levels 5 assemblages

2- Joining the coils: the parameters related to this stage could include the following:
a- Type of joining: the coil is placed against the previous one either in abut or levelled type of joining.
b- Methods of joining:
- pressing the coils against each other that leaves a : shallow horizontal recess at different horizontal spatial interval; these recesses are observed either on both surfaces or on the external one.
- by a slight smoothing on the joining area: in this case the wall of the pot presents horizontal voids on the coil binding area, or a shallow groove, the size of a finger width.

3- Thinning operation
Discontinuous pressing: relatively deep vertical finger recess at variuos horizontal spatial intervals.

4- Shaping operation
a- Scraping the clay with fingers while supporting the opposite side with the other hand causes plastic, coarse, horizontal finger striations which covering the whole surface.
b- Curving the pot wall by pressing the coiled face which results in relatively deep recesses on the inside of the pot and in the curve of the body (**Fig. 64**).
c- Different coil thickness to control the profile of the pot.

Fig. 64: Curving the pot wall by pressing on the coil-surface

5- Evenness operation
It involves smearing clay inside and outside on an already shaped surface. This action has been identified by:
a- plastic finger striations partly visible on the pot wall that has not been subjected to clay smearing (**Fig. 65 b,c**)
b- two overlapped clay layers (**Fig. 65 a,d**).

a. b. c. d.

Fig. 65: Smearing clay at one or both surfaces, sometimes clay smearing is partially conducted

II.1.2.6.3 Identification of the rim forming and shaping methods

1- Shaping the coil: rolling a ball of clay between the palms. The segment size most used in forming the rim varies betzeen 10 and 20 mm (**Fig. 66**), the frequent one being ca. 10 mm.

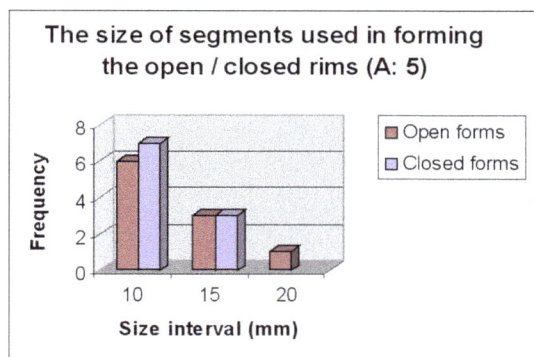

Fig. 66: The size of the segments used in forming the rims

2- Joining the coils:
a- type of joining: abut
b- joining methods:
- pressing the coil against the previous one: shallow horizontal recess at different horizontal spatial interval; these recesses are observed either on both surfaces or on the outside one.
- by a slight smoothing at the joining area (**Fig. 67**).

Fig. 67: The joining of the rim segment by slightly smoothing

3- Thinning operation
Finger pressing at the surface of the coils at different horizontal interval.

4- Shaping operation
Two methods have been used:
a- pinching between fingers: This is recognized by the decrease of the rim thickness compared with the body one, and the dominance of recesses at variuos horizontal spatial intervals.

b- horizontal shaping between fingers on the surface of the coils, followed by perpendicular smoothing on the lip, and finally by folding the clay on the rim surfaces. This shaping action has been identified by the folded clay on one of the rim faces and the surfaces that present clay ridges that have not been subjected to folding (**Fig. 68 a,b**). Similar technical features have been observed by potters in northern Jordan when they were forming the rim.

Fig. 68: Clay ridge on the rim part that was produced when the rim was shaped

5- Evenness operation
The rim-body part is levelled by smearing the clay. In some cases, the smeared clay appears as applied knots. When it is the case, a clear micro-relief (recess) between the rim and body is present. Evenness operation is sometimes applied on one surface of the rim.

II.1.2.6.4 Identification of the body finishing operation

The following static macro-traces have been defined:

1- finishing on humid clay
a- wet hand finishing: medium coarse, rounded set of striations.
b- tool finishing: striations that have a deep and raised edge, and a coarse texture.

2- finishing on leather-hard clay
a- hand finishing: very soft face, slipped-like one, striations sets very fine and shallow, drag marks obliterated that seem filled with fine clay.
b- finishing with a tool: very even and soft facets, relatively shallow and sharp-edge striations.

3- slip: clay suspension covers one surface of the pot (**Fig. 69 a,b**).

a. 1 cm

b. 1 cm

Fig. 69: Surface of a pot covered with clay suspension

II.1.3 Pinching technique

II.1.3.1 Identification of the body forming technique

Pinching technique is mainly used to shape small to hand size bowls. The following diagnostic features can be correlated with this technique:

1- No clear evidence of coil joining either in section or on the surfaces.

2- vertical–oblique pattern of shallow finger indentations or recesses.

3- predominance of plastic state fingerprints on the inside surface.

4- continuous profile between the base and the body.

5- irregular pattern of pinching that causes differentiation in wall thickness – horizontally – within a small area of the body.

6- fracture pattern of the sherd which is more vertical-diagonal or oblique rather than horizontal as it is when a coiling technique has been used.

7- sharp decrease of the rim thickness compared with the body one.

8- pointed or/and rounded bases.

II.1.3.2 Forming methods and operations

1- Identification of the forming and shaping operation
a- Forming a ball / cylindrical clay mass, by rolling a clay mass between the palms.

b- Thinning the clay: pressing a hole into the mass of clay; repeatedly squeezing the clay between the thumb and fingers.

c- Shaping the walls with a discontinued fingers scraping / smoothing pattern. This action could delimit partly the recesses of fingers resulted during thinning.

2- Identification of the rim forming operation
The rim is shaped by pinching slightly the clay between fingers. This shaping operation has been identified by the shallow recess present on the rim surfaces, it shows a horizontal distribution pattern and a decrease in rim thickness.

II.1.4 Moulding technique

The use of a mould – concave or convex – to shape a pot has been attested for medium size bowls. The use of moulding has been identified according to the following diagnostic features (**Fig. 70 b,c**):

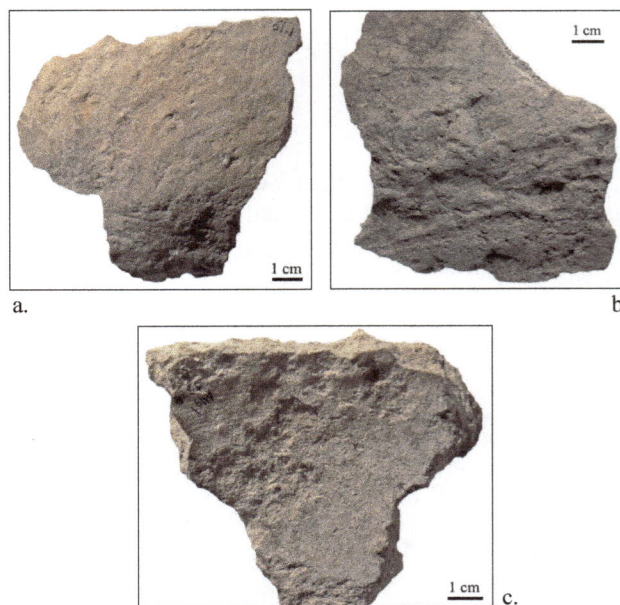

a.   b.

1 cm

1 cm

1 cm c.

Fig. 70: Technical features related to the use of mould in pot shaping

1- the external surface of the sherd shows a negative impression. This is relatively deep in the body and is not regular.

2- absence of recess of coil joining / thinning pattern at both pot surfaces.

3- the inside surface has a smoothed and even surface compared to the external one. It lacks evidence of finger recesses.

4- absence of joining area in the wall section.

5- relative regular wall thickness.

II.2 The pottery forming methods and techniques of the Middle Levels (A: 3)

The technological characteristics of this pottery assemblage show significant similarities as well as differences with the previous ones. These are mostly subjected to intensive finishing operation which has deliberated most of the fashioning chains. Nonetheless, it was possible to identify the following fashioning techniques.

II.2.1 The clay body

Based on the observations that were made on radiographic images, the clay body or paste found in Levels 3 is characterized by the following features:

1- high density of non-plastic inclusions.
2- the non-plastic inclusions are characterized by their medium-coarse size.
3- low to medium degree of voids.

II.2.2 Forming technique(s)

The pottery sherds that have been studied show that the pots (restricted or open forms) have been shaped with *coiling technique*. There have been no trances of regular, parallel and continuous striations at internal or external faces of the pot's body.

II.2.2.1 Identification of the forming techniques

As for the Levels 5 and 4 potteries, the use of the coiling technique in shaping the pots has been identified based on the following surface features:

1- Coils are preserved on one face: these have not been subjected to thinning or/and shaping (**Fig. 71**).
2- The base has an undercut with the body.
3- Horizontal corrugations between coils (**Fig. 72**)
4- Horizontal voids at face (see **fig. 71**).
5- Voids in section.

Fig. 71: Technical feature showing the use of coiling in pot forming

Fig. 72: Horizontal corrugation at pot's surface following the use of coiling in pot forming

6- Irregular wall thickness at regular intervals: at the binding areas, the pot walls subjected to either an increase or decrease in thickness.
7- Presence of recess at internal and external faces which have a horizontal pattern following the binding area (**Fig. 73**)

Fig. 73: Horizontal recesses pattern between the coils

8- The fracture pattern of sherds has more straight horizontal fracture.

II.2.2.2 Identification of the roughout technique

This stage of body fashioning refers to the techniques of joining and thinning the segmental coils that are used in building the pot wall. The studied pottery sherds which showed the evidence of this stage illustrate that:

1- coils were joined by
a- a discontinuous pressing at the binding area: relative shallow recesses which has a horizontal pattern and distributed with different spatial intervals at pot's faces.
b- discontinuous smoothing of the joining area: the coil's binding area is still clear at one face, and has plastic smoothing with fingers.

2- coils were thinned by discontinuous pressure with a hand:
a- discontinuous vertical–diagonal scraping pattern: finger width size clay scraping is conducted at the coil's face at irregular vertical spatial interval, and leaves a dent at

face.
b- irregular faces characterized by micro-relief morphology.

II.2.2.3 Identification of the preform techniques

The pottery sherds that have been analyzed from these levels show that the technique of shaping the roughout can be distinguished in the variuos pot's phases, that is, between the pots' walls and their rims. This separation has its justification as the roughout of these two phases have been subjected to two different shaping techniques:

1- Discontinuous shaping technique
All the pottery *body* sherds (those with no rims nor bases), show no traces of the use of rotative kinetic energy. This is evident on their inside and outside surfaces. Therefore, it seems that the roughout has been subjected to shaping with a discontinuous pressure. The few sherds left evidence of this stage, sharing the technical characteristics of Levels 5 and 4 tradition (see above). This stage of fashioning might have been performed by a discontinuous pressure of either hand or a tool. The latter left in some cases a hard tool impression of lunate shape at pot face.

a.

b.

Fig. 74: Showing the use of rotative method of rim shaping

2- Shaping with the use of RKE
In contrast to the discontinuous shaping technique and its associated pot phase, it might be that some kind of rotative method (rotative kinetic energy) was used in shaping the *rim* part. The use of this movement in shaping the rim has been attested based on the following surface features:
a- parallel, regular striations on the rim part (**Fig. 74 a,b**).
b- regular rim wall.
c- regular rim faces either internal or external without recesses.
d- relatively, deep striations on the rim which might have been left when the clay was still plastic.
e- regular height of the rim.

II.2.2.4 Identification of the finishing technique

Two finishing techniques have been identified on the basis of the pot phases. these are 1) discontinuous finishing operation and 2) with the use of rotative kinetic energy.

1- Discontinuous smoothing technique
This finishing technique has been performed at the body of the pot as well as the rims. either hand or tool finishing were used.
a- Hand finishing: the smoothing has been identified according to the following macro-traces:
- matte appearance surface (**Fig. 75 a,b**)
- fine-medium set of shallow striations, rounded edge, left when the clay was leather hard state.
- self-slip facets characterized by the dominance of fine, shallow and random striations.

a.   b.

Fig. 75: Hand-smoothing at leather hard clay

b- Tool finishing
- soft and matte (**Fig. 76 a**)
- relative to high shiny facets (**Fig. 76 b**).
- relative shallow and sharp edge striations distributed randomly, left when the clay was leather hard.

a.   b.

Fig. 76: Technical features associated with hard-tool smoothing

2- Use of RKE for finishing

This finishing technique has only been used in the rims of bowls and certain types of jars. This technique has been recognized in the following macro-traces:
a- parallel, regular and continuous striations (**Fig. 77a,b**).
b- shallow striations which indicate that the pressure applied by RKE has slightly changed the preform of the rim.

a.

b.

Fig. 77: Finishing the rim with rotative technique

II.2.3 Identification of pottery forming methods and operations

II.2.3.1 Identification of the base forming operation

Three types of bases have been identified: flattened, concave, and disc ones. The forming of these bases is based on the following sequences:

1- forming a ball of clay: a mass of clay rolled between the palms
2- thinning the ball of clay between the palms or on a flat surface
3- placing the clay disc on the supporting tool. This can be made of matt or soft material (**Fig. 78 a,b**).
4- shaping the inside surface of the base by smoothing with wet hands.
5- the base external face is subjected to:
a- evenness with clay smearing. The type of supporting tool is absent (**Fig. 78 c**).
b- scraping with hard tool.

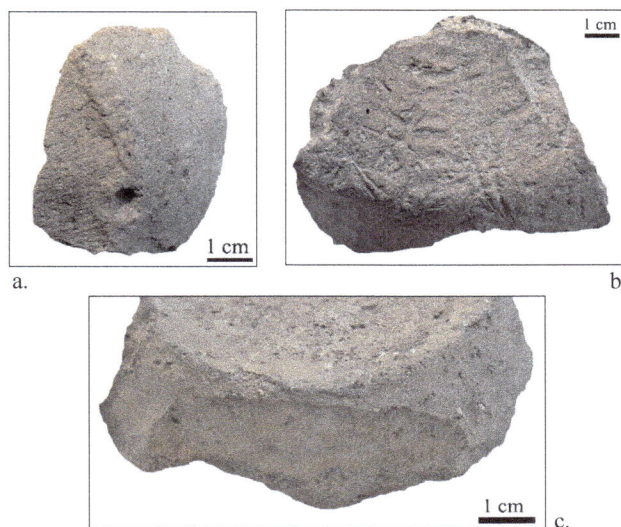

a.   b.

c.

Fig. 78: Technical features associated with base shaping

II.2.3.2 Identification of the body forming methods and operations

1- The coils: range from 10-15 mm (**Fig. 79**). This size meets the closed form as well as the open forms pots.

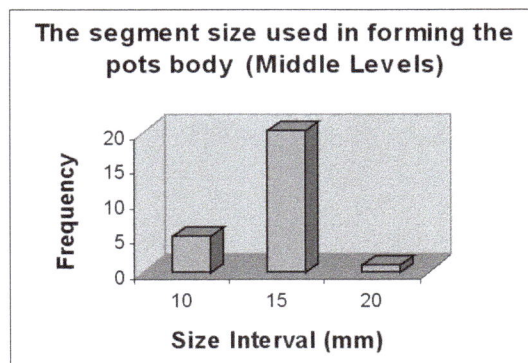

Fig. 79: The size of the segment used in body forming – Middle Levels assemblage

85

2- Joining the coils:
a- joining type: abut.
b- joining methods:
- pressing the coils against each other: shallow horizontal recess at different horizontal spatial interval.
- by slightly smoothing the joining area.

3-Thinning operation
Discontinuous finger pressing: vertical shallow recesses at wall faces that take different spatial intervals.

4- Shaping operation
The pot's roughout has been subjected to shaping operation with discontinuous scraping pattern. These are conducted in two ways:
a- hand scraping
- Horizontal–diagonal direction: medium-coarse striations, left on humid clay at the internal face.
- Irregular and discontinuous clay scraping; in an either horizontal–diagonal or/and vertical direction.
- Curving the body with pinching: slight or deep recesses of finger at the curving area of the pot.
b- shaping the wall with a tool: hard tool that left relatively even and regular faces without micro-relief morphology.

5- Evenness operation
This operation is conducted to level or and increase the thickness of the pot's wall. It is conducted by adding clay and smearing it at the wall's face. It involves additional clay out of the clay wall itself. This action has been identified at pot's walls according to the following features:
a- superimposed clay layers at pot face: one layer rose out of the original face. This is evident in the case where the smeared layer is conducted partly at the original face (**Fig. 80 a,b**).

Fig. 80: Clay smearing at either internal or external pot's surface

b- two clear layers visible in wall section.
c- differences in the regularity of the wall thickness: this occurs when the surfaces of the pot have been parley levelled.

The levelling of pot face (s) has been conducted at one face of the pot or at both faces (**Fig. 81**). In the most observed cases, both faces have subjected to levelling operation by smearing thick clay layer at the faces (>4 mm) or a thin one (<4 mm). Meanwhile, very few sherds have been not subjected to a levelling operation. This indicates that the original face of the pot is based on the preforming stage to finishing one without the evenness stage.

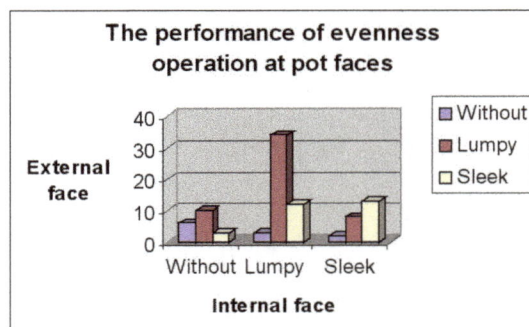

Fig. 81: The frequency of levelling operation at pot faces and the type of clay used

II.2.3.3 Identification of the rim forming methods and operations

1- Shaping the coil: the potters used coils of 10-15 mm thick (**Fig. 82**).

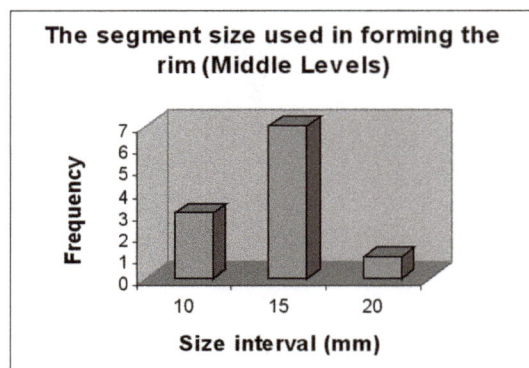

Fig. 82: The identified coil sizes used in rim shaping

2- Joining the coils:
a- joining type: either levelled or abut.
b- joining method: by pressing the coil against the previous one: shallow horizontal recesses at a different horizontal spatial interval.

3- Thinning operation
Finger pressing at the coil's face at different horizontal interval.

4- Shaping operation
The shaping of the roughout of the rim has been obtained

either by discontinuous scraping and smoothing or the aid of rotative kinetic energy. The latter being used for closed and open forms. Two dominant rim profiles have been shaped by this technique. These are tapered or pinched rims (in case of bowls) and thickened outward rims in case of jars. The use of RKE in the shaping operation has been identified by the continuous, parallel striations which cover the rim part. These are more conducted at humid clay that resulted in relative deep striations.

The shaping of the rim, by discontinuous hand scraping, has resulted in tapered rims with recesses on their faces, or rims with folded clay on one face (**Fig. 83 a,b**).

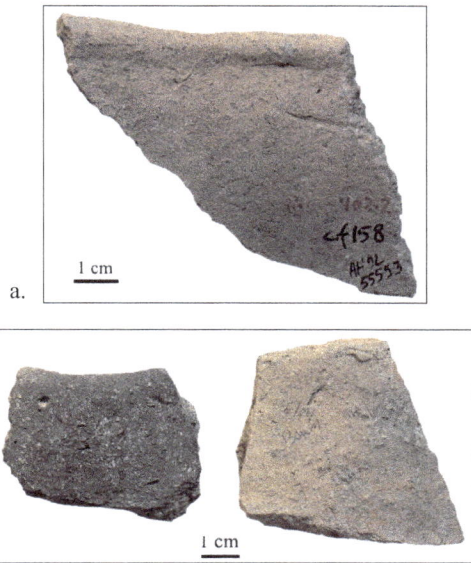

a.

b.

Fig. 83: Shaping the pot's rim with discontinuous pressure

a- The tapered rims have been shaped by strong/ weak pinching the clay between fingers: The later is identified by a relative shallow recess on the rim face. The strong pinching has been recognized by the decrease of rim thickness compared with the one of body wall, and the dominance of recesses at a different horizontal spatial interval.

b- Horizontal shaping between fingers at the coil's face is followed by perpendicular smoothing at the lip, and finally folding and/or smoothing the clay at the rim faces. This shaping action has been identified by the folded clay at one of the rim faces and the ones' that have clay ridges and have not been subjected to folding at the rim face.

II.2.3.4 Identification of the body finishing operation

The assemblage of these levels shows a great difference in the finishing operations compared with the previous ones. However, following is a description of the identified finishing operations that are conducted at either internal or external faces of the pots' body.

Finishing on leather hard clay:

1- Hand smoothing
Leather hard state: fine rounded edges striations, these have (see **Fig. 75**):
a- horizontal direction.
b- vertical striations.
c- diagonal-horizontal pattern.

2- Tool smoothing (see **Fig. 76 a, b**)
a- leather hard state finishing:
- horizontal sharp fine-to medium striations cover most of the face
- fine, sharp, random striations, cause a soft relative shiny face: this action resulted by smoothing the face with hard smoothed tool.
b- soft tool smoothing: medium-coarse striations, has a distribution between bands, and cause a relative matte face (**Fig. 84 a, b**)

a.

b.

Fig. 84: Soft-tool smoothing at leather hard clay

c- slip: clay-suspension (**Fig. 85**); and pigment: red colour

Fig. 85: Coating the pot surface with fine clay slip

III. Summary and discussion

The identification of the type and kind of the surface features observed on the pottery assemblages that have been studied from Abu Hamid enables the reconstruction of their forming methods and techniques. Each pottery assemblage has been studied so as to identify the set of actions and gestures embedded in transforming the clay body into a final shape.

It has been noted that during the Levels 5, the pottery repertoire has been fashioned with three different techniques (**Fig. 86**): coiling, moulding and pinching. Assembled elements like coils are used in fashioning different pot forms such as jars and bowls. Several diagnostic surface features such as joining patterns, fracture one and horizontal corrugation are the indication that the pots were fashioned in parts. Moreover, the characteristics of surface features show that the different forming stages after pot's phases were performed by discontinuous pressure. The type of pressure is applied on the coils with hands, fingers or with the use of a hard tool. It is the main source of energy employed in fashioning the different forming stages.

The analysis of the pottery fashioning methods enabled reconstruct the different steps of production: size of segments used for the body or the rim, type and method of segments joining. Moreover, it has been possible to identify the set of gestures associated with thinning and shaping operations.

The other two forming techniques, pinching and moulding, were used in fashioning two main pot shapes. Pinching to fashion only small bowls and cups, while the use of moulding was restricted to medium size bowls.
The same can be said concerning the pottery assemblage of Levels 4 (**Fig. 86**). Here too, the identified technical features showed that the assembled elements – coils – were a main forming technique. It has also been employed in fashioning either jars or bowls. The similarities in fashioning techniques with previous Levels (A: 5) is strong. The same type of pressure was applied at clay body to transform it into final pot shape.

The significant change in pot fashioning has been identified in the Middle Levels(A:3). Pots are still formed out of coils, but subjected to two operation sequences, *chaînes opératoires* (**Fig. 87**). These two operation sequences differ mainly in the type of pressure that has been applied in fashioning the pot forming stages. The first pot forming sequence showed that discontinuous pressure was applied on the coils in order to transform the clay into final shape. This type of pressure is applied at different phases of pot such as the base, the body and the rim. The second forming sequence showed that two types of pressures were applied at coils according to the pot phases. First, coils were the main clay mass that have been used in forming. Secondly, the discontinuous pressure of hands or fingers was applied at different forming stages in fashioning the bases and the body. Third, the main difference is in the use of continuous pressure with different source of energy to fashion only the rim. In the identified cases, finger or hands combined with rotative kinetic energy were applied against the rim fashioning. This technique has been used at two forming stages: the preform and finishing.

A further comparison between the pottery repertoires of Levels 5, 4 and 3 can be made in terms of the clay body characteristics and the surface finishing. The former technical features have been identified by studying the radiographic images of pottery sherds. These images have shed light on the density of the non-plastic inclusions, their sizes and the degree of voids in pot's walls. The results showed that the pots that related to Levels 5 and are characterized by clay body of low density of non-plastic inclusions. On the contrary, during the Middle Levels the most pottery sherds are characterized by high density of non-plastic inclusions. These inclusions have an angular shape which can be a hint that they were added to the clay, which means a cultural practice, rather than being natural. The size of these inclusions is coarse in comparison with the ones found in the clay body of the Lower Levels pottery. The interesting result that was obtained by the radiographic images is the degree of voids in the clay body. The sample related to Levels 5 show that most of the sherds have a high degree of voids which are elongated and do not have a regular size and pattern. The case differs during the Middle Levels, despite the pastes coarse texture. They mostly have low degree of voids. These differences might indicate that during the Lower Levels potters did not subject the clay body to enough kneading compared to what was done by the potters during the Middle Levels.

The analysis of the three pottery repertoires shows both similarities and differences in terms of pots' surface finishing (**Fig. 88**). During Levels A: 5, it seems that pots were subjected mainly to hand smoothing on leather hard clay. This method seems to dominate the analysed pottery. The second finishing method is the use of a hard-tool. If we compare this method with the ones used in Levels 4 and 3, this finishing method seems to be less performed (**Fig. 88**). The main differences in surface finishing are found in using soft-tool to finish the pot surface. This seems to have been employed frequently at the Middle Levels assemblage (A: 3). Meanwhile,during Levels 5 and 4 show differences which are obvious in the way the surface of the pot was finished: much more sherds show burnishing and the use of pigment to cover the surfaces.

Preparing the clay body for shaping

Without RKE

Discontinues pressure at assembled elements forming and thinning the coils.

Discontinues pressure at mass of clay. molding and pinching.

The roughout

Discontinues scraping with fingers or tool

The preform

Smearing clay

Smoothing with hand / tool

Finished pot

Fashioning the Roughout

Fashioning the preform

Evenness operation

Finishing

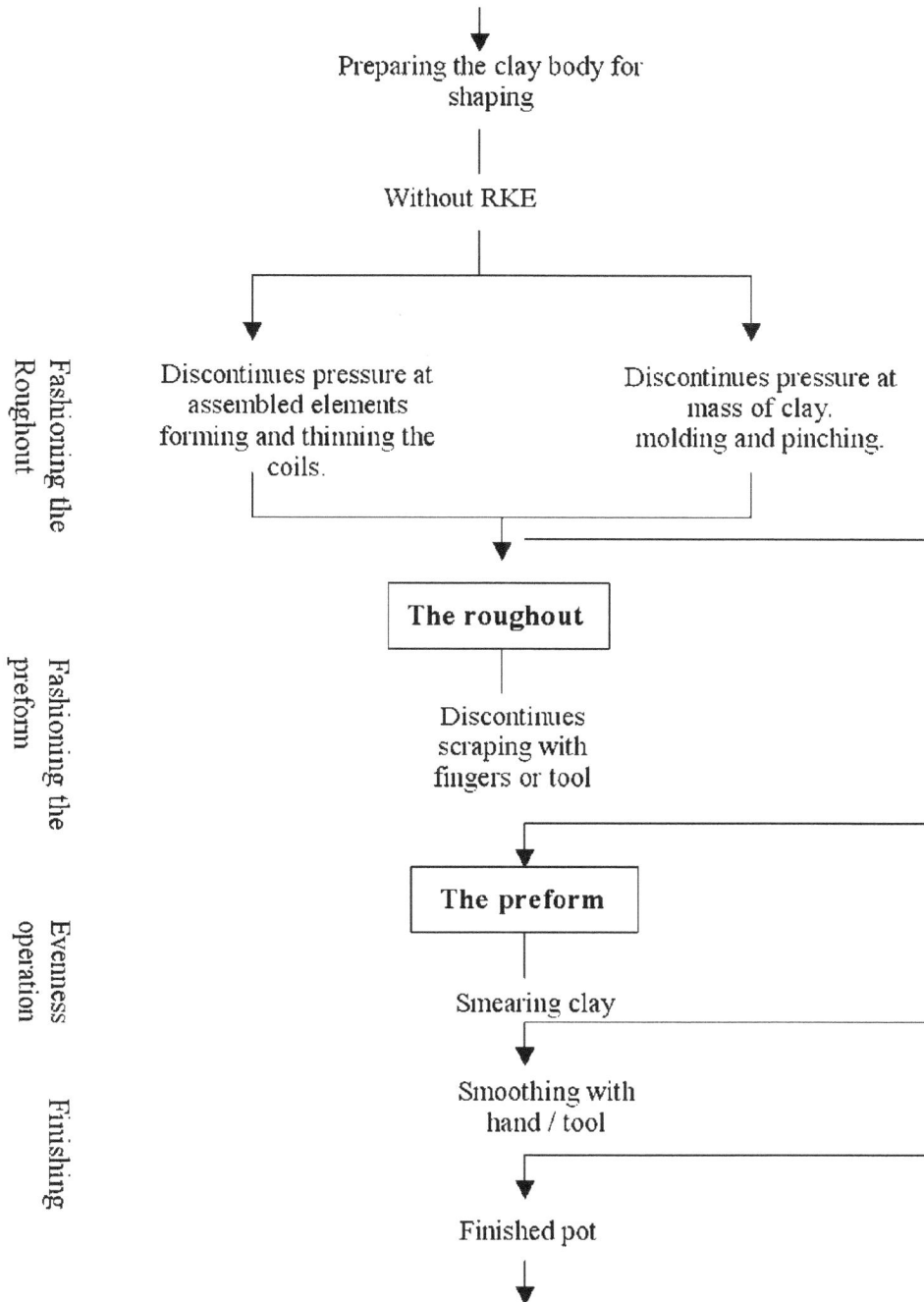

Fig. 86: The schema of fashioning techniques of pottery assemblages (Levels 5 and 4)

Fashioning the roughout

Preparing the clay body
for pot shaping

↓

*Discontinuous pressure on
assembled elements.*
Joining and thinning the coils.

↓

Roughout

Fashioning the preform

Without RKE.
Shaping with discontinues
hand / tool scraping

With RKE – shaping on
tournette. Only the rim

Preform

↓

Evenness operation

Without RKE
coating, clay smearing

↓

Finishing

Without RKE
Smoothing, burnishing

With RKE
smoothing

Finished pots

↓

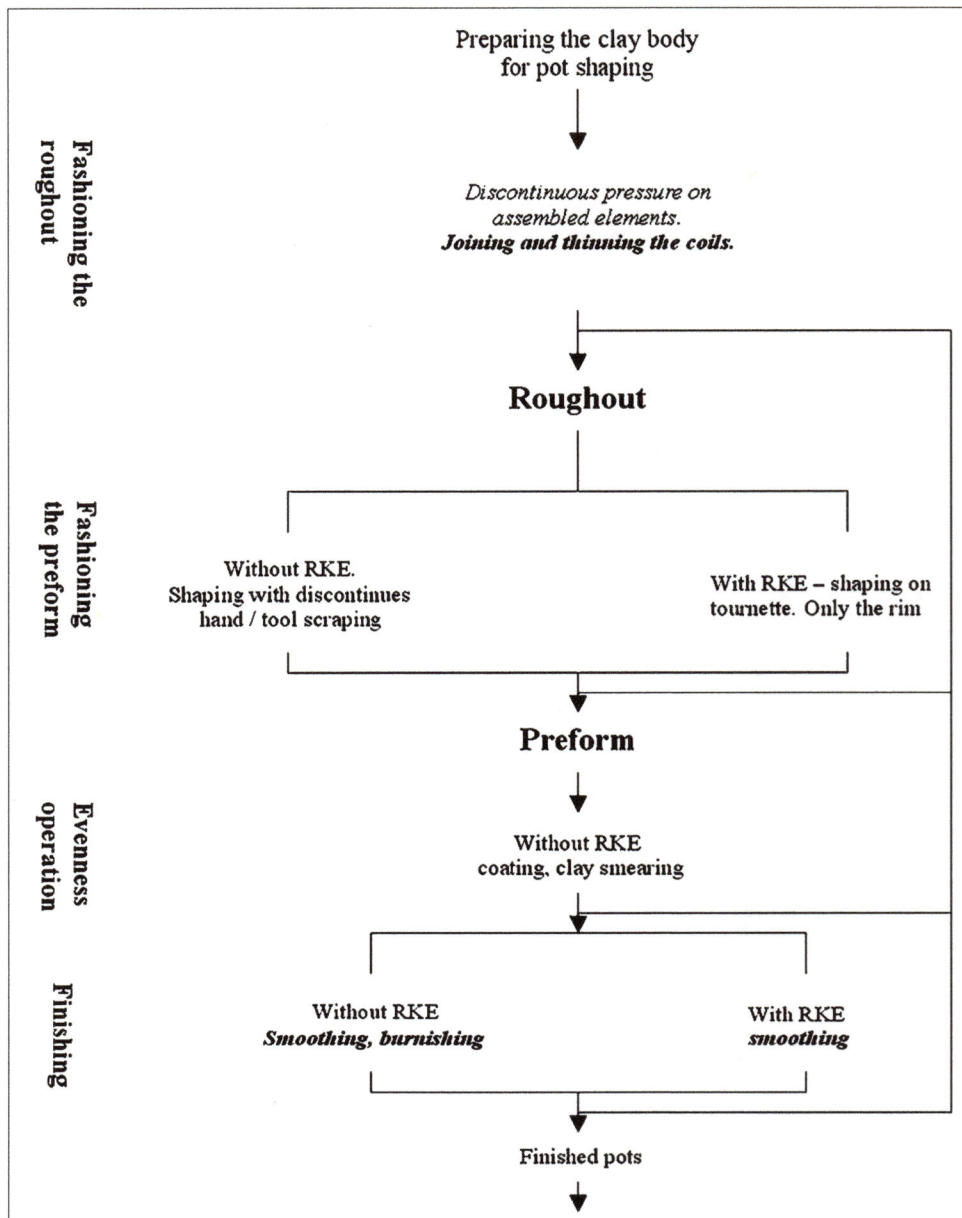

Fig. 87: The operation
sequences schema of pot
shaping as identified in
the Middle Levels (A: 3)

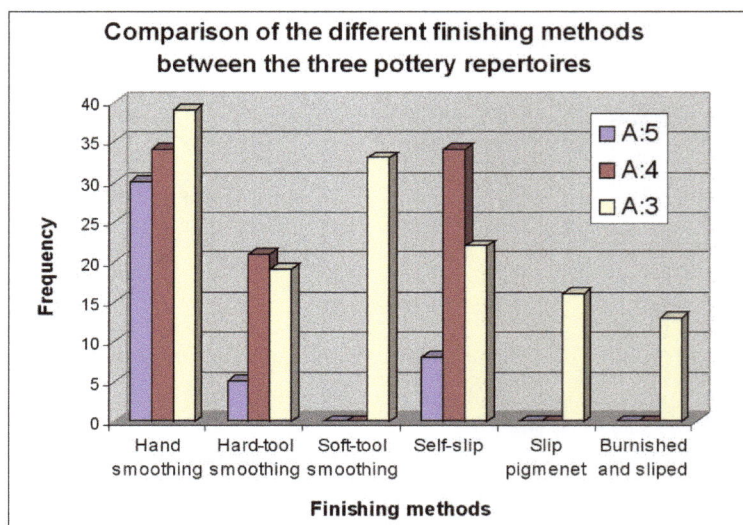

Fig. 88: The different
methods employed in
finishing the surface of the
pots

**Comparison of the different finishing methods
between the three pottery repertoires**

Chapter Nine: Technological classification and measuring variation
of pottery shaping at Abu Hamid

In the previous chapter, it was possible to identify the various techniques used in shaping the pottery assemblages at Abu Hamid, as well as the respective forming sequences. The aims in this chapter are a) to define a set of parameters that will aid in classifying the technical variability within each pottery assemblage at the site, and b) to measure variation within each identified technical group.

I. Background

Pottery can be assigned as artefacts that enhance the richness and variability of attributes. These characteristics call for two archaeological procedures; a) identifying and classifying these attributes and b) correlating them with human behaviour in order to establish an explanatory framework (Hayden 1984: 80). In this way, classification becomes an analytical tool rather than an interpretative procedure (Rice 1987, 1996). It is a hypothesis about the ordering of data for a specific problem (Dunnell 1971: 117). This conceptual aspect is a pre-requisite for selecting a set of attributes, as each research problem is solved on the basis of a different set of attributes or criteria. For example, defining the dates of pottery sherds required a different set of attributes comparing with using pottery to infer the specialization of production. In this way, the research design or nature of the problem constrains the set of attributes or criteria selected for classification.

This chapter aims to measure technical *variability* and *variation* within the pottery assemblages of the different cultural phases observed at Abu Hamid. To achieve this goal, it is necessary to identify how this process will be expressed in the surface features – shaping techniques used in a given assemblage. This involves two procedures. First, theoretical units must be identified that allow to categorize objects into groups. Second, objects must be sorted into these units. In dealing with classification problem, Rouse (1960) has postulated these two lines as class and type. A class is defined as a "series of objects which are grouped together". Type is defined as a "series of attributes – modes – which are shared by a class and which distinguish them as a class" (Rouse 1953: 62). Classes are thus recognized as empirical entities whereas types define as theoretical units. If the theoretical unit is identified, it facilitates the choice of criteria that aids in sorting pottery objects / sherds. In this way, it is linked to the problem that needs to be solved (Lyman *et al.* 1997: 118-119). In a similar way, other scholars like Franken (1995) maintain a direct correlation between pottery classification system and identification of the processes of pottery making. Like Rouse (1960), Franken emphasizes identification of the behavioural pattern of pottery making as a prerequisite for further typological schema. As a conceptual framework, the type will be a set of objects that will be furthered an explanatory framework rather than static entities.

In the previous chapter, the identification of operational sequences – *chaîne opératoire* – in terms of the methods and techniques employed in pot fashioning help in the determining the different stages of pot production. This is the first step in establishing a technological classification based on the different stages of manufacture. It also helped in establishing a correlation between a given forming stage and the material actions, defined as cultural, undertaken in its forming. Hence, this recognition makes it possible to differentiate the variability of a set of actions undertaken in transforming a given forming stage. The detailed description of the *chaîne opératoire* facilitates identification of this technical variability / group within a given pottery assemblage, on the one hand, and measuring technical variation within each group, on the other. Each technical group constitutes then a theoretical unit, that shares similarities in the set of forming and finishing techniques.

II. Methodological consideration

If the researcher's aim plays a constraint on the selection of a set of attributes that might answer his or her question, then what are those attributes that might help classifying the pottery assemblages at Abu Hamid as manifested in the pot shaping operations? In chapter 4, we have observed that variation among pottery assemblages can be evaluated based on either their morphological attributes, the metric analysis or technological features. The first two indexes can be of significance when archaeologists deal with complete vessels. We have seen that morphological and technological indexes are closely related to each other, and that technological index concerned with shaping operations can be a useful tool to classifying the pottery assemblage. This is especially true when we are dealing with pottery sherds, which is the case at Abu Hamid, rather than with complete or intact objects. The classification can be proceeded using the observations made on those surface features that correlated with the different stages of pot forming (such as pot wall roughout, preform, evenness, and finishing). The technique used in performing each stage has been selected as a primary parameter to establish technical groups. Technical group is then represented as a set of pottery objects / sherds that share similar techniques with respect to forming and finishing operations.

Each technical group includes variation related to the forming and finishing methods. The analysis of the surface features on both internal and external surfaces would enable measuring the variation in the performance of fashioning methods within the technical groups. A set of parameters, therefore, can be selected to achieve such an end. Based on the ethnographic study, these parameters can include:

1. morphology of the pot walls.
2. modification of the initial roughout walls when thinning: this modification can be either strong, average or weak: a weak modification hardly changes the coil thickness; an average action moderate the coil thickness in a medium stand and a strong modification reduces the coil thickness. These modifications can be measured in terms of the degree of pressure applied at the coil faces which maintained either a relative deep, medium or shallow recess.
3. the regular or intermittent thinning operation.
4. modification of the shape of the roughout during the shaping stage: this modification can be also weak, average or strong: a weak modification does not change the shape of the roughout; an average one moderate slightly the roughout wall, and a strong modification changes the shape of the roughout.
5. evenness of the walls of the pot: it refers to the levelling of the pot faces by the use of clay out of the clay wall.
6. intensity of finishing: this refers to the degree of performance of a finishing method on one or on the two surfaces of the pot.
7. variation on wall thickness – referring to difference in the percentage of the pot's wall thickness. A parameter assumed to have a direct relation to the shaping operation.

Based on the above methodological framework, the three pottery assemblages at Abu Hamid have been classified at two scales. One deals with classifying each pottery repertoire into technical groups, whereas the second scale of classification represents the classification of each group into sub-groups. The following are the results of the classification procedures.

III. The results of technological classification of the pottery assemblages

Presentation of the classification results has been organized for each pottery repertoire separately. This will include the type of technological group and then the technical variation within each group.

III. 1. Technological classification of the Levels 5 and 4

Based on the forming technique, as a classifying parame-

ter, the pottery assemblages of Levels 5 and 4can be classified into three different technical groups. These include:

- Group 1: represents vessels that have been formed with a coiling technique.
- Group 2: vessels that have been formed with a moulding technique.
- Group 3: represents vessels that have been formed with a pinching technique.

In both repertoires, technical group 1 is dominant. Therefore, only this group has been subjected to further classification to measure the variation in the forming methods. This has been conducted for A: 5 and A: 4 repertoires separatel in order to see if we can note some differences.

III.1.1 Technical classification of A: 5 pottery assemblages into sub-groups

A finer classification of technological group I is based firstly on defining the relationship between sherd and the shape it belongs to. It is assumed that the degree of face evenness with respect to the regulation of the face during the preform stage reflects the probable pot shape. Therefore, if the internal face of a vessel is subjected to a higher degree of evenness and finishing in comparison with the external face, then the sherd is classified as belonging to the open-forms repertoire. Based on this assumption, pottery sherds related to group 1 are classified into two functional categories: open vs. closed forms. Each functional repertoire is then further classified into technical sub-groups.

III.1.1.1 Technical classification of open forms

The probable open forms repertoire, dating to the Late Neolithic 2 period (A: 5), has been classified into three main technical sub-groups, with a sum of 50 sherds. This classification is based on the forming stages and operations carried out on the internal face. This repertoire includes the following sub-groups:

1- Sub-group I
This sub-group represents 10% of the open forms repertoire (**Fig. 89**). The morphology of the walls is characterized by an internal surfaces where the roughout has been modified due to a later shaping stage. The operation on these surface is not pronounced (a weakly average), and traces of the roughout are evident. The external surfaces are also moderately changed by a later shaping operation. It reveals a discontinuous downward pressure of thinning operation, as well as relatively deep recesses resulting from irregular thinning of the coils. Moreover, the joining pattern of the coil show recesses at different horizontal, spatial intervals. This sub-group is further characterized

by a remarkable variation in wall thickness.

Concerning the finishing, the pot surfaces related to this sub-group show low to middle intensity of smoothing with the hands.

2- Sub-group II

This is the dominant sub-group of the open forms assemblage. It is represented by 61% of the pottery sherds that have been analysed. The internal surfaces received shaping of moderate intensity, as it shown by the presence of relatively shallow micro-relief recesses, though they are not as prominent as in the previous sub-group. The external surfaces can be classified into those subjected to a) a weak shaping operation and b) to an average shaping operation. In the case of the latter, the external surface is subjected to more or the less the same intensity of the internal surface, but they are differentiated by the later finishing operation. The internal surface is given a smooth middle to high intensity relative to the external surface, using either the hands or a tool.

3- Sub-group III

This sub-group represents 29% of the assemblage. The morphology of the internal surface lacks the traces of a roughout stage; it is characterized by a strong intensity of shaping that leaves few very shallow recesses. The result is a relative regular internal surface. The external surfaces have the morphological characteristics as the ones of sub-group II, and, to a lesser extent, those of sub-group I. The internal surface has been highly smoothed, either by hand or with a tool. The wall thickness shows relative regularity, as reflected in its minimal variation.

The analysis of these morpho-technical sub-groups shows that the material actions characteristics of sub-group II are dominant (**Fig. 89**). This is true for the fashioning stages of both the internal and external faces. It has been evident that almost 26% of the sherds have an external face

similar to those found in sub-group I. The roughout wall has been weakly subjected to a shaping operation. This means that the potters paid more attention to shaping and levelling of the internal face, the assumed functional face, compared with the external one.

III.1.1.2 Technical classification of Closed forms

The analysis of sherds potentially derived of closed forms show that three main technical sub-groups can be recognized (n=61 sherds). These are:

1- Sub-group I

This sub-group makes up 18% of the closed- form assemblage (**Fig. 90**). The morphology of the external surface is characterized by relatively deep recesses, resulting in an irregular micro-relief surface which is due to a weakly shaping operation. To a large extent, this sub-group is characterized by variation in wall thickness. The internal face is subjected to a weak- to- average shaping operation, levelling in part the discontinuous recess pattern caused by the thinning operation.

2- Sub-group II

74 percent of the analysed pottery sherds belong to this sub-group. The morphology of the external wall shows an average scraping pattern with respect to modification of the roughout face. The result is a medium recess depth, producing a micro-relief face. The internal surface of this group shows variation in its forming. In some cases, it was subjected to a weak shaping operation, resulting in a relatively deep, discontinuous recess surface. In others, it shows a shaping operation as the external surface, resulting in a medium micro-relief surface.

3- Sub-group III

This sub-group makes up only 8 percent of the assemblage. It is characterized by an external wall with a morphology featuring very shallow recesses and a regular surface. These are the result of a strong shaping action applied

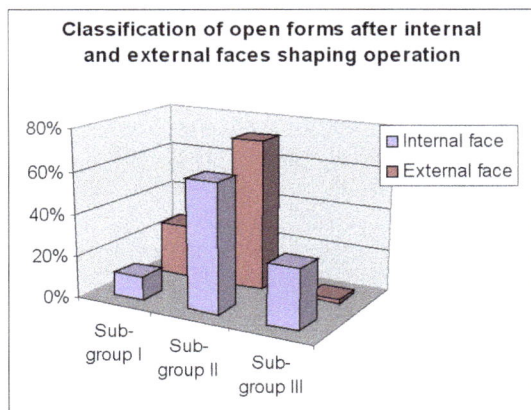

Fig. 89: The frequency of technical sub-groups of levels 5 open forms

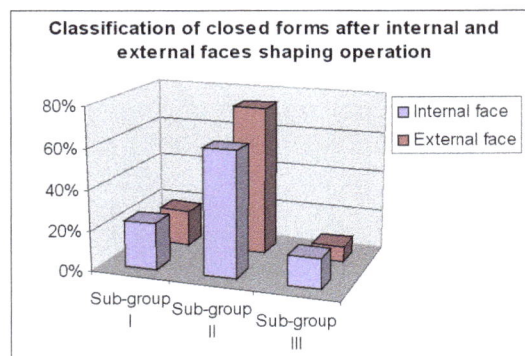

Fig. 90: The frequency of technical sub-groups of the closed forms within levels 5 pottery assemblage

to the roughout surface. Internal faces have the characteristics of either sub-group II or III. However, wall thickness is characterized by less variation. With respect to the finishing stage, both the internal and external surfaces show an intensive smoothing operation.

III.1.2 The technical classification of A: 4 pottery assemblages into sub-groups

The following are the results of classifying technological group 1 into sub-groups.

III.1.2.1 Open forms technical classification

Pottery sherds most probably related to open forms have been classified into two main sub-groups (with a sum of 57 sherds) on the basis of their internal face-forming sequences.

1- Sub-group II
This technical sub-group represents 47 % of the Level 4 open forms assemblage (**Fig. 91**). In some respects, it is similar to sub-group II of the A: 5 assemblage with respect to internal surface morphology. The internal surface is characterized by recesses of medium depth caused by the discontinuous pressure of the thinning operation. The roughout face might have been the object of an average shaping that did not completely erase the marks of the pressure of the thinning operation. Meanwhile, the morphology of the external surface shows a) a weak shaping operation that slightly changed the roughout face; b) an average shaping operation that modified the roughout face and resulted in a medium-shallow micro-relief face. The latter shaping operation is prevalent than the first. This indicates that most of the objects were subjected to an average shaping operation that changed the roughout face.

The surfaces of the sherds analysed were subjected to various levels of intensity in terms of finishing. The internal surfaces were subjected to an average to high smoothing, while the external surfaces to a low to high degree of smoothing. Those with an average degree of smoothing either by hand or with a tool outnumber the others.

2- Sub-group III
This sub-group is also isomorphic to group III of the A: 5 open forms. It represents 53% of the sherds. The internal surface morphology shows very shallow recesses and is regular. On the surface took place a strong shaping operation that changed the roughout wall, and is the witness of a corresponding discontinuous pressure pattern. Moreover, the wall thickness shows less variation as far as differences in thickness at varying interval. The internal surfaces, for the most part, received a middle to high intensive smoothing either by hand or with the use of a hard tool.

An average shaping intensity that did not completely erase the effect of the discontinuous pressure of the thinning operation has been made on the external surface of the pot. This is similar to the shaping pattern of sub-group II. Additionally, they share similarities with the internal faces of their own sub-group with respect to shaping intensity. Regarding the smoothing operation, the external faces have been subjected to either self- slip smoothing or middle to high intensity smoothing, either by hand or using a tool. However, the state of the finishing operation is dominated for the most part, by a middle smoothing intensity.

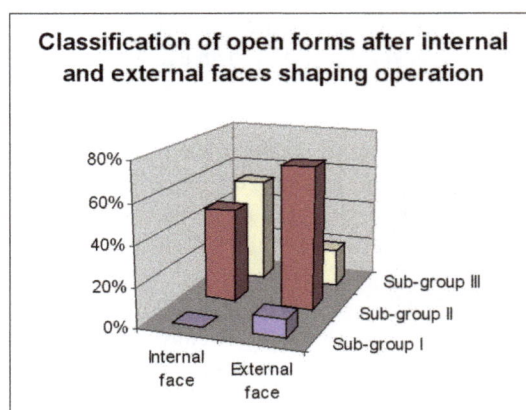

Fig. 91: The percentage of technical sub-groups of open forms (level 4 pottery assemblage)

III.1.2.2 Closed forms technical classification

The pottery repertoire designated as closed forms are classified on the basis of differences in the shaping sequences between the internal and external faces. The classification process is based on the forming sequence of the external surface. Three main sub-groups have been identified (n= 50). These are:

1- Sub-group I
Sub-Group I represents 6% of the sherds (**Fig. 92**). The morphology of the external surface is characterized mainly by a weak modification of the roughout face. Hence, the face is irregular and is dominated by relatively deep recesses that have been weakly modified during the preform stage. This also applies to the internal surface. This sub-group is characterized by irregular wall thickness and variations in thickness at short intervals. Moreover, the finishing of both faces shows a low intensity of smoothing.

2- Sub-group II
This sub-group dominates the assemblage and represents 53% of the sherds. The external surface received an average shaping that partly delimited the roughout face. Its morphology is characterized by relative irregularity, and

is dominated by a micro-relief, or recesses, consequence of the thinning operation. The internal surface, however, less often shows either an average shaping of the roughout face, or relatively shallow recesses that were strongly modified by the shaping operation. The latter is less prevalent among the sherds. The thickness of the walls are irregular at differing intervals. Both faces, for the most part, exhibit a middle intensity smoothing operation, done by hand or with a tool.

3- Sub-group III
The closed forms related to this sub-group makes up 41% of the assemblage. The external face is characterized by a regular morphology with relatively shallow recesses. It indicates that the roughout face was subjected to a strong shaping operation which delimits the discontinuous pressure applied during the coils' thinning operation. By contrast, the internal face was subjected to an average shaping pressure. The result is a relative micro-relief morphology. However, in a few cases, the internal face was subjected to a degree of shaping similar to that applied to the external face, thus reducing the pressure resulting from the thinning operation. This sub-group is characterized by regular walls , with less thickness variation over intervals. Moreover, for this sub-group, the external face was subjected to a middle to high smoothing intensity.

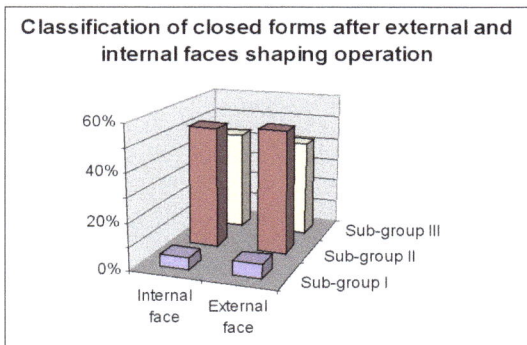

Fig. 92: The frequency of the technical sub-groups of closed forms (level 4 pottery assemblage)

III.1.3. A comparison between A: 5 and A: 4 pottery assemblages

Despite the considerable similarities between the pottery assemblages of the two phases (A: 5 and A: 4), some differences exist:

III.1.3.1 The frequency of the technical sub-groups

The pottery assemblages from Levels 5 and 4 share the same shaping operation sequences whether we consider the open or the closed forms. However, technical classification of the assemblages show that there are differences

in the frequency of practicing the forming sequences after the technical sub-groups. In pottery assemblages of Levels 5 and 4 the forming sequence for sub-group II dominates (**Fig. 93**). The differences are particularly notable with respect to the frequencies of sub-groups I and III. In the A:4 pottery assemblage, sub-group I is less prevalent than is the case for the A: 5 pottery assemblage. By contrast, sub-group III is more prevalent in the A:4 assemblage than the A:5 assemblage.

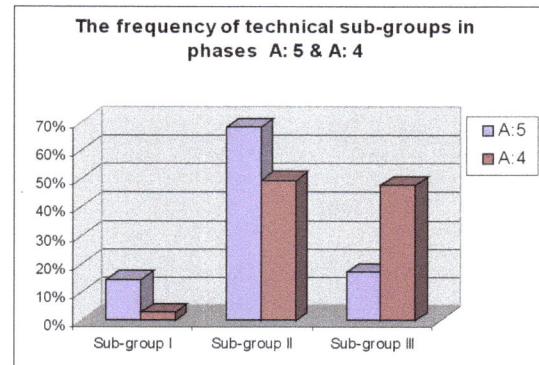

Fig. 93: The frequency of technical sub-groups in both pottery assemblages (Levels 5 and 4)

III.1.3.2 Wall thickness

This parameter refers to the median thickness of the pottery sherds. It is more informative if it is correlated with the pot shape. Regarding the so-called open forms, the diagram (**Fig. 94**) shows that the thickness of this repertoire can be classified into four groups. Most of the sherds fall within groups 2 (7-10 mm) and 3 (10-13 mm). The diagram also shows that the frequency of sherds in group 1 (4-7 mm) is increasing in Level 4. In Level 4 the frequency of group 4 (more than 13 mm) sherds is less relative to that for the A:5 phase. This indicates that fewer open forms with thick walls were produced during this phase compared with the older one.

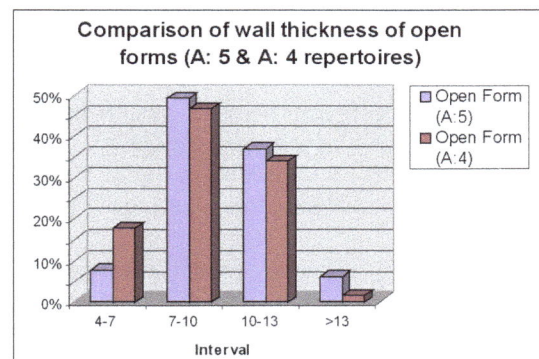

Fig. 94: The comparison of wall thickness of open forms repertoire of Levels 5 and 4

The closed forms vessels have been also compared based on the median thickness of their walls (**Fig. 95**). The dominant median thickness for Levels 5 and 4 fall within group II (7-10 mm) and group III (10-13 mm). and the frequency of sherds belonging to group II outnumber.

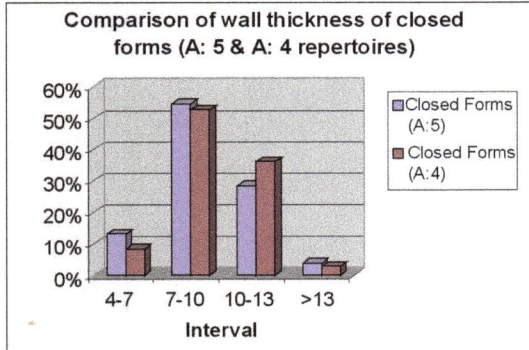

Fig. 95: A comparison of closed form between Levels 5 and 4 on the basis of wall thickness

III.1.3.3 Thickness variations

This parameter refers to differences in the sherds wall thickness at different spots. At least four measurements were taken for each sherd. The distribution of these measurements ranged to opposite ends of the sherds. Measurement variation was calculated based on the following formula:

$$200*ABS(M1-M2)/(M1+M2)$$

whereas M_n refers to the number of measurements undertaken for each sherd.

The main aim of this step is to measure a degree of control for the pot wall with respect to the different forming sequences. Such measurements were undertaken for both, the closed and open forms. The analysis of thickness variation for closed forms from Levels 5 shows a tendency towards wall irregularity (**Fig. 96**). Variation in wall thickness increases and takes a wide base form in the diagram. Meanwhile, the analysis of thickness variation for the A: 4 pottery sherds shows a sharp decline in variation as one moves in the diagram from left to right. This indicates that the pots from A4 level show minor variation in thickness similar to that found in Levels 5.

An analysis of wall thicknesses for the open forms reveals the same pattern as for the closed forms. The walls of the pots in the assemblage from Levels 5 show a remarkable variation in wall thickness (**Fig. 97**). The variation pattern takes a wide base form in the diagram, indicating an increase in the number of sherds exhibiting a higher number of differences in thickness. The case differs for the A:

4 assemblage. These pots exhibit a decrease in wall thickness variation in terms of their percentage. Most of the sherds have a relatively regular wall thickness; correspondingly, there is a sharp decline in the number of sherds that exhibit a great variation in thickness. This might be correlated with the frequency of the technical sub-groups in each phase. The frequency of technical sub-groups II and III in Level 4 is greater than that in Levels 5. These two sub-groups exhibit a remarkable advance in terms of the performance of the forming operation as reflected in the relatively regular pot walls.

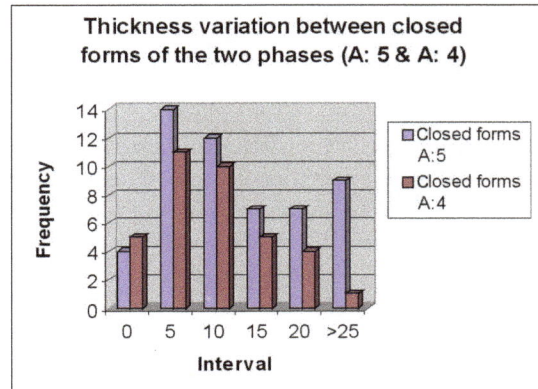

Fig. 96: A comparison of thickness variations of closed forms repertoires of Levels 5 and 4

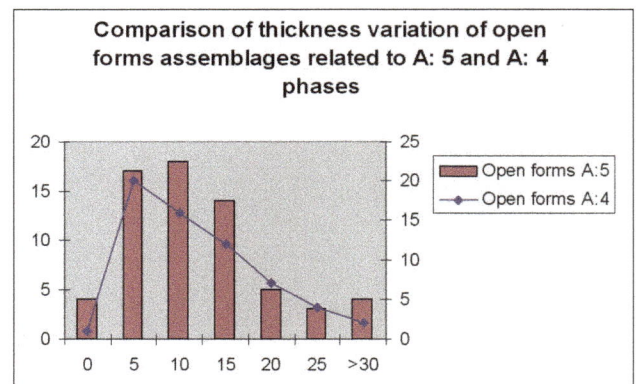

Fig. 97: The comparison of thickness variation of open forms (Levels 5 and 4)

III.2 The technological classification and metric analysis of Middle Levels pottery assemblages

III.2.1 Technological classification of Middle Levels (A: 3) pottery assemblages

The pottery from these Levels are characterized by more homogeneity compared with the assemblage from Levels 5 and 4. The pottery assemblage related to these levels has been classified into technological groups based on the forming and finishing techniques. Three main groups have been identified:

- Group 1: vessels formed and finished without rotative kinetic energy (RKE).
- Group 2: upper part of the vessels shaped with the use of RKE.
- Group 3: upper part of the vessels has been finished with the use of RKE.

These three groups share in common that their *roughouts* are formed by coiling. Group 1 is the major one, whereas group 2 and 3 are the minor ones. The restricted use of RKE in shaping / finishing the rims makes difficult the correlation between the rims and their related body sherds. However, this innovative technique has not been employed in shaping the body of the pot.

III.2.2 Technical classification of the pottery assemblages of the Levels 3 into sub-groups

Technological group 1 enhances variation in terms of its forming and finishing methods. This group has been firstly classified into general functional repertoires. That is to say, open forms vs. closed forms. Then, each form repertoire has been classified into technological sub-groups based on the variation in performing the operational sequences of body forming (the serial of subgroups follows the ones that have been already described).

III.2.2.1 Open forms technical classification

This morphological repertoire has been classified into three main sub-groups (n= 54). These are:

1- Sub-group II
This sub-group is represented by 21% of the studied sherds (**Fig. 98**). The degree to which the roughout of the internal face has been changed is accounted for as a primary grouping parameter. Related body sherds show that the wall roughout has been subjected to average pressure during the preform stage. The result is an internal surface characterized by a medium- regular face and by traces of thinning recesses that were not modified by later shaping. The external surface for this sub-group, is characterized by varying degrees of shaping in the roughout stage. Among these are sherds that were a) subjected to a weak shaping operation, and thus have similar characteristics to those in sub-group I (of levels 5 and 4) ; b) subjected to average pressure during shaping (and thus have similar characteristics to the respective internal face); and c) subjected to a strong shaping operation, resulting in relatively regular walls with relatively shallow recesses. The most common methods of surface finishing are hand-smoothing and self-slip ones.

2- Sub-group III
This is the dominant sub-group, and is represented by 75% of the studied sherds. The internal surface of these sherds was subjected to strong pressure, such that the *roughout* wall was modified. This in turn resulted in a regular internal face, with respect to which recesses are more shallow and less frequent. Almost 69% of the external surfaces of these sherds is similar to the internal surfaces in terms of degree of shaping. Meanwhile, the rest of the sherds are shaped in the same manner that characterized sub-group II. That is with an average pressure at their external surfaces. In general, the sherds related to this subgroup are characterized by relative regular wall thickness, on the one hand, and of minor variation in their walls regularities, on the other.

In terms of finishing methods, hard- and soft-tools smoothing are the major finishing methods, whereas hand smoothing and self-slip have been less frequently performed. Slip burnished finishing or the use of slip have minor occurrence in the studied sample.

3- Sub-group IV
The number of sherds related to this sub-group are few. They represent only 4% of the sample. This sub-group is characterized by an internal face that was subjected to strong pressure during the shaping operation. The result is a regular and even internal wall. It is also characterized by the rare presence of very shallow and random recesses. The external face of this sub-group was subjected to either an average or strong shaping operation. It is also characterized by minor variation in wall thickness. Burnished slip is a major finishing method.

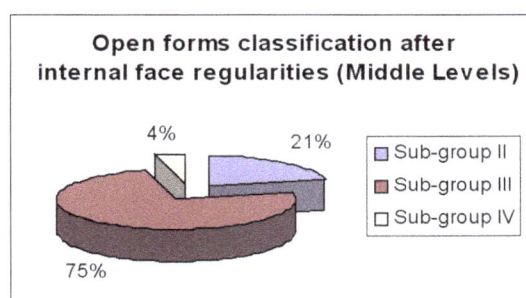

Fig. 98: The frequency of the technical sub-groups of open forms – Middle Levels

III.2.2.2 The technical classification of closed forms (Fig. 99)

This techno-morphological repertoire is primarily classified on the basis of the operational sequences used in forming the external face. Three main sub-groups have been identified (n= 132). These are:

1- Sub-group II
This technical sub-group is represented by 23% of the sample. It is characterized by a collection of pottery sherds that their external surfaces received an average shaping operation, and have a relative dominance of recesses or dents. The internal surfaces were subjected to different degree of shaping. Almost 53 % of them were subjected to a similar degree of shaping as the external faces. 4 % of the sherds, by contrast, resemble those of sub-group I in this respect (see above III.1.1.1), whereas 43% those of sub-group III.

In terms of finishing methods, the majority of the external faces related to this sub-group have been subjected to either hand smoothing or self-slip. The minority of performed finishing methods include hard or soft tool smoothing, slip and burnishing on slip.

2- Sub-group III
This technical sub-group was dominant, constituting 71 % of the pottery sherds studied. It is characterized by external surfaces that were subjected to a strong shaping operation and changed the morphology of the roughout faces. They are characterized by a relatively regular surface, dominated by very shallow recesses. The internal surface generally shows the same morphological characteristics as the external one. These constitute almost 52% of the sherds related to this sub-group. The remaining 47% shares similar characteristics with sub-group II sherds in this respect.
The majority of the external surfaces of this sub-group have been subjected to finishing with, soft-tool (e.g. textile) (30%), hand smoothing (20%), self-slip (18%), and to less extent hard-tool smoothing and slip (red colour). Only 5% of this sub-group has been subjected to slip burnishing at their external surfaces.

3- Sub-group IV
This sub-group is poorly represented in the assemblage. It makes up only 6% of the studied sherds. These have a regular external face with relatively few shallow recesses.

The internal face was subjected to a forming operation similar to that found in sub-group III sherds. Concerning the pot's thickness, this technical sub-group is characterized by objects that have minor variation in wall thickness. In terms of finishing methods, the majority of sherds received slip burnishing and in less cases either a soft or hard tool smoothing.

III.2.3 Metric characteristics of Middle Levels pottery assemblages

III.2.3.1 Technical sub-groups frequency

Most of the sherds 72% fall within sub-group III (**Fig. 100**). They are either related to closed or open forms, and are characterized a having at least one face with relatively shallow recesses and less variation in thickness.

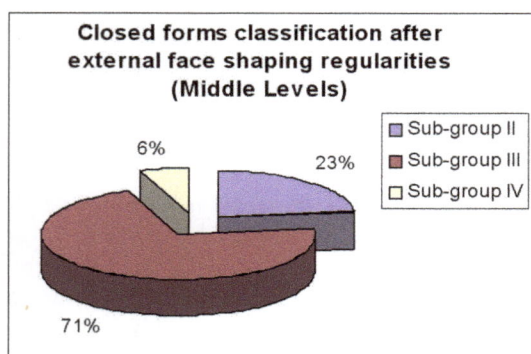

Fig. 100: The frequency of technical sub-groups in the Middle Levels

III.2.3.2 Wall thickness

Pottery sherds studied from the Middle Levels show that the median wall thickness of the assemblage falls mainly within two groups. Thickness measurements for open forms (**Fig. 101**) are related mainly to group 1, with a thickness interval between 7-10 mm. This group also dominates the repertoire of closed forms (**Fig. 102**). The second group ranges in its thickness interval between 4-7 mm. This one is also found in both closed and open forms.

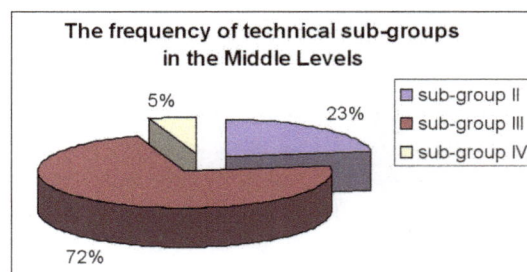

Fig. 99: The frequency of the technical sub-groups of closed forms – Middle Levels

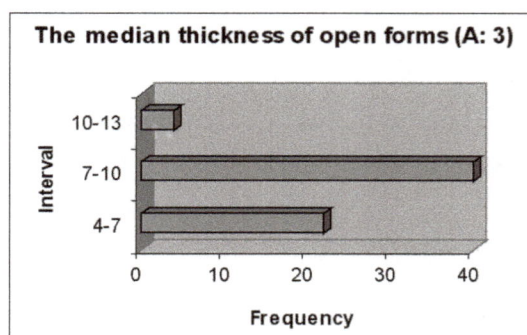

Fig. 101: The median thickness of open forms walls for Middle Levels assemblages

Median thickness of A: 3 closed forms

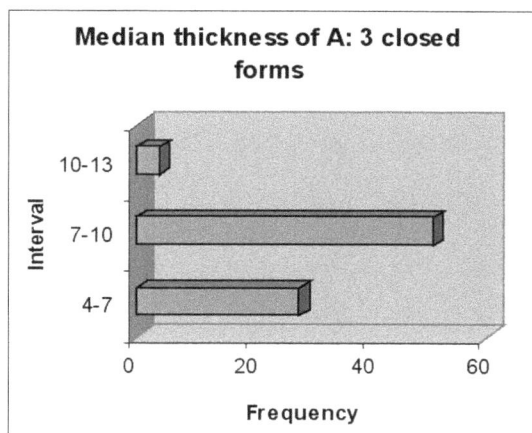

Fig. 102: The median thickness of closed forms
(Middle Levels)

Thickness variations of closed forms (A: 3)

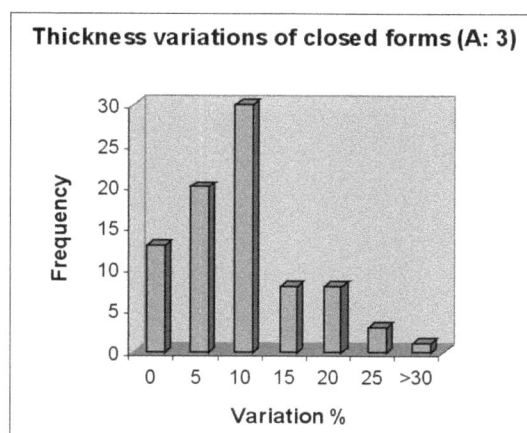

Fig. 104: The variation percentage of closed forms walls
(Middle Levels)

The least frequent group is that which ranges between 10-13 mm. This group is less evident in both morpho-stylistic repertoires.

III.2.3.3 Thickness variation

In addition to measuring the wall thickness of each sherd, an attempt was made to measure variations in wall thickness for each individual sherd. This was measured using the same formula applied in the A: 5 and A: 4 assemblages (see III.1.3.3). The result of this analysis shows that the repertoires for both open and closed forms (**Fig. 103** and **Fig. 104**) are mainly characterized by minor wall variation. Wall measurements for the open forms show a variation of less than 10% on average. This means that the related sherds had relatively regular wall thicknesses when measured at different points.

The same can be said in the case of closed forms (**Fig.**

Thickness variations of open forms (Middle Levels)

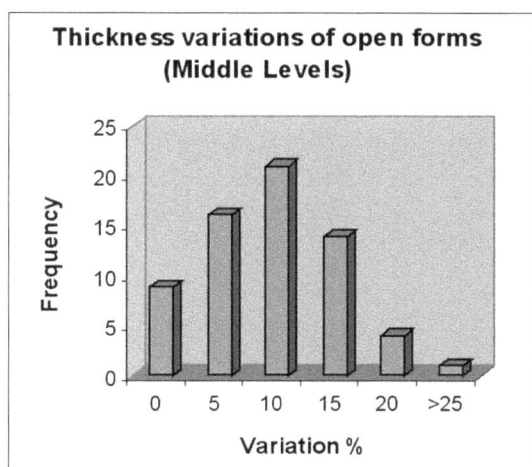

Fig. 103: Variations in thickness for the open forms repertoire (Middle Levels)

104). These are mainly dominated by sherds showing minor variation in thickness over different points. This indicates that most sherds have relatively regular walls.

IV. Summary

The aim in this chapter was to group or sort out the pottery assemblages according to the technical attributes. Each assemblage has been subjected to grouping after identifying the technical operations of shaping (Chapter 9). These forming operations or tradition (Franken 1995) or mode (Rouse 1960) is the sum of total actions and gestures that potters performed in shaping their pots. Grouping process has been pre-perceived with the set of parameters that can reflect the differentiations of performing the technical operations.

Grouping process enables us not only to identify technical groups at the synchronic scale, but also to measure the differences and similarities between the assemblages diachronically. It was then possible to classify the entire assemblages in a cross-cut pattern in which both continuity and discontinuity of performing technical actions appear within or between the assemblages. For example, the identification of sub-group IV was only attested within the Middle Levels pottery assemblages. In the same level, technical sub-group I was absent in open vessels as well as in the closed ones. Meanwhile, sub-groups II & III have been attested in all assemblages. The next step was to estimate the frequency of performing each technical gesture after their associated group. This in turn enables measuring the relative dominance of technical sub-groups within and between the pottery assemblages. This showed the development of technical sub-group performance. For example, technical sub-group I decreases in frequency from Level 4 and iddisappears in Levels 3. Whereas, technical sub-group III shows an increase in performance from Level 4 and dominate the assemblage of Middle Levels (Levels 3). So, an important result is to see that

Level 4 still shares most of the characts of Levels 5 which on a technical point of view offer also for the first time some features that will be developed in the Levels 3.

Chapter Ten: Explaining technical variation in pottery shaping at Abu Hamid

This chapter focuses on the causes of pottery variation observed in the assemblages of Abu Hamid. The term "variation" refers mainly to morpho-types and technical differences within a given pottery repertoire. These kinds of variation are thought to shed light on the potter's behaviour with respect to the technical, economic and to large extent social organisations.

I. Background

The dual anthropological approaches to technology – materialist and social – have increased the archaeological inferences that can be provided by material culture. Whereas materialist approach considers technology more as an economic activity, the social one considers it more as a socially constructed activity. The first approach views technology as being directed to fulfil human needs. Emphasis is placed on the functional manifestations of technology and the material constraints that affect technological performance. Then pottery production is viewed as a process that responds in a way or the other to human functional requirements. Therefore, more attention is paid to identify the material constraints of the technology used, such as the relationship between types of clay and shaping technique, and the distribution of raw materials. Such studies enrich the inferences that can be made using technical attributes and providing an explanation to the human behaviour embedded in the technique.

The social anthropology of technology defines the relationship between technology and material culture in another way that focuses on the relationship between material culture, techniques and technology, within a wider socially and culturally informed context (Lemonnier 1986, 1989, 1993; Pfaffenberger 1992). Moreover, this approach attempts to define manufacturing techniques as technological *styles*. The conceptual tool utilized in this approach derives from the *chaîne opératoire* one. In pottery studies, this approach expands the kinds of inferences that can be derived from either of the technical attributes of the pottery or from the operational sequences. Several ethnoarchaeological studies emphasize the choices available to potters in pot manufacture (Mahias 1993; van der Leeuw 1993), as opposed to seeing pottery as merely a response to functional requirements. This kind of study makes possible to correlate different social groups with the technical operations embedded in pottery manufacture (Gelbert 2000, Livingstone-Smith 2000, Gosselain 1998, 2000).

The anthropology of technology is significant in that it emphasises the social context of techniques. Addressing

manufacturing techniques as a reflection of technological style is one approach-toward this objective. It can enhance our understanding of the cognitive structure underlying a given technology (van der Leeuw 1994), the roles of apprenticeship and skill, and of the different levels of know-how, as the basis of pottery variation (Roux 1990). As one approach would be insufficient for fully understanding all that can be derived from pottery, both approaches were used in examining the pottery assemblages from Abu Hamid (Levels 5, 4 and 3)

II. Techno-economic factors and pottery variability at Abu Hamid

The probable correlation between techno-economic factors and artefact variability has been attested at the archaeological site of Abu Hamid. Two lines of evidence have been selected as base-lines for testing the validity of this assumption. The first is represented by the kind of architecture; the second, by the pottery assemblages from the three Levels that have been identified at the site.

As mentioned in chapter 6, the archaeological sequence at Abu Hamid, during the Lower and Middle Levels, represents two different settlement structures. The Lower Levels (Levels 5) are characterized by a system of a non-permanent settlement, residential mobility. The inhabitants of the site during this period seem to have been pit-dwellers. The micro-morphological studies show that these pits were occupied more than once during the late sixth millennium BC (Hourani 1997). At the end of this period (Level 4), the excavated part of the site shows no evidence of dwellings in pits. But the people still come to the site as it is evidenced by the hearths, plastered basins, pits, etc. At least in this area, it seems that we are in presence of more mobile groups

Both types of residencies are indicative of a temporary, may be seasonal, settlement pattern rather than a permanent one. If this is the case, the main question to be raised is the following: to what extent the choice of this system affected various technologies and more specifically the pottery. The pottery assemblages collected in these levels (5 and 4) show that two main pot functional-types dominate: bowls and, to a lesser extent, jars. The analysis we made with a technological approach of these types show that these assemblages can be classified into three technical groups (see chapter 9). Further classification of group 1 (the pots shaped by coiling technique), the dominant group, showed that sub-groups I and to a larger extent II are outnumbered sub-group III. However, the pottery related to these three groups is characterized by light weight.

The pottery types and the dominance of these two technical sub-groups (I & II) may be due in part to the mode of settlement and the related economic activities that have been carried out at the site. Seasonal occupation, if it was the case, might have determined the functional-type variability and performance characteristics of pottery assemblages. These are characterized by a limited variation in the types of pottery used (bowls and less frequent jars); the vessels might have had a multi-function and been used for various purposes. Further, the light weight of these pots and the quality of production – in terms of production sequences – would seem to provide strong evidence of a temporary settlement (the publication of the flora and faunal remains will provide us with more insight on the kinds of activities that have been carried out during this period at Abu Hamid. This is going to be published in 2006 by R. Neet, J. Desse and C. Tonie).

The correlation between residential mobility and pottery technical characteristics has been emphasized (Arnold III 1999; Schiffer and Skibo 1997). It has been assumed that the restricted variability of pot shapes can be an indication of residential mobility whereas close-vessel might have been produced to fulfil multi-uses (Arnold III 1999). Others see a correlation between residential mobility and the formal characteristics of the pottery. If so, potters would more likely produce pottery objects that had less weight and would be easy to move from the place of production to the place the pots are used (Schiffer and Skibo 1997: 38). To these two aspects we could add the forming technique and the performance of various operational sequences of pot shaping. Ethnoarchaeological observation in Jordan can support these two new aspects. Usually in the Ajlun mountains, potters use coiling technique in forming of the bowls. But, in the cases observed, some potters would employ the moulding technique to make the same kind of pot. They ascribed such a shift from coiling to moulding technique as a means to reduce the time in forming the bowls. This specially takes place before moving to seasonal site for the summer.

The time it takes to shape a pot might be directly related to the context of production. So we argue that at Abu Hamid what is thought to be a non-permanent occupation of the site affected not only the pottery variability but also the "operational sequences" of pot shaping. The latter has a direct relation with the intended use of the pots and their life-expectancy. Pots in this case seem not to have been shaped in advance, but could depend more on the situational factors. Moreover, possibly the use of moulding technique in forming small to medium size bowls was a means to reduce the time needed in shaping the pots.

With the Middle Levels (Levels 3) at Abu Hamid, we obs-

erve a great change in the mode of settlement and in the pottery assemblage as well. During this phase, that covers the second part of the 5th millennium, the dwellings become mud-brick, well built houses complexes consisting of living rooms, storage ones and open areas where domestic activities were taking place. Changes in the pottery assemblage occur as shown by the variety of functional-types of pots and the organization of the production as well. The pottery shapes of the middle Levels, are characterized by a great variability in the products. In addition to the shape such as bowls, hole-mouth jars and neck jars, other functional types appear in the first time during this phase, including "churns" and pedestal bowls. Moreover, the frequency of closed forms such as jars (neck or hole mouth ones) seems to increase in this phase if we compare the assemblage with what was found in Lower Levels.

If we consider the technology, differences as well as similarities with the techniques used previously occur. Technical similarities are represented mainly by the continuous use of coiling technique, and of the forming methods and operations. The main differences concern the use of different kinds of temper, of rotative kinetic energy, the finishing methods, the reduction of walls thickness, and the improvements leading to fewer variations in wall thickness.

During the permanent settlement, early Chalcolithic (Middle Levels), it seems that potters produced not for direct and short use of the vessels but for a longer time. It has been shown that technical sub-group III dominates the assemblage; the operation sequences embodied in the production of this sub-group show that potters spent more time in the shaping and finishing operations than of the other sub-groups I and II. This appears in the technical characteristics of production, in terms of the vessels surfaces evenness, regularity in wall thickness and finishing operations.

Another dimension related to the organization of production during the early Chalcolithic at Abu Hamid is the technical skills embedded in the operational sequences of pot fashioning. The classification of the pottery assemblages into three technical groups (chapter 9: III.2) indicates the use of rotative kinetic energy in pot production (esp. in shaping and finishing the upper part of the pot). This new technique embedded different skill and experience comparing with the use of discontinuous pressure in pot shaping (cf. Roux 1990; Roux and Courty *in press*). Further distinction based on skill can be made when comparing the frequency of technical sub-groups. We have noted that among the material we studied coming from the Middle Levels the technical group 1 dominates the pottery assemblage. The classification of this group into sub-groups revealed that sub-group III which is characterized by an "operation sequence" indicative of a high time-expenditure in pot shaping and finishing operations is predominent.

By contrast, sub-group II is indicative of a less time expenditure with respect to the shaping operations; and resulting pot bodies had relatively shallow recesses.

What we have just showed might suggest that technological organization related to the Middle Levels is quite different from the previous one. It might be that in Levels 5 and 4 at Abu Hamid, the scale of pottery production was at the level of a small social unit. There is a high probability that each of these units would produce its own pottery-needs. The scale of production had changed by the period indicated by the Middle Levels. The organization of the settlement with its multicellular houses and permanent occupation had most probably a direct effect on the organization of the pottery production. The specialized skill in pottery production indicated by the first use of RKE and the predominance of technical sub-group III hints at the concentration of production for certain types of vessels within a limited number of potters. It is probable that not all households produced their own needs. The variety of techniques observed in this phase can be an indication of two modes of production. First, a number of households could have produced and consumed their own products (technical sub-group II; see chapter 9: III). The second mode of production would be the image of a number of households whose production was not only for their direct needs but also to the households that were not producers. This is what we could call *specialized* household production. It is represented by the pots related to technical sub-groups III and IV.

III. From the economic to the social context of pottery production

Recent anthropological studies on technology uphold a strong tradition of defining a close relationship between technology and society (Lemonnier 1986; Pfaffenberger 1992; Creswell 1990). The locus of technique is assumed to be looked at in the social domain. Thus, attention in technological studies shifts from a focus only on material constraints to the identification of the cultural factors that affect technological choices made by a given social group. In other words, cultural factors, rather than natural ones are seen as having a primary influence in determining technique and technological choices. It is in this realm that technology has been considered as a social activity and technique as a socialized action on matter (Lemonnier 1980: 1 cited in Schlanger 1994: 145).

This theoretical stand has had an influence on the study of material culture variation. The dominant discourse in this regard defines the nature of material culture in dualistic terms, constituting both style and function. A social approach to technology lessens the gap between these two

aspects by considering them within the context of the production system. That is, stylistic attributes can be best understood when studied within the context of production sequence, understanding here as a cultural manifestation of material cultures. The role of the maker in this context is defined as that of an active participant within the cultural system.

Based on this theoretical approach, looking at the combination of technology and technique, archaeologists or/and anthropologists are able to expand the kind of cultural inferences they can make from material objects. To start with, there is an increased focus on the evaluation of cultural factors that might have influenced technology; secondly, the cognitive structures underlying a given technology are analysed – that is technological knowledge. Thus, object manufacture is approached as a cognitive activity (Ingold 2000; Schlanger 1994; Karlin and Julian 1994; Pelegrin 1990; van der Leeuw 1991, 1993, 1994; Roux 1990). This approach to artefact manufacturing works on the assumption that object forms pre-exist in the makers' minds, as geometric representations that the maker impress upon the material in making the intended objects (Schlanger 1994; Pelegrin 1990). Such an assumption runs contrary to an approach that sees the form of the intended object as *emerging* "through a pattern of skilled movement, and it is the rhythmic repetition of that movement that gives rise to the regularity of form" (Ingold 2000: 57).

The view of technology as a cognitive activity stems methodologically and theoretically from the *chaîne opératoire* approach. There are three aspects of material manufacture that are focused on in this approach. These include gestures and operations (technical processes), the employment of objects as a means of action on matter; and lastly the existence of a specific knowledge (Lemonnier 1980, 1989). This methodology allows for a fine analysis of the technical processes involved in tool or object becoming. It allows for a fine reconstruction of the sequence of gestures and actions undertaken to transform an object from its raw material state to that of the finished product. The second dimension involves the identification – based on the technical processes employed – of the cognitive elements possibly underlying the reconstructed operation sequences. These two dimensions in the manufacture have been distinguished at two levels: the technological knowledge (*connaissances*) and the technological know-how (*savoir-faire*) (Pelegrin 1990: 118). In other words, archaeologists who focus on technology strive to define in some fashion the "thinking mind" and the "doing mind" of the maker (Schlanger 1994:144).

The application of this approach with respect to material culture study, has until recently, focused on lithic tools (Pelegrin 1990; Karlin and Julian 1994). However, more recently, it has been applied to pottery studies, both in archaeological and ethnoarchaeological ones (van der Leeuw 1994; van der Leeuw *et al.* 1992; Roux 1990). The pioneering work of van der Leeuw is worth mentioning. It is a cross-cultural study which derives its data from throughout the world. This, in turn, has enabled a conceptualisation of the relationship between the thinking mind and the doing mind. He focuses on three aspects in bridging this dualism: conceptualisation, executive function, and raw materials (van der Leeuw 1994: 136). The first refers to the fact that the potter might have in mind a mental representation of the pot's form he or she wishes to produce. This representation may be considered as consisting of three conceptual elements – topology, partonomy, and sequence. Each element can be correlated with a set of gestures and actions performed by the potter.

Approaching pottery technology as the product of a cognitive activity addresses other dimensions of pottery variation and its causes. Emphasis is placed on different levels of technical know-how (Roux 1990). This kind of study seeks to establish a correlation between variations in technique and the artisan's skill or experience (Courty and Roux 1998).

In sum, the social approach to technology is significant in explaining two dimensions of pottery technology. The first concerns explaining the technological knowledge that participated in by a given potter population. The second concerns the different levels of technical know-how (i.e., skills). In our study, these two dimensions have been evaluated with respect to the pottery assemblages exposed at the archaeological site of Abu Hamid as the test. The modality of these dimensions stems from the following two assumptions:

The potter population within a given social group might adapt and consequently share the same technological knowledge and information pool of pot shaping necessary for sustaining their cultural needs. The second part of this assumption is based on the fact that these potters will participate in this technological knowledge differently depending on their socio-cultural environment.

III.1 Pottery making as a cognitive activity

To approach pot shaping as a cognitive activity means to define the technical knowledge that the potter has in his or her mind while transforming the clay body into a final product. This knowledge can be defined as a sum of the different cognitive orders that together form the conceptual operative schema or strategy (Pelegrin 1990; Karlin and Julien 1994). The components of this operative strategy are assumed to include intentions, concepts, the evaluation of problems during shaping, and technical decisions (Karlin and Julien 1994: 154). The inference of such

technical knowledge is based on a reconstruction of the *chaînes opératoires* that can be identified within a given pottery assemblage. Such chains are linear and represent the succession of the different stages employed in object formation. They also reveal the fundamental (and often repetitive) movements that potters perform at each forming stage.

The pottery assemblages analysed at Abu Hamid are related to three Levels. The assemblage of each Level has been analysed in a separate way. This procedure aims at identifying the various stages of pot forming as well as the basic movements that are undertaken at each stage. That is, we are more interested in the way potters achieved the pot shapes than the shapes themselves. This involves an understanding of the technical patterns that potters learned within a given social group to transform the clay body into final shape. The pattern refers to the set of technical decisions that potters performed when transforming the clay body into its final shape. After our research and our observation in the villages of the Ajlun region, we tried to figure out the way the Abu Hamid pots were conceptualised.

The reconstruction of the *chaînes opératoires* of the three pottery assemblages at Abu Hamid seems to show that there are similarities in terms of the *conceptualisation* of pot shape. This refers to the mental representation of pot shape in terms of topology, partonomy and sequence.

a) Topology
With respect to this cognitive component, the following considerations or elements are significant: whether pot shape is horizontal or vertical; whether the shape was achieved by stretching or compressing; and, finally, whether there is a distinction between internal and external faces of pot. The pottery assemblages from Abu Hamid that we studied were mainly formed by coiling. The wall of the pot in this case is formed by stretching the coils. This entails two main operations: thinning and shaping. The main point is that potters during pot forming made a distinction between the internal and external faces of the pot, and gave much more attention to the inner face of the open forms than to the outer or external one. This is due to the optimal fashioning stages that the internal face was subjected to, with respect to shaping, re-shaping (or evenness) and finishing operations. This is an indication that the shape of the pot pre-existed in the mind of its maker and guided his or her physical actions.

b) Partonomy
This refers to the partition of pots into parts. It has been noted that a pot was not formed as a whole, but rather consisted of different parts. Each part was made out of a number of coils that were then worked together. In a few cases observed, the potter shaped three of these coils at

once. This division of pots into spatial parts is designed to prevent the collapse of the pot's body. This is particularly significant, for example, with respect to the shaping of neck jars. The neck, in the cases we observed, has been shaped when the clay of the pot walls was at already a leather hard state. Additionally, it has been strengthened internally by smearing clay where the neck joins the body. Finally, the partitioning of the pot's body promoted wall thickness and the controlling of the shaping operation. It has been noted that the thicker the wall and the greater the number of worked coils, the more irregular the surface becomes.

However, the partition of pots into parts does not mean that they were seen as discontinuous entities. The profile of the pot was hemispherical and this is an indication that its shape was seen as a continuous conception.

c) Sequence
The pottery assemblages from Abu Hamid show that potters shaped the pots from the bottom upwards. The base is formed first, then the body, and finally the opening. This sequence of pot shaping fits well with the argument that the shaping of the pot from bottom to top eventually gave way to the use of the wheel (van der Leeuw 1994: 137). This is attested by the assemblage from the Middle Levels, where some of the pots rims were either re-shaped or finished using RKE.

The studied pottery assemblages at Abu Hamid demonstrate a consistent stream of pot conceptualisation. Despite morpho-stylistic variability between the Lower and Middle Levels, the assemblages show a continuation in the cognitive components of pot conceptualisation.

III.2 Defining the different levels of know-how

It has been shown that technical activity manifests both knowledge and know-how as well. Technical knowledge includes both the conceptualisation of the intended pot shape and the modalities of know-how. Regarding the conceptualisation of the pot shape, we have seen that the potters' population at Abu Hamid shared the same conceptual schema of shaping with respect to sequence, partition, and the spatial conception of shape. These cognitive components of shape can be learned in much less time than the operative ideational know-how. The latter involves the acquisition of a set of gestures and actions needed to transform the clay body into a final product. Moreover, it involves the organization of these movements both temporally and spatially (i.e. with respect to the different phases of the pot). To what degree modalities of the know-how are transformed into actual practice varies with each individual potter. The causes of technical variation within synchronically defined pottery assemblage can be assumed to be seen as a result varying levels of knowledge and

know-how in pot shaping. The actual application of know-how is an indication of the level of technical skill. The technical skill required for pot-shaping has been evaluated as a cause of *variation* in pottery production. The parameters utilized for measuring skill include the source of learning, the duration of the craft practice, and the age at which the craft was learned (see chapter 5). Personal capabilities are another parameter considered inasmuch as it influences the proficiency of the individual in acquiring both the knowledge and ideational know-how. The materialization of these parameters can be measured in pottery product depending on (after Ploux 1990; cited in Karlin and Julian 1994) the following criteria:

1. the complexity of the conceptual schema – that is the mental construction which guides the execution.
2. the degree of preconception of the *chaîne opératoire* – i.e., the precision of the forward planning.
3. the discrepancy between a project and its achievement, referring here to all the data concerning the problem which has to be solved.
4. the quality of production – the correlation between technical skills and the planned work.

1- The complexity of the conceptual schema
The technical groupings of the pottery assemblages at Abu Hamid have been evaluated based on different parameters that combine the above mentioned criteria. It has been shown that for the Levels 5, the classification of the dominant technical group (Group 1) into three sub-groups which most probably relate to three different skill levels. Objects related to technical sub-group I may have been formed by potters with a lower level of proficiency in terms of acquiring the operative know-how. Their product is characterized by a sharp contrast between the internal and external faces of the pot. The assumed functional face was subjected to the lower level of forming stages like the thinning, shaping and finishing operations. The opposite surface by contrast had, in most cases, not been subjected to shaping operation and the finishing operation is performed at the thinning state. The application or non-application of motor know-how may be a reflection of the conceptual pattern of the maker. Thus, in the case noted, it may be that the potters had a minimal or reduced conceptual schema of the forming stages.

The case seems to differ with the potters responsible for the technical sub-group II repertoire. The conceptual pattern that guided them during the forming stages is relatively complex, and the potter maintained the topology of both the internal and external faces. In most cases, they give both faces the same extent of shaping operation. Nonetheless, they do not expand the operation to the end, with the result that the faces have the recesses or dent pattern of average shaping. The gestures and movements of the potters reflect a time expenditure of sufficient if not excessive length in the application of fashioning methods. At the same time, they reflect better control on the way to work with the clay if we compare it to the products of the potters of sub-group I.

The potters who produced the pottery repertoire of sub-group III demonstrated a much more complex and organized conceptual pattern with respect to the different forming stages. The technical schema incorporate all the forming stages for both sides of the pot. At each stage, the operation of each stage was achieved to its end resulting in regular pot surfaces.

2- The degree of preconception of the chaîne opératoire – the precision of the forward planning
This refers to the precision of planning forward the different forming stages. The identified technical sub-groups III and IV show that the potters had worked out a complete and detailed estimate of the whole operative process. It seems that they conceived their work precisely at each stage of the *chaîne opératoire*. On the contrary, technical sub-group II shows that the potters who formed these pots had only the basic details of the planning associated with each stage of the forming. The work of sub-group I assemblage seems to reveal some irregularities in the planning by the potters during the different stages of forming.

3- The discrepancy (difference) between the object form and its achievement
This mainly refers to the way that potters solved the problems that were raised while they working with clay to accomplish their product. The product of the potters related to technical sub-group I shows that their conceptual pattern did not pre-determine the kinds of movements they used. Their works reflect an insufficient control of the plastic clay during the shaping operation. This is exemplified by certain incorrect movements or gestures on the surfaces which demonstrate the lack of a rhythmic pattern. The product of the potters related to sub-group II show that they forced some difficulties in controlling the worked part at both surfaces. The transformation of the one surface affected the shaping of the other. Their works reflected an average technical knowledge of shaping the intended function of the surface of the pot. The pottery sherds related to technical sub-groups III and IV reflect an assemblage where its makers have achieved what they intended to achieve at both surfaces of the pot.

4- The quality of production
The relationship between technical skill and the planned work might be expressed in the *quality* of the product. The technical skills involved in the production of technical sub-groups III and IV are remarkable. The works are defined by the long time spent in their forming, as well as in the finishing. By contrast, technical sub-group II shows average time expenditure in the stage of shaping the pots,

reflected in the basic movements involved in shaping. These technical sub-groups, however, are clearly distinct from sub-group I, which shows short time expenditure in the forming stages.

To sum up, it has been possible to correlate between the techno-economical changes at Abu Hamid with the changes in pottery production. The change from residential mobility to permanent one might have affected the conditions under which pottery was produced and used. The change of settling in permanent houses was accompanied by the production of new pot forms and an increase in the frequency of others previously produced. These changes affect the organization of pottery production. The technological attributes associated with the operational sequence of pot shaping are positively affirmed by the change from a domestic household production to a specialized household production. Specialization in pottery production has been inferred from the use of rotative kinetic energy in pot fashioning, which required a different technical skill. Moreover, it has been reflected in the majority of pottery products that enhance the optimal *chaîne opératoire* of pot fashioning.

Conclusion

The prime aim of this work is to investigate, based on pottery, the organization of technology dating from the late sixth to the fifth millennium BC in Jordan. Such an attempt evaluates the interrelation between the form of technological organization and the socio-cultural one.

The justification of choosing the subject – pottery – stemmed from the fact that pottery is not only a by-product of a given society–environment interrelationship, but it has also its manifestations in the social and economical realms. Hence, analysing pottery from this angle would enable the discussion of different relevant socio-cultural points.

The justification of choosing the time span from the late sixth to the fifth millennium stemmed from the significant of this period as a middle point between the origins of agriculture and the rise of socially and politically complex societies. It is a significant point in our discussion for it explains the socio-political evolution in the southern Levant. The site of Abu Hamid, located in the Jordan Valley, fulfils a diachronic dataset to attest such a cultural development or evolution.

At the methodological scale, this study depends largely on an ethonarchaeological research as a source of reference to evaluate the above stated interrelationships between technology and socio-cultural dimensions. This study has been conducted in Jordan, and took the form of a regional one. Such a source of reference hopes to state the kinds and types of variables that might be significant in testing the hypothesis: to which extent the techno-economical factors can affect the socio-cultural variability.

The analytical style of the archaeological as well as the ethnoarchaeological data is based on the concept of *chaîne opératoire*, a conceptual tool of analysis that tackled the different operation sequences undertaken by the artisans to transform raw material into a finished product. Not only does this concept enable the identification of general technological style(s) participated in, but also the variation within it/them, on the one hand, and the development or evolution of such a style over time, on the other. Both macro-features examination and X-radiographic analysis have been employed to achieve such a result.

The ethnoarchaeological regional-scale study of pottery production in northern Jordan allows one to infer the modalities of the economical as well as the social interrelationships of pottery production, on the one hand, and the effect of these two dimensions on the pottery technology (especially in shaping *techniques*) on the other hand. The

main economical strategies of the villages visited could be described as a mixed-farming subsistence strategy. To a large extent, the inhabitants depend on agriculture and animal husbandry as the source of their income. These economical practices have been reflected into two settlement systems: the permanent – village – and the seasonal camp. With respect to pottery production, it can be described as a small-scale one. It is a part-time activity, conducted by women, and it is restricted to the summer season due to environmental conditions.

Two main technological styles have been identified among the observed potters in Jordan. The first is characterized by using coiling technique in pot forming with grog as the main non-plastic or temper. The second forming technique is moulding which is mainly employed in the forming of cooking pots with calcite as the main temper. To a lesser extent, this technique is also used in forming bowls but with grog as the temper. These two production styles can be distinguished through techno-functional manifestations rather than through social differentiation. The use of the moulding technique has been correlated with the *positive* performance characteristic of the cooking pots, e.g. thermal shock resistance and heating effectness. On the other hand, the occasional use of moulding in shaping medium sized bowls has a relation with energy expenditure in forming. This technique reduces the time needed for pot shaping. This in turn has been correlated with the short-time use of the object. Potters who employ this technique intended to use the pots in the seasonal camp rather than as household repertoire.

Another significant characteristic of these pottery technological styles is their spatial distribution. At the regional scale, all potters are accustomed to producing pots using the coiling technique (style I). Although style II (the moulding technique) has not been found among all potters, it should be noted that in any particular village, these two styles could be practiced in co-existence. In villages where style II is absent, the inhabitants and the potters depend on the *exchange* to secure their need for cooking pots. This spatial restriction of style II is evident despite the acculturation process between the potters. However, the cause is a technological one in terms of both the shaping and, to a large extent, the firing techniques.

On the intra-village scale, it has been possible to attest a set of parameters that can be used for measuring variation among the product of different potters. This stemmed from the assumption that different potters will *participate* in the performance of a given technological style differently. These parameters derived from three indexes: the morphological analysis, the metric analysis (co-efficient of variation) and the technological one. For example, technical parameters related to the roughing out of the coils, shaping them, evenness and finishing the pots' surfaces have been of value in distinguishing the products of different potters. These sets of parameters are significant when dealing with pottery sherds like in the case of archaeological ones. The causes of pottery variations within and among the potters have been correlated with the potters' motor habit and their level of know-how.

This actualistic study has positively attested the direct interrelationships of the technological with the socio-cultural factors on the one hand, and the methods of identifying and defining the parameters that can testify these interrelationships and their materialization in the final product (pottery), on the other.

Archaeologically speaking, the pottery assemblages from the archaeological site of Abu Hamid have been chosen to attest the validity of the ethno-archaeological results. The pottery assemblages from the Lower Levels (Levels 5 and 4) and the Middle Levels (Levels 3), cover two main archaeological periods at the site, have been analyzed. That of the Lower Levels are related to the "post Yarmoukian" Horizon (Late Neolithic 2 or early 5th millennium BC), while of the Middle Levels one are related to the Wadi Rabah Horizon (Early Chalcolithic or second part of the 5th millennium BC). The pottery assemblages of the Lower Levels have been contextually recovered from what can be ascribed as seasonally like camp-associated features. Part of the first assemblage (A:5a-b) has been recovered from "pit-dwellings", whereas another part (A:4) from an exposure that did not contain any permanent structures but different features such as hearths and basins. These have been also associated with more mobile groups coming at certain seasons to the site. The Middle Levels pottery assemblage has been uncovered in archaeological deposits which contain permanent architecture or houses.

Examining the above mentioned pottery assemblages has shown that the Lower Levels assemblages have been formed by using three distinct techniques: coiling, pinching and moulding whereas in the Middle Levels, coiling was the main technique of pot building. The fashioning of the pot body, in terms of forming methods and operations, has been performed with discontinuous pressure, either with a tool like a scraper or with the fingers, in the all studied pottery repertoires. However, in the Middle Levels at Abu Hamid, it seems that rotative kinetic energy (RKE) was used, though only in the fashioning of rims of bowls and jars.

The technological classification of the studied pottery assemblages at Abu Hamid enabled us to measure the technical variations that occur in one group as well as among the various identified technical groups. These groups and their associated technical characteristics might reveal economical as well as social manifestations. As an example, during the Lower Levels, the residual mobility of Abu Hamid's inhabitants seems to have affected the technical characteristics of their products. The identified technical groups might be an indication that pots were made only when they were in need and not in advance. This is reflected in the level of energy expenditure in pot shaping. It has also been possible to correlate the three technical sub-groups with different levels of know-how or skills.

The case differs in the assemblage of the Middle Levels (Early Chalcolithic or second part of the 5th millennium BC) when the permanent settlement has been established. From this time on, the pottery assemblage shows that two main technical categories can be identified. One is fashioned with the use of RKE, and the other sustained the technical actions of the older tradition. The technical groups and the two various fashioning techniques we have identified might be a hint that the organization of pottery production has changed. Instead of being produced at the domestic scale, as in the Lower Levels, pottery producers and consumers might have not been the same. The technical actions embedded in pot shaping show that pottery production might be a result of a specialized production. This could be a shift in the production organization from the domestic household to a more *specialized household* pottery production. Such a change in the organization of pottery production raised the main issue of a parallel change in the socio-political organization. In other words, whether this would suggest an emergence of socio-economical differences during the Early Chalcolithic period or the second part of the 5th millennium BC. The archaeological record of Abu Hamid during this period lacks any direct evidence – architecture or other artefacts – that could be an indication of the presence of such socio-political institution. However, what this change of production organization indicates is that there was craft specialization but this is an independent rather than an attached one, a one that might be correlated with a re-organization of economic activities within the site's inhabitants.

List of references

Ahmad, A.A.
1989 Jordan Environmental Profile: Status and Abatement. Amman: United States Agency for International Development.

Aikens, M.
1995 First in the world: The Jomon pottery of early Japan. In: Hoopes, J., and Barnett, W. (eds.).*The Emergence of Pottery: Technology and Innovation in Ancient Societies:* 11-21. Washington, DC: Smithsonian Institution Press.

Al-Eisawi, D.
1985 Vegetation in Jordan. In: Hadidi, A. (ed.). *Studies in The History and Archaeology of Jordan*, II.: 45- 57. Amman: Department of Antiquity.

Ali, N.
1998 Procédé de fabrication d'une jarre ayant 6000 ans: approche expérimentale. *Nouvelles Scientifiques:* 82-90.
2005 The relationship between subsistence strategies and pottery production areas: an ethnoarchaeological study in Jordan. *Leiden Journal of Pottery Studies.* November 2005.

Al-Saa'd, Z., Abu-Jaber, N. and Bataineh, S.
1997 Provenance and Technology of Late Neolithic Pottery from Wadi Shu'eib, Jordan. In: Gebel, H-G., Kafafi, Z. and Rollefson, G. (eds.).*The Prehistory of Jordan, II: Perspectives from 1997*: 615-624. Berlin: *ex oriente*.

Annis, M.
1984 Pots in Oristano: A lesson for the archaeologist. *Newsletter of the Department of Pottery Technology (Leiden University)2:* 32-51.

Arnold, D.E.
1985 *Ceramic Theory and Cultural Process.* Cambridge: Cambridge University Press.
1989 Patterns of learning, residence, and descent among potters in Ticul, Yucatán, Mexico. In: Shennan, S. (ed.). *Archaeological Approaches to Cultural Identity*: 174-184. London: George Allen and Unwin.
1993 *Ecology and Ceramic Production in an Andean community.* Cambridge: Cambridge University Press.
2000 Does the Standardization of Ceramic Pastes really mean specialization? *Journal of Archaeological Method and Theory* 7 (4): 333-375.

Arnold, D. and Nieves, A.
1992 Factors affecting ceramic standardization. In: Bey, G. and Pool,C. (eds.). *Ceramic Production and Distribution: An Integrated approach*: 93-113. West-view, Boulder, Co.

Arnold, D., Neff, H. and Bishop, R.
1991 Compositional Analysis and sources of pottery: An ethnoarchaeological approach. *American Anthropologist* 93: 70-90.

Arnold, P. III
1999 *Tecomates*, residential mobility, and Early Formative occupation in coastal lowland Mesoamerica. In: Skibo, J., and Feinman, G. (eds.). *Pottery and People: A Dynamic Interaction*: 157-170. Salt Lake City: University of Utah Press.
2000 Working without a net: Recent trends in ceramic ethnoarchaeology. *Journal of Archaeological Research* 8(2): 105-133.

Ascher, R.
1961 Analogy in archaeological interpretation. *Southwestern Journal of Anthropology* 17: 317-25.
1962 Ethnography for Archaeology: A case from the Seri Indians. *Ethnology* 1: 360-369.
1968 Time's arrow and the archaeology of contemporary community. In: Chang, K. (ed.). *Settlement Archaeology:* 43-52. Palo Alto: National Press Book.

Balfet, H.
1965 Ethnographic observation in North Africa and archaeological interpretation: The pottery of the Magreb. In: Matson, F. (ed.). *Ceramic and Man*: 161-177. Chicago: Aldine Publishing Co.

Balfet, H., Fauvet-Berthelot, M. and Monzon, S.
1989 *Pour la normalisation de la description des poteries.* Paris : Ed. du CNRS.

Banning, E.
2002 Consensus and debate on the Late Neolithic and Chalcolithic of the southern Levant. *Paléorient* 28 (2) : 148-155.

Beaumont, P.
1985 Man-induced Erosion in Northern Jordan. In: Hadidi, A. (ed.). *Studies in The History and Archaeology of Jordan*, II : 291-296. Jordan: Amman.

Bender, F.
1974   The Geology of Jordan. Trans. M. K. Khdeir. Berlin: Gebruder Borntaeger.

Bettinger, R., Boyd. R. and Richerson, P.
1996   Style, Function, and Cultural Evolutionary Processes. In: Maschner, H. (ed.). Darwinian Archaeologies: 133-164. New York and London: Plenum Press.

Binford, L.
1962   Archaeology as Anthropology, *American Antiquity* 28 (2): 217-225.
1965   Archaeological systematic and the study of cultural process. *American Antiquity* 31: 203-210
1967   Smudge pits and hide smoking: The use of analogy in archaeological reasoning. *American Antiquity* 32 (1): 1-12.
1968   Methodological considerations of the archaeological use of Ethnographic data. In: Lee, R., and DeVore, I. (eds.). *Man the Hunter*:268- 273. New York: Aldine Publishing Company.
1977   General Introduction. In: Binford, L. (ed.).*For Theory Building in Archaeology*: 1-10. New York: Academic Press.
1978   *Nunamiut Ethnooarchaeology*. New York: Academic Press.
1983   *In Pursuit of the Past: Decoding the archaeological record*. New York: Thames and Hudson Inc.

Bintliff, J.
1991   Postmodernism, Rhetoric and Scholasticism at TAG : The current state of British archaeology. *Antiquity* 65: 274-278.

Bril, B.
1991   Les gestes de percussion: analyse d'un mouvement technique. In : Chevallier, D. (ed.). *Savoir faire et pouvoir transmettre*, Collection d'Ethnologie de la France, Cahier 6. Paris : Editions de la Maison des Sciences de l'Homme.

Carr, C.
1990   Advances in ceramic radiography and analysis: Potentials. *Journal of Archaeological Science* 17: 13-34.
1993   Identifying individual vessels with X-Radiography. *American Antiquity* 58 (1): 96-117.

Carr, C. and Riddick, E.
1990   Advances in ceramic radiography and analysis: Laboratory methods. *Journal of Archaeological Science* 17: 35-66.

Carr, C. and Neitzel, J. (eds.)
1995   *Style, Society, and Person*. New York: Plenum Press.

Childe, G.
1951   *Man makes himself.* New York: Mentor Print, New American Library.
1956   *Society and Knowledge*. New York: Harper.

Clarke, D.
1968   *Analytical archaeology*. London: Methuen.

Conkey, M.
1990   Experimenting with style in archaeology: Some historical and theoretical issues. In: Conkey, M. , and Hastorf, C. (eds.). *The Uses of Styles in Archaeology*: 5-17. Cambridge: Cambridge University Press.

Conkey, M. and Hastorf, C. (eds.)
1990   *The Uses of Styles in Archaeology*. Cambridge: Cambridge University Press.

Costin, C.L.
1991   Craft Specialization: Issues in Defining, Documenting, and Explaining the Organization of Production. In: Schiffer, M. (ed.). *Archaeological Method and Theory*, vol.3: 1-56. Tucson: University of Arizona Press.
2000   The Use of Ethnoarchaeology for the Archaeological Study of Ceramic Production. *Journal of Archaeological Method and Theory* 7(4): 377-403.

Costin, C. and Hagstrum, M.
1995   Standardization, Labor Investment, skill and the organization of ceramic production in Late Prehispanic Highland Perue. *American Antiquity* 60 (4): 619-639.

Courty, M.-A. and Roux, V.
1995   Identification of wheel throwing on the basis of ceramic surface features and micro-fabrics. *Journal of Archaeological Science*, 22: 17-50.

Creswell, R.
1990   "A New Technology" Revisited. *Archaeological Review from Cambridge* 9 (1): 30-54.
1996   *Prométhée ou Pandore? Propos de technologie culturelle*. Paris : Kim.

Dark, K.R.
1996   *Theoretical Archaeology*. Ithaca: Cornell University Press.

Davidson, T. and McKerrell, H.
1976   Pottery analysis and Halaf period trade in the Khabur Headwaters region. *Iraq* 38 (1): 45-56.
1980   The Neutron Activation analysis of Halaf and 'Ubaid pottery from Tell Arpachiyah and Tepe Gawra. *Iraq* 42 (2): 155-167.

Davis, W.
1990   Style and history in art history. In: Conkey, M. , and Hastorf, C. (eds.). *The Uses of Styles in Archaeology*: 18-31. Cambridge: Cambridge University Press.

Deal, M.
1988   An ethnoarchaeological approach to the identification of Maya domestic pottery production. In: Kolb, Ch. (ed.). *Ceramic Ecology Revisited 1987*: 111-142. Oxford: BAR International Series 436(i).
1998   *Pottery Ethnoarchaeology in the central Maya Highlands*. Salt Lake City: University of Utah Press.

Deetz, J.
1965   *The Dynamics of Stylistic Change in Arikara Ceramics*. Studies in Anthropology No. 4, Urbana: University of Illinois.
1968   The Inference of Residence and Descent Rules from Archaeological Data. In: S., and L. Binford. (eds.). *New Perspective in Archaeology*: 41-48. Chicago: Aldine.

Dietler, M. and Herbich, I.
1998   *Habitus*, Techniques, Style: An integrated approach to the social understanding of material culture and boundaries. In: *The archaeology of social boundaries*, Stark, M. (ed.).Pp. 232-263. Washington DC: Smithsonian Institution Press

Dollfus,G. and Kafafi, Z.
1986   Abu Hamid, Jordanie. Premiers Résultats. *Paléorient* 12 (1): 91-100.
1993   Recent Researches at Abu Hamid. *ADAJ* 37: 241-263.
2001   Jordan in the Fourth Millennium. In: *Studies in the history and archaeology of Jordan, VII*, (ed.).Pp. 163-172. Amman: Department of Antiquities.

Dollfus, G. and Kafafi, Z. (eds.)
1988   *Abu Hamid, village du 4e millénaire de la Vallée du Jourdain*. Amman: Centre culturel français et Department of antiquities of Jordan.

Dollfus, G., Kafafi, Z. et al.
1988   Abu Hamid, an Early Fourth Millennium Site in the Jordan Valley. In: Garrard, A. and Gebel, H-G. (eds.). *The Prehistory of Jordan:* The State of research in 1986. British Archaeological Reports-Intern. Series 396.2: 567-601. Oxford, B.A.R.

Dunnell, R.
1971   Comment on: Sabloff and Smith's "The Importance of both analytic and taxonomic classification in the type-variety system. *American Antiquity* 36 (1) 115-118).
1978   Style and function: A fundamental dichotomy. *American Antiquity* 43: 192-202.

1980   Evolutionary Theory and Archaeology. In: Schiffer, M. (ed.). *Advances in Archaeological Method and Theory*, vol. 3: 35-99
1986   Issues in Americanist artifacts classification. In: Schiffer, M (ed.). *Advances in Archaeological Method and Theory*, vol. 9: 149-208. New York: Academic Press.
1989   Aspects of the application of evolutionary thought in archaeology. In: Lamberg-Karlovsky, C. (ed.), *Archaeological Thought in America*, New York: Cambridge University Press.

Flannery, K.
1972   The Cultural evolution of civilizations. *Annual Review of Ecology and Systematic* 61: 380-392.

Franken, H.J.
1974   *In Search of the Jericho Potters*: North-Holland Ceramic studies in Archaeology, Volume 1, Leiden.
1995   Theory and practice of ceramic studies in archaeology. *Newsletter of the Department of Pottery Technology (Leiden University)* 13: 81-102.

Franken, H.J. and Kalsbeek, J.
1975   *Potters of the Medieval Village in the Jordan Valley*, Amsterdam: Elsevier.
1983   Iron Age pottery from Haren (Northern Brabant, The Netherlands). *Newsletter of the Department of Pottery Technology (Leiden University)* 1: 27-31.

Fritz, J. and Plog, f.
1970   The nature of archaeological reasoning. *American Antiquity* 35(4): 405-12.

Gamble, C.
2001   *Archaeology: The Basic*. London: Routledge.

Garfinkel, Y.
1992   *The Pottery Assemblages of the Sha'ar Hagolan and Rabah Stages from Munhata (Israel)*. Cahiers du Centre de Recherche Francais de Jerusalem 6. Paris : Association Paléorient.

Gelbert, A.
1994   Tour et tournette en Espagne : recherche de macrotraces significatives des différentes techniques et méthodes de façonnage. In : Binder, D. et Courtin. J. *Terre cuite et Société. La céramique, document technique, économique, culturel*: 59-74. Juan-les-Pins : Editions APDCA. XIVe Rencontres Internationales d'Archéologie et d'Histoire d'Antibes.
2000   *Etude ethnoarchéologique des phénomènes d'emprunts céramiques. Enquêtes dans les haute et moyenne vallées du fleuve Sénégal (Sénégal)*. Paris X – Nanterre. Ph.D. dissertation.

Gilead, I.
1987   A new look at Chalcolithic Beer-Sheba. *Biblical Archaeologist* June: 110-117.
1990   The Neolithic-Chalcolithic Transition and the Qatifian of the Northern Negev and Sinai. *Levant* 22: 47-63.

Gosselain, O.P.
1998   Social and Technical Identity in a Clay Crystal Ball. In: Stark, M. (ed.). *The Archaeology of Social Boundaries*: 78-106. Washington and London: Smithsonian Institution Press.
2000   Materializing identities: an African perspective. *Journal of Archaeological Method and Theory*, 7(3), p. 187-218.

Gould, R.
1968   Living archaeology: The Ngatatjara of Western Australia. *Southwestern Journal of Anthropology* 24: 101-22

Graves, M.
1991   Pottery production and distribution among Kalinga: A study of household and regional organization and differentiation. In: Longacre. W. (ed.). *Ceramic Ethnoarchaeology*, Tucson: University of Arizona Press.

Hardin, M.
1991   Sources of ceramic variability at Zuni Pueblo. In: Longacre, W. (ed.). *Ceramic Ethnoarchaeology*: 40-70. Tucson: University of Arizona Press.

Harris, M.
1968   *The Rise of Anthropological Theory*, New York: Crowell.
1987   *Cultural anthropology*. New York: Harper & Row, Publisher, Inc.

Hayden, B.
1984   Are emic types relevant to archaeology. *Ethnohistory* 31 (2): 79-92.

Hayden, B. and Cannon, A.
1984   Interaction inferences in archaeology and learning frameworks of the Maya. *Journal of Anthropological Archaeology* 3: 325-367.

Hegmon, M.
1992   Archaeological research on style. *Annual Review of Anthropology* 21: 517-536
1998   Technology, Style, and Social Practices: Archaeological Approaches. In: Stark, M. (ed.). *The Archaeology of Social Boundaries*: 264-279. Washington and London: Smithsonian Institution Press.

Hennessy, J.
1982   Teleilat Ghassul and its place in the Archaeology of Jordan. In *Studies in the History and Archaeology of Jordan I*: 55-58. Amman: Department of Antiquity

Hill, J.
1977   Individual variability in ceramics and the study of Prehistoric social organization. In: Hill, J. and Gunn, J. (eds.). *The individual in Prehistory*: 55-109. New York: Academic Press

Hill, J. and Gunn, J. (eds.)
1977   *The individual in Prehistory*, New York: Academic Press.

Hodder, I.
1982   *Symbols in Action: Ethnoarchaeological Studies of Material Culture*. Cambridge: Cambridge University Press.
1986   *Reading the Past: Current research approaches and interpretations in archaeology*. Cambridge: Cambridge University Press.
1990   Style as historical quality. In: Conkey, M., and Hastorf, C. (eds.). *The Uses of Styles in Archaeology*, Pp. 44-51. Cambridge: Cambridge University Press.
1991   Interpretive archaeology and its role. *American Antiquity* 56: 7-18.
1997   "Always Momentary, Fluid and Flexible": Towards a reflexive excavation methodology. *Antiquity* 71: 691-700.

Hole, F.
1979   Rediscovering the Past in the Present: Ethnoarchaeology in Luristan, Iran. In: Kramer, C. (ed.). *Ethnoarchaeology: Implications of ethnography for archaeology*: 192-218. New York: Columbia University Press

Hoopes, J. and Barnett, W. (eds.)
1995   *The Emergence of Pottery: Technology and Innovation in Ancient Societies*. Washington, DC: Smithsonian Institution Press.

Hourani, F.
1997   Natural constraints, space organization models and rhythm of occupation at Abu Hamid during the Seventh and the Six Millennium BP. A Geo-archaeological Study. In: Bisheh, G., Zaghloul, M., and Kehrberg, I. (eds.). *Studies in the History and Archaeology of Jordan VI*: 67-76. Amman: Department of Antiquities.
2002   *Le cadre paléogéographique des premières sociétés agricoles dans la vallée du Jourdain: Etude de l'impact des événements climatiques de l'Holocène ancien sur la dynamique du peuplement humain*. Paris: Institut National Agronomique Paris-Grignon. Ph.D. Thesis.

Hourani, F. and Courty, M.,-A.
1997   L'evolution Morpho-Climatique de 10 500 à 5 500 BP dans la Vallée du Jourdain. *Paléorient* 23/2 :95-105

Hütteroth, W.-D. and Abdulfattah, K.
1977   *Historical Geography of Palestine, Transjordan and Southern Syria in the Late 16ᵗʰ century.* Erlangen: Palm and Einke.

Ibrahim, M., Yassine, Kh. and Sauer, J.
1976   The East Jordan Valley Survey, 1975. *Bulletin of American School of Oriental Research* 222: 41-66.

Ingold, T.
2000   Making culture and weaving the world. In: Graves-Brown, P. (ed.). *Matter, Materiality and Modern Culture*: 50-71. London: Routledge.

Joffe, A. and Dessel, J.P.
1995   Redefining chronology and terminology for the Chalcolithic of the southern Levant. *Current Anthropology* 36: 507-518.

Kafafi, Z.
1982   *The Neolithic of Jordan.* Unpublished Ph.D. dissertation. Berlin: Freie Universität Berlin.
1988   Jebel Abu Thawwab: A pottery Neolithic village in Northern Jordan. In: Garrard, A., and Gebel, H-G. (eds.). *Prehistory of Jordan*: 451-471. BAR International Series 396 (ii). Oxford.
1993   The Yarmoukian in Jordan. *Paléorient* 19 (1): 101-113.
1995   Decorative elements on the excavated Neolithic pottery at 'Ain Ghazal. In: 'Amr, K., Zayadine, F. and Zaghloul, M. (eds.). *Studies in the History and Archaeology of Jordan.* 545-555. Amman: Department of Antiquities.
1998   The Late Neolithic in Jordan. In: Henry, D. (ed.). *The Prehistoric Archaeology of Jordan*: 127-138. BAR International Series 705. Oxford.

Karlin, C. and Julian, M.
1994   Prehistoric technology: A cognitive science? In: Renfrew, C., and Zubrow, E. (eds.).*The ancient mind: Elements of cognitive archaeology:* 152-164.Cambridge: Cambridge University Press.

Kenyon, K.
1979   *Archaeology in the Holy Land.* 4ᵗʰ ed. London: Benn.

Kerner, S.
2001   Das Chalkolithikum in der südlichen Levante. Die Entwicklung handwerklicher Spezialisierung und ihre Beziehung zu gesellschaftlicher Komplexität. Orient Archäologie Band 8. Deutsches archäologisches Institut Orient – Abteilung.

Kleindienst, M. and Watson, P.
1956   "Action archaeology: The archaeological inventory of a living community". *Anthropology Tomorrow* 5: 75-78.

Kolb, Ch.
1989a   Ceramic Ecology in retrospect: A critical review of methodology and results. In: Kolb, Ch. (ed.). *Ceramic Ecology, 1988: current research on Ceramic Materials*: 261-376. BAR international series: 513.
1989b   The Current Status of ceramic studies. In: Kolb, Ch. (ed.). *Ceramic Ecology,1988: current research on Ceramic Materials*: 377-421. BAR international series: 513. Oxford.

Kolb, Ch. and Lackey, L. (eds.)
1988   *A Pot for All reasons: ceramic Ecology Revisited*, Philadelphia: Temple University, Laboratory of Anthropology.

Kramer, C.
1979   Introduction. In: Kramer, C. (ed.). *Ethnoarchaeology: Implications of ethnography for archaeology*: 1-20. New York: Columbia University Press.
1985   Ceramic Ethnoarchaeology. *Annual Review of Anthropology* 14: 77-102.
1997   *Pottery in Rajasthan: Ethnoarchaeology in Two Indian Cities.* Washington, DC.: Smithsonian Institution Press.

Kramer, C. and David, N.
2001   *Ethnoarchaeology in Action.* Cambridge: Cambridge University Press.

Kvamme, K., Stark, M. and Longacre, W.
1996   Alternative procedures for assessing standardization in ceramic assemblages. *America Antiquity* 61(1): 116-126.

Lechtman, H. and Merrill, R. (eds.)
1977   Material Culture: Styles, Organization, and Dynamic of Technology. Minnesota: West Publishers.

Lemonnier, P.
1980   *Les Salines de l'ouest – logique technique, logique sociale.* Paris / Lille, Maison des Sciences de l'Homme / Presses Universitaires de Lille.
1986   The study of material culture today: Towards an anthropology of technical systems. *Journal of Anthropological Archaeology* 5:147-186.
1989   Bark capes, arrowheads and Concorde: On social representations of technology. In: Hodder, I. (ed.). *The*

Meanings of Things: Material culture and symbolic expression: 156-172. Hammersmith: HarperCollins Academic
1993 (Ed.) *Technological choices: Transformation in material cultures since the Neolithic*. London and New York: Routledge.

Lewis, N.
1987 *Nomads and settlers in Syria and Jordan*, 1800-1980. Cambridge: Cambridge University Press.

Livingstone-Smith, A.
2000 Processing clay for pottery in northern Cameroon: social and technical requirements. *Archaeometry*, 42 (1), p. 21-42

Loney, H.
1995 *The Development of Apennine Ceramic Manufacturing Technology: Xeroradiographic Analysis*. Unpublished Ph.D. dissertation. Department of Anthropology, University of Pennsylvania
2000 Society and technological control: A critical review of models of technological change in ceramic studies. *American Antiquity* 65 (4): 646-668.

Longacre, W.
1968 Some aspects of prehistoric society in east-central Arizona. In: S. and L. Binford (eds.). *New perspectives in archaeology*: 89-102. Chicago: Aldine Publishing Company.
1981 Kalinga pottery: An ethnoarchaeological study. In: Hodder, I., Isaac, G., and Hammond, N. (eds.). *Pattern of the Past: Studies in Honor of David. L, Clarke*: 49-66. Cambridge: Cambridge University Press.
1991 *Ceramic ethnoarchaeology*. Tucson: University of Arizona Press.
1999 Standardization and Specialization: What's the Link? In: Skibo, J. and Feinman, G. (eds.). *Pottery and People: A Dynamic Interaction*: 44-58. Salt Lake City: The University of Utah Press.

Lovell, J.
2001 The Late Neolithic and Chalcolithic Periods in the Southern Levant. New Data from the site of Teleilat Ghassul, Jordan. Oxford: BAR International Series 974.

Lovell, J., Kafafi, Z. and Dollfus, G.
1997 A Preliminary note on the ceramics from the Basal Levels of Abu Hamid. In: Gebel, H-G., Kafafi, Z., and Rollefson, G. (eds.). *The Prehistory of Jordan, II. Perspectives from 1997*: 361-370. Studies in Early Near Eastern Production, Subsistence and Environment 4 (1997). Berlin: *ex oriente*.

Lovell, J., Dollfus, G. and Kafafi, Z.
n.d The Middle Phases at Abu Hamid and the Wadi

Rabah Horizon. In *Studies in the History and Archaeology of Jordan*, VIII. Jordan: Department of archaeology.

Lyman, R., O'Brien, M. and Dunnell, R.
1997 *The rise and fall of culture history*. New York and London: Plenum Press.

Mahias, M.-C.
1993 Pottery techniques in India; Technical variants and social choice. In: Lemonnier, P. (ed.). *Technological choices: Transformation in material cultures since the Neolithic*: 157-180. London and New York: Routledge

Matson, F.
1939 Further technological notes on the pottery of the Younge site, Lapeer Country, Michigan. Papers of the Michigan Academy of Science, Arts and Letters 24 (4): 11-23.
1965 Ceramic ecology: An approach to the study of the early cultures of the Near East. In: Matson, F. (ed.). *Ceramics and Man*: 202-217. Chicago: Aldine.

Mellaart, J.
1956 The Neolithic site of Ghrubba. *Annual of the Department of Antiquities of Jordan* 3:24-40.

Mershen, B.
1985 Recent Hand-Made Pottery from Northern Jordan. *Berytus* XXXIII: 75-87.
1992 Settlement history and village space in Late Ottoman Northern Jordan. In: Zaghloul, M., and Amr, Kh., (eds.) *Studies in The History and Archaeology of Jordan*, IV: 409-416. Amman: Department of Antiquities.

Mittmann, S.
1970 *Beiträger zur Siedlungs- und Territorialgeschichte des Nördlichen Ostjordanlandes*. Wiesbaden: Otto Harrassowitz.

Moore, A.
1995 The inception of potting in Western Asia and its impact on economy and society. In: Hoopes, J., and Barnett, W. (eds.). *The Emergence of Pottery: Technology and Innovation in Ancient Societies*: 39-53. Washington, DC: Smithsonian Institution Press.

Morgan, L.
1877 *Ancient Society*. New York: Holt.

Muller, J.
1977 Individual variation in art styles. In: Hill, J. and Gunn, J. (eds.). *The individual in Prehistory*: 23-39. New York: Academic Press.

Mundy, M.
1994   Village land and Individual Title: Mush'a and Ottoman land registration in the Ajlun District. In: Rogan, E. and Tell, T. (eds.). *Village, Steppe and State*: the social origins of modern Jordan. 58-79. London: British Academic Press.

Neff, D.
1993   Theory, sampling, and analytical techniques in the archaeological study of prehistoric ceramics. *American Antiquity* 58(1): 23-44.

Neff, D., Larson, O. and Glascock, M.
1997   The evolution of Anasazi ceramic production and distribution: Compositional evidence from a Pueblo III site in south-central Utah. *Journal of Field Archaeology* 24: 473-492.

Neupert, M.
2000   Clay of Contention: An ethnoarchaeological study of factionalism and clay composition. *Journal of Archaeological Method and Theory* 7(4): 249-272.

O'Brien, M.
1996   The historical development of an evolutionary archaeology: A selectionist approach. In: Maschner, H. (ed.). Darwinian Archaeologies: 19-32. New York: Plenum Press.

Peacock, D.P.S.
1982   *Pottery in the Roman World: An ethnoarchaeological approach*. London: Longman.

Pelegrin, J.
1990   Prehistoric Lithic technology: some aspects of research. *Archaeological Review from Cambridge* 9(1): 116-125.

Perrot, J.
1964   Les deux premiéres campagnes de fouilles à Munhata. *Syria* 41 :323-345.
1968   Munhata 1967 (Chronique archéologique). *Revue Biblique* 75 :263-264.

Perrot, J., and Zory, N
1967   Neve Ur, un nouvel aspect du Ghassoulien. *Israel Exploration Journal* 17: 201-32.

Pfaffenberger, B.
1992   Social Anthropology of Technology. *Annual Review of Anthropology* 21: 491-516.

Ploux, S.
1991   Technologie, Technicité, Techniciens: méthodes de détermination d'auteurs et comportement technique individuel. In *25 ans d'études technologiques en préhis-toire, bilan et perspectives, XIe rencontres internationales d'archéologie et d'histoire d'Antibes* : 201-214. ADPCA, Juan-les-Pins.

Preucel, R.
1991   The Philosophy of Archaeology. In: Preucel, R. (ed.). *Processual and Postprocessual Archaeologies: Multiple ways of knowing the past*: 17-29. Carbondale: Centre for Archaeological Investigations Occasional Paper No. 10, Southern Illinois University.
1995   The Postprocessual Condition. *Journal of Archaeological Research* 3: 147-175.

Renfrew, C.
1994   Towards a cognitive archaeology. In Renfrew, C., and Zubrow, E. (eds.). *The ancient mind: Elements of cognitive archaeology* : 3-12. Cambridge: Cambridge University Press

Rice, P.
1981   Evolution of specialized pottery production: A trial model. *Current Anthropology* 22: 219-240.
1984   Change and conservatism in pottery-producing systems. In: van der Leeuw, S. and Pritchard, A. (eds.). *The Many Dimensions of Pottery*: 231-293. Amsterdam: Universiteit van Amsterdam.
1987   *Pottery Analysis: A Sourcebook*. Chicago: University Chicago Press.
1996   Recent ceramic analysis 2: Composition, production, and theory. *Journal of Archaeological Research* 4: 165-202.
1999   On the Origin of Pottery. *Journal of Archaeological Method and Theory* 6: 1-54.

Rogan, E.
1999   *Frontiers of the State in the Late Ottoman Empire: Transjordan*, 1850-1921. Cambridge: Cambridge University Press.

Rouse, I.
1953   The strategy of culture history. In: Kroeber, Al. (ed.). *Anthropology Today*: 57-76. Chicago: University of Chicago Press.
1960   The Classification of Artifact in Archaeology. *American Antiquity* 25 (3): 313-323.

Roux, V.
1990   The Psychosocial analysis of Technical Activities: A contribution to the Study of Craft Specialization. *Archaeological Review from Cambridge* 9: 1: 142-153.
1994   La technique du tournage: définition et reconnaissance par les macro-traces. In: Binder, D. et Courtin, J. (eds.). *Terre cuite et Société. La céramique, document technique, économique, culturel* : 45-58. Juan-les-Pins : Edition APDCA. XIVe Rencontres Internationales

d'Archéologie et d'Histoire d'Antibes.

Roux, V. and Courty, M-A.
1997   Les bols élaborés au tour d'Abu Hamid : Rupture technique au 4e mill. av. J.-C. dans le Levant sud. *Paléorient* 23 (1) : 25-43.
1998   Identification of wheel-fashioning methods: technical analysis of 4th-3rd millennium BC oriental ceramic. *Journal of Archaeological Science* 25: 747-763.
forth   Identifying social entities at a macro-regional level: Chalcolithic ceramics of South Levant as a case study. In: Bosquet, D., Livingstone-Smith, A., and Martineau, R. (eds.), *Pottery Manufacturing Processes: Reconstruction and Interpretation*. B.A.R., Oxford.

Roux, V. in coll. with Corbetta, D.
1989   *The potter's wheel : craft specialization and technical competence*. New Delhi: Oxford and IBH Publishing.

Roux, V. and Corbetta, D.
1990   Technique du tournage et spécialisation artisanale. In *Le tour du potier: Spécialisation artisanale et compétences techniques*, Roux, V. and Corbetta, D., p. 19-100. Paris : CNRS (monographie du CRA, 4).

Rye, O.
1977   Pottery manufacturing techniques: X-ray studies, *Archaeometry 19*: 205-211
1981   *Pottery Technology: Principles and Reconstruction*. Washington D.C: Taraxacum Press.

Sackett, J.
1982   Approaches to style in lithic archaeology. *Journal of Anthropological Archaeology* 1: 59-112.
1990   Style and ethnicity in archaeology: the case for isochrestism. In: Conkey, M., and Hastorf, C. (eds.). *The Uses of Styles in Archaeology:* 32-43. Cambridge: Cambridge University Press.

Shehadeh, N.
1985   The Climate of Jordan in the Past and Present. In: Hadidi, A. (ed.). *Studies in The History and Archaeology of Jordan*, II : 25-37. Jordan: Amman

Schiffer, M.
1983   Review of Cultural Materialism: The Struggle for a Science of Culture, by M. Harris. *American Antiquity* 48 (4): 190-194

Schiffer, M. and Skibo, J.
1997   The Explanation of Artifact Variability. *American Antiquity* 62(1): 27-50.

Schiffer, M., Skibo, J., Boelke, T., Neupert, M. and Aronson, M.
1994   New Perspectives on Experimental Archaeology: Surface Treatments and Thermal Response of the Clay Cooking Pot. *American Antiquity* 59 (2): 197-217.

Schlanger, N.
1994   Mindful technology: unleashing the *chaîne opératoire* for an archaeology of mind. In: Renfrew, C., and Zubrow, E. (eds.). *The ancient mind: Elements of cognitive archaeology*: 143-151.Cambridge: Cambridge University Press.

Service, E.
1985   *A century of controversy: Ethnological issues from 1860 to 1960*. London: Academic Press.

Shepard, A.
1965   *Ceramics for the Archaeologists*. Washington, D.C.: Carnegie Institution of Washington.

Skibo, J., Schiffer, M. and Kowalski, N.
1989   Ceramic Style Analysis in Archaeology and Ethnoarchaeology: Bridging the Analytical Gab. *Journal of Anthropological Archaeology* 8: 388-409.

Stark, B.
1985   Archaeological identification of pottery production locations: Ethnoarchaeological and archaeological data in Mesoamerica. In: Nelson, B. (ed.). *Decoding Prehistoric Ceramics*: 158-194. Carbondale: Southern Illinois University Press

Stark, M. (ed.)
1998   *The Archaeology of Social Boundaries*. Washington and London: Smithsonian Institution Press

Stark, M., Bishop, R. and Miksa, E.
2000   Ceramic technology and social boundaries: Cultural practices in Kalinga clay selection and use. *Journal of Archaeological Method and Theory* 7(4): 295-331.

Stekelis, M.
1951   A new Neolithic Industry: the Yarmoukian of Palestine. *Israel Exploration Journal* 1:1-19.
1972   *The Yarmoukian Culture of the Neolithic Period*. Jerusalem: Magnes Press.

Steponaitis, V.
1984   Technological studies of Prehistoric pottery from Alabama: Physical properties and vessel function. In: van der Leeuw, S., and Pritchard, , A. (eds.). *The Many Dimensions of Pottery*: 79-127. Amsterdam: Universiteit van Amsterdam.

Steward, J.
1955   *The theory of cultural change.* Urbana: University of Illinois Press.

Thagard, P.
1996   *Mind: Introduction to cognitive science.* Cambridge, Mass: MTT Press.

Thompson, R.
1958   *Modern Yucatan pottery making.* Memories of the Society for American Archaeology 15. Washington, DC: Society for American Archaeology.
1991   The archaeological purpose of ethnoarchaeology. In: Longacre, W. (ed.). *Ceramic Ethnoarchaeology*:231-45. Tucson: University of Arizona Press.

Trigger, B.
1989   *A History of Archaeological Thought.* Cambridge: Cambridge University Press.

Tylor, E.B.
1871   *Primitive Culture.* London: Murray.

Van As, A. and Wijnen, M.-H.
1989/90 Neolithic and early Chalcolithic pottery from Ilipinar (Phases X-VIII), in Northern Anatolia. *Newsletter of the Department of Pottery Technology (Leiden University)*7/8: 21-68.

Van As, A., Jacobs, L. and Wijnen, M.-H.
1996/97 Further technological research on the Chalcolithic pottery of Ilipinar, Phase VB. *Newsletter of the Department of Pottery Technology (Leiden University)* 14/15: 60-84.

Van der Leeuw, S.
1977   *Studies in the Technology of ancient Pottery*, 2 vols. Ph.D. dissertation.
1984   Dust to dust: A transformational view of the ceramic cycle. In: van der Leeuw, S., and Pritchard, A., (eds.). *The Many Dimensions of Pottery: Ceramics in Archaeology and Anthropology*: 707-773. Amsterdam: Universiteit van Amsterdam.
1991   Variation, variability, and explanation in pottery studies. In: Longacre, W. (ed.). *Ceramic Ethnoarchaeology*: 11-39, Tucson: University of Arizona Press.
1993   Given the potter a choice: Conceptual aspects of pottery techniques. In: Lemmonier, P (ed.). *Technological Choices: Transformation in Material Culture Since the Neolithic*: 238-288. London: Routledge
1994   Cognitive aspects of "technique". In: Renfrew, C. and Zubrow, E. (eds.).*The ancient mind: Elements of cognitive archaeology*:135-142. Cambridge: Cambridge University Press.

Van der Leeuw, S., Papousek, R. and Coudart, A.
1992   Technological Traditions and unquestioned assumptions: The case of pottery in Michoacan. *Techniques et Culture* 16-17: 145-173.

Vandiver, P.
1986   The production technology of earthenware ceramics, ca. 4900-2800 B.C., In: Lamberg-Karlovsky, C. and Beale, T. (eds.). *Excavation at Tepe Yahya, Iran, 1967-1975: the Early Periods*: 91-100. American School of Prehistoric research, Bull 38. Cambridge: Peabody Museum, Harvard University.
1987   Sequential slab construction; A conservative southwest Asiatic ceramic tradition, ca. 7000- 3000, *Paléorient 13 (2)*: 9-35.

Van Pool, Ch. and Van Pool, T.
1999   The scientific nature of postprocessualism. *American Antiquity* 64 (1): 33-53.

Vitelli, K.
1984   Greek Neolithic pottery by experiment. In: Rice, P. (ed.). *Pots and Potters: Current Approaches in Ceramic Archaeology*:113-131. Los Angelos: University of California.

Watson, P.
1979   *Archaeological ethnography in western Iran.* Tucson: University of Arizona Press.
1980   The theory and practice of ethnoarchaeology with special reference to the Near east, *Paléorient* 6: 55-64

Watson, P. and Gould, R.
1982   A dialogue on the meaning and use of analogy in ethnoarchaeological reasoning, *Journal of anthropological archaeology* 1 (4): 355-81.

Watson, P., Le Blanc, S. and Redman, R.
1984   *Archaeological Explanation: The scientific method in archaeology.* New York: Colombia University Press.

Whallon, R.
1968   Investigations of Late Prehistoric social organization in New York State. In: Binford S. and L. (eds.). *New perspectives in archaeology*: 223-244. Chicago: Aldine Publishing Company.

White, L.
1949   *The science of culture: a study of man and civilization.* New York: Farrar Straus.
1959   *The evolution of culture.* New York: McGraw-Hill.

Wiessner, P.
1983   Style and social information in Kalahari San projectile points. *American Antiquity* 49: 253-276.
1990   Is there a unity to style? In: Conkey, M., and Hastorf, C. (eds.). *The Uses of Styles in Archaeology*: 105-112. Cambridge: Cambridge University Press.

Wobst, H.
1977   Stylistic behavior and information exchange. In: Cleland, C. (ed.). *Papers for the Director: Research Essays in Honor of James B. Griffin*: 317-334. Anthropological Papers No. 61. Ann Arbor: Museum of Anthropology, University of Michigan.
1978   The archaeo-ethnology of hunter gatherers or the tyranny of the ethnographic record in archaeology. *American Antiquity* 43: 303-309.

Wright, R.
1993   Technological style: Transforming a natural material into cultural object. In: Lubar, S., and Kingery, W. (eds.). *History from Things: Essay on material culture*: 242-269. Washington and London: Smithsonian Institution Press.

Wyle, A.
1985   An analogy by any other name is just as analogical: A commentary on the Gould - Watson dialogue, *Journal of Anthropological Archaeology* 1: 382-401.

Yellen, J.
1977   *Archaeological approaches to the present*. New York: Academic Press.

www.ingramcontent.com/pod-product-compliance
Lightning Source LLC
Chambersburg PA
CBHW061001030426
42334CB00033B/3316